Microsoft® Office® XP

fast&easy®

Check the Web for Updates

To check for updates or corrections relevant to this book and/or CD-ROM, visit our updates page on the Web at **http://www.prima-tech.com/support**.

Send Us Your Comments

To comment on this book or any other PRIMA TECH title, visit our reader response page on the Web at **http://www.prima-tech.com/comments**.

How to Order

For information on quantity discounts, contact the publisher: Prima Publishing, P.O. Box 1260BK, Rocklin, CA 95677-1260; (916) 787-7000. On your letterhead, include information concerning the intended use of the books and the number of books you want to purchase. For individual orders, turn to the back of this book for more information.

Microsoft Office® XP

fast&easy®

Diane Koers

A DIVISION OF PRIMA PUBLISHING

A Division of Prima Publishing

Prima Publishing and colophon and fast & easy are registered trademarks of Prima Communications, Inc. PRIMA TECH is a trademark of Prima Communications, Inc., Roseville, California 95661.

Publisher: Stacy L. Hiquet
Managing Editor: Sandy Doell
Acquisitions Editor: Debbie Abshier
Project Editor: Kezia Endsley
Technical Reviewer: Jacqueline Harris
Copy Editor: Kezia Endsley
Interior Layout: Marian Hartsough
Cover Design: Prima Design Team
Indexer: Johnna Dinse
Proofreader: Mitzi Foster

Microsoft, Windows, Office XP, Word, Excel, Access, PowerPoint, and Internet Explorer are either registered trademarks or trademarks of Microsoft Corporation in the United States and/or other countries. Netscape is a registered trademark of Netscape Communications Corporation in the U.S. and other countries.

Important: Prima Publishing cannot provide software support. Please contact the appropriate software manufacturer's technical support line or Web site for assistance.

Prima Publishing and the author have attempted throughout this book to distinguish proprietary trademarks from descriptive terms by following the capitalization style used by the manufacturer.

Information contained in this book has been obtained by Prima Publishing from sources believed to be reliable. However, because of the possibility of human or mechanical error by our sources, Prima Publishing, or others, the Publisher does not guarantee the accuracy, adequacy, or completeness of any information and is not responsible for any errors or omissions or the results obtained from use of such information. Readers should be particularly aware of the fact that the Internet is an ever-changing entity. Some facts may have changed since this book went to press.

ISBN: 0-7615-3388-5
Library of Congress Catalog Card Number: 2001086686
Printed in the United States of America

00 01 02 03 04 DD 10 9 8 7 6 5 4 3 2 1

To Tresee and Spencer

Welcome to our family!

Acknowledgments

I am deeply grateful to the many people at Prima Publishing who worked on this book. Thank you for all the time you gave and for your assistance.

While I can't name everyone involved, I'd like to especially thank Debbie Abshier for the opportunity to write this book and her confidence in me; to Jacqueline Harris for her assistance in making this book technically correct, and to Kezia Endsley for all her patience and guidance in pulling the project together. It takes a lot of both to work with me! Also, a special note of thanks to Stacey Hiquet, Sandy Doell, Marian Hartsough, Johnna Dinse, Mitzi Foster, and the Prima Design Team for all their help behind the scenes.

Lastly, a big hug and kiss to my husband, Vern, for his never-ending patience during those very late nights spent writing this book.

About the Author

DIANE KOERS owns and operates All Business Service, a software training and consulting business formed in 1988 that services the central Indiana area. Her area of expertise has long been in the word processing, spreadsheet, and graphics area of computing as well as providing training and support for Peachtree Accounting Software. Diane's authoring experience includes 14 other Prima Publishing Fast & Easy books including *Windows Millennium Fast & Easy*, *WordPerfect 9 Fast & Easy*, *Paint Shop Pro 7 Fast & Easy*, *Office 2000 Fast & Easy*, *Word XP Fast & Easy*, and has co-authored Prima's *Essential Windows 98*. She has also developed and written software training manuals for her clients' use.

Active in her church and civic activities, Diane enjoys spending her free time traveling and playing with her grandson and her three Yorkshire Terriers.

Contents at a Glance

Contents

Introduction

Welcome to the world of Microsoft Office.

This new *Fast & Easy* guide from Prima Publishing will help you master the many and varied features of one of Microsoft's most popular products—Microsoft Office XP. Microsoft Office is a powerful and popular suite of programs that will support many aspects of your everyday work style. For example, information is provided to help you write a letter, create a spreadsheet, produce a professional-looking presentation, and manage your schedule and electronic mail.

Each of the individual programs interact with the other programs in the suite. For example, you might need to prepare a business report in Word that contains graphs and charts based on data you enter in an Excel spreadsheet. Perhaps later, after you have delivered your report (possibly using Outlook's e-mail), you might need to prepare and schedule a PowerPoint presentation. In addition, you'll learn how to use Office products to interact with the Internet.

Through this book you learn *how* to create Office documents, however *what* you create is totally up to you! Your imagination is the only limit to what you can do with them after that. This book cannot begin to teach you everything you can do with Microsoft Office, nor will it give you all the different ways to accomplish a task.

What I *have* tried to do is give you the fastest and easiest way to get started with this fun and exciting suite of programs.

I've divided the book into seven parts and two appendixes. In Part I, I show you how to use basic Office commands; things that are common among most Office applications. Although it's not the most exciting part of the book, it's certainly the most practical. Look out then! Things start to be lots of fun! In Parts II, III, IV, V, and VI, you learn the basics of five of the most popular Office applications: Word, Excel, PowerPoint, Outlook, and Access.

While some versions of Microsoft Office XP will also include other products such as Microsoft FrontPage, we didn't include them in this *Microsoft Office XP Fast & Easy* guide, however Prima Publishing has a number of books available dedicated exclusively to those special products. Some titles you might want to investigate include *Microsoft FrontPage XP Fast & Easy* (ISBN #0761533907) or *Create FrontPage XP Web Pages In A Weekend* (ISBN #0761534474).

The final part, Part VII, teaches you how to use Office's state of the art technological features to create Web documents, save time with the Office Shortcut Bar, and the newest and most exciting feature—Speech. Speech lets you talk to your computer, allowing your voice to do the work instead of your fingers!

I've even included two helpful appendixes to show you how to install Microsoft Office and how to save your valuable time with keyboard shortcuts!

Who Should Read This Book?

Whether you are computer challenged or have used Microsoft products before, you will be able to quickly tap into the user-friendly integrated design and feature-rich environment of Microsoft Office XP.

Prima Publishing *Fast & Easy* guides use a step-by-step approach with illustrations of what you will see on your screen, linked with instructions for the next mouse movements or keyboard operations to complete your task. Computer terms and phrases are clearly explained in non-technical language, and expert tips and shortcuts help you produce professional-quality documents.

This book can be used as a learning tool or as a task reference. The easy-to-follow, highly visual nature of this book makes it the perfect learning tool. No prerequisites are required from you, the reader, except that you know how to turn your computer on and how to use your mouse.

In addition, anyone using a software application always needs an occasional reminder about the steps required to perform a particular task. By using the *Microsoft Office XP Fast & Easy* guide, any level of user can look up steps for a task quickly without having to plow through pages of descriptions.

Added Advice to Make You a Pro

You'll notice that this book uses steps and keeps explanations to a minimum to help you learn faster. Included in the book are a few elements that provide some additional comments to help you master the program, without encumbering your progress through the steps:

- Tips offer shortcuts when performing an action, or a hint about a feature that might make your work in Word quicker and easier.
- Notes give you a bit of background or additional information about a feature, or advice about how to use the feature in your day-to-day activities.

Read and enjoy this *Fast & Easy* book. It certainly is the *fastest and easiest* way to learn Microsoft Office XP.

—Diane Koers

PART I

Getting Started

1

Welcome to Office XP

If you're relatively new to using a computer, not understanding the basic elements you see on-screen can be frustrating. What's a dialog box? Where is that pop-up menu coming from? The good thing about Microsoft Office products is that the elements are the same in each program.

Throughout Part I, you will learn the common ways you can approach tasks, regardless of the Office program you are using or the document in which you are working.

The basic premise of each *Fast & Easy* guide is that people learn best by doing. In this chapter, you'll learn how to:

- Understand the different Office programs
- Start and exit an Office XP program
- Identify common screen elements

Discovering Office Applications

Microsoft Office includes multiple applications; each designed to accomplish a particular task. Although each application operates independently of the others, all are designed to tightly integrate so information you enter in one application can be shared among the others. The Office applications covered in this book include:

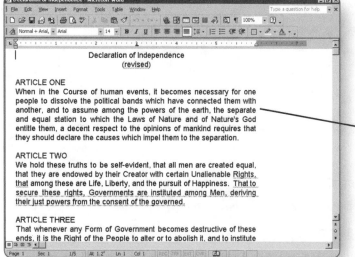

- **Word**—The Microsoft Office word-processing application. You'll learn about Word in Part II of this book.

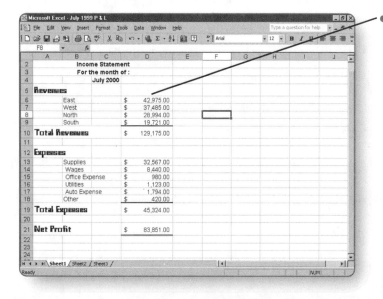

- **Excel**—The Microsoft Office spreadsheet application. You'll learn about Excel in Part III of this book.

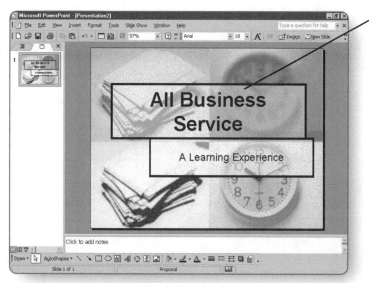

PowerPoint—The Microsoft Office graphics and presentations application. You'll learn about PowerPoint in Part IV of this book.

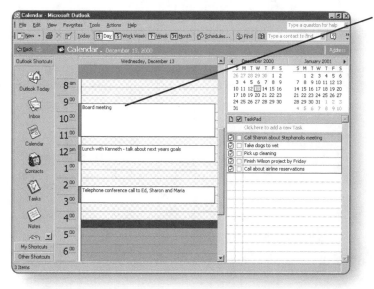

Outlook—The Microsoft Office e-mail and personal information management application. You'll learn about Outlook in Part V of this book.

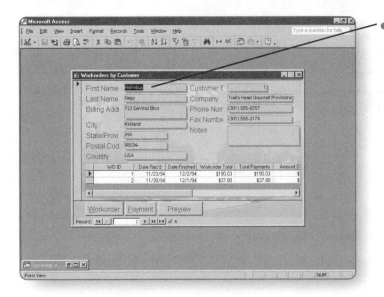

● **Access**—The Microsoft Office database application. You'll learn about Access in Part VI of this book.

Starting a Program

Starting a program (also called an *application*) is simple to do—and it's the first, necessary step toward getting anything done. Because computers can be set up differently, you might not see the icons on your Desktop or the menu choices on the Programs menu that you see in this example.

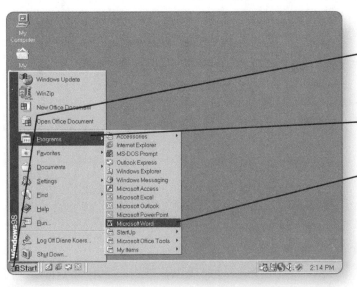

1. Click on the **Start button** on the Windows Taskbar. The Start menu will appear.

2. Click on **Programs**. The Programs menu will appear.

3. Click on the Office program name (in this instance, **Microsoft Word**) that you want to start. The Welcome screen for the program will appear briefly before the main program window opens.

If this is the first time you have accessed a Microsoft Office application, the Activation Wizard will appear. You can only access Microsoft Office a total of 50 times without using the Activation Wizard. After the 50 uses, you will not be able to access Office until you register your product with the Activation Wizard.

Microsoft Office Beta 2 Activation Wizard

Welcome to the Microsoft Office Activation Wizard
This wizard will guide you through the product activation process.

You have not yet activated your copy of Microsoft Office Beta 2. This product will run 49 more times before you will be required to activate it. For more information, click the Help button.

Would you like to activate through the Internet or by other means?

- Activate by using the Internet
- Activate by using the telephone

If you are not already connected, the Microsoft Office Activation Wizard will use your default Internet connection to process your information. Or, you can connect to the Internet manually and then continue with the wizard. If you do not have access to the Internet, choose the option to use the telephone.

Help   < Back   Next >   Activate Later

4. Click on the **Activate Later button**. The Office application you selected will appear.

TIP

If you're asked for a user name, type your name and initials in the dialog box and click on OK.

Identifying Common Screen Elements

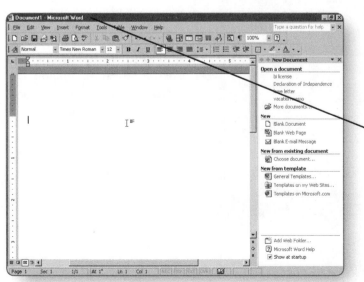

All Office programs contain common screen elements. You'll learn more about the following elements as you work in individual programs in this book:

- **Title bar**—A bar displayed at the top of a document that displays the name of the current Office program and document.

Menu bar—A group of all available features in the selected Office program.

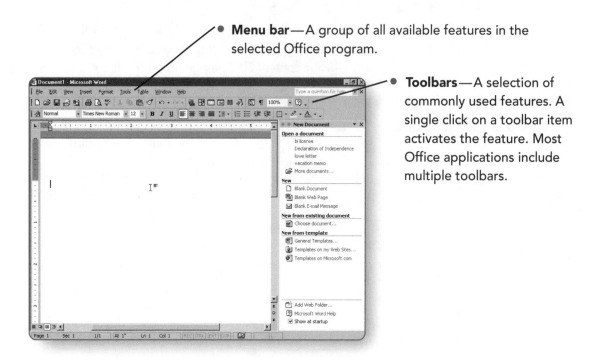

Toolbars—A selection of commonly used features. A single click on a toolbar item activates the feature. Most Office applications include multiple toolbars.

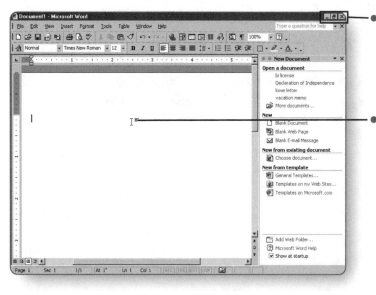

Window control buttons—Three buttons, Minimize, Maximize/Restore, and Close, used to control the size of a document window.

Mouse pointer—The mouse pointer, which will change shape as it moves to different locations on the screen.

Working area (also called the Document screen)—The white area of the screen where the text will appear.

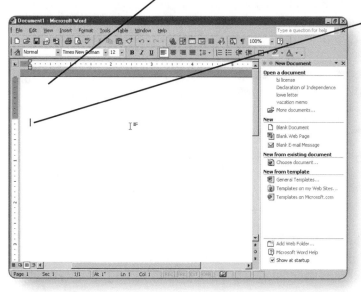

Insertion point—The blinking vertical line in the document screen that indicates where text will appear when you begin typing.

The insertion point appears in different locations in the various Office programs. On your screen, it flashes. The insertion point represents the location at which text will appear when you start typing. As you type, the insertion point moves to the right.

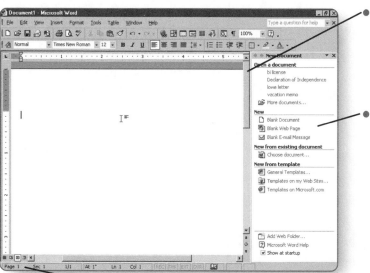

Scroll bars—Horizontal and vertical bars on the bottom and right sides of the screen that allow you to see more of a document.

Task Pane—Small windows that assist you in working with Word. Task panes store collections of important features and present them in ways that are much easier to find and use. There are several different task panes.

Status bar—A bar at the bottom of the screen indicating document information such as the current page or the location of the insertion point.

Exiting a Program

When you no longer want to work in a program, you should follow the proper procedures for exiting the program to ensure that you don't damage files.

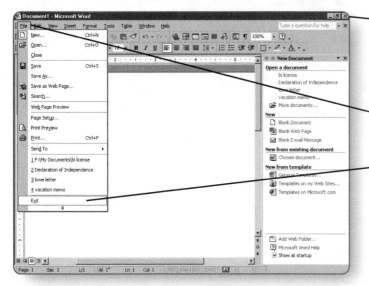

1a. **Click** on the **Close button**. The program will close.

OR

1b. **Click** on the **File menu**. The File menu will appear.

2. **Click** on **Exit**. The program will close.

NOTE

If you did any work in a document, a dialog box will appear asking whether you want to save your work. In Chapter 3, "Finding Common Ways to Work," you'll learn how to save documents.

2

Choosing Commands

You use commands to communicate with programs—
commands are your way of telling a program what you want it
to do. Most often, you issue commands by choosing them from
menus, but you also can issue commands using toolbars,
shortcut menus, and keyboard shortcuts. In this chapter, you'll
learn how to:

- Use the menu and keyboard to choose commands
- Make selections in dialog boxes
- Work with shortcut menus and toolbars
- Use the standard toolbar to fix mistakes
- Understand SmartTags

Discovering Personalized Menus

All Windows programs use menus to select commands and options from, but Office has a functionality called *personalized menus*. When the menu is first accessed, only the most common features are displayed. If you pause the mouse pointer over the main menu selection, or move it down to the double arrows at the bottom of a menu, the menu will expand to include all available features for that menu.

TIP

If you find you don't like using personalized menus, see "Separating Toolbars" later in this chapter for a tip on turning off the personalized menu feature.

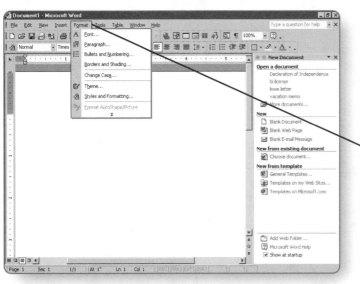

In this chapter, you'll use the Microsoft Word application. Start Word by clicking on the Start button in Windows and choosing Programs, Microsoft Word.

1. **Click** on **Format**. The Format menu will appear with eight options.

2. Pause the **mouse pointer** over the Format menu. The Format menu will expand to include more items.

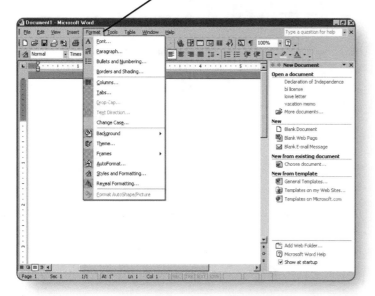

TIP

Click on the main menu selection (Format, in this example) to close a menu without making any selection.

When you see a right-pointing arrowhead in a menu (such as in the Background command), it means another menu is available.

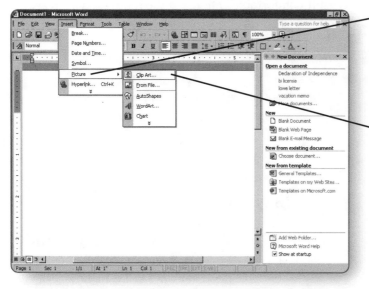

3. Move the **mouse pointer** down a menu to select any item with an arrow. The item will be highlighted and a submenu will appear.

4. Move the **mouse pointer** to the right of your selection in step 3. The first item in the submenu will be highlighted.

5. Click on a **selection** in the submenu. The feature associated with that menu item will be activated.

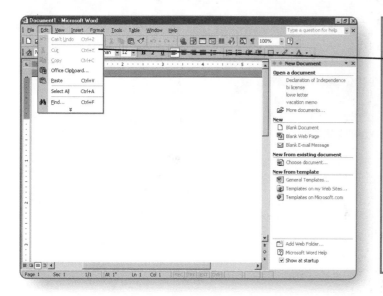

NOTE

Some options in a menu can appear *dimmed*, meaning that they are not available at this time. You probably need a document open or text selected before you can use items that are dimmed. For example, the Cut command is dimmed here because nothing is selected to be cut.

Choosing Commands with the Keyboard

If you're not comfortable with using the mouse, you can also open menus and choose commands using the keyboard.

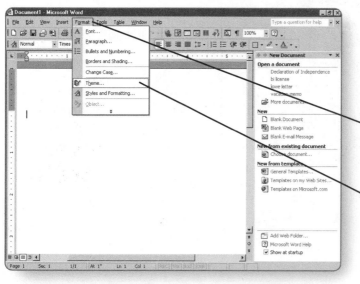

1. Press the **Alt key** on your keyboard. The menu bar will become active and a box will appear around the word "File" on the menu bar.

2. Press the **underlined letter** of a menu name. The menu will appear.

3. Press the **underlined letter** of a command name. The command will execute.

Press the Esc key twice to cancel out of the menu.

Using Shortcut Menus

Shortcut menus contain a limited number of commands. The commands you see on a shortcut menu depend on what you're doing at the time you open the shortcut menu. You always click the right mouse button (called a *right-click*) to open a shortcut menu.

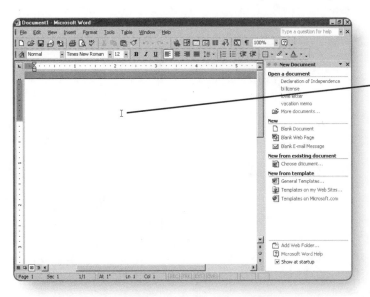

1. **Move** the **mouse pointer** into the document area. The pointer will appear as an I-beam.

2. **Press** the **right mouse button** (right-click). The mouse pointer will change to an arrow and the shortcut menu for regular text will appear in the working area of the document.

3. **Click** on a **menu selection**. The menu action will take place.

TIP

Press the Esc key or click on the working area to close a shortcut menu without choosing a command.

Working with Dialog Boxes

Many selections in the menu are followed by three periods, called *ellipses*. Selections followed by ellipses indicate that, if you select one of these items, a dialog box will appear with the next group of options. Word's Page Setup menu selection will display an example of such a dialog box.

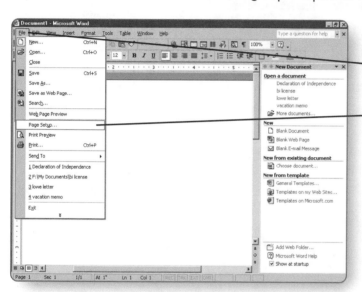

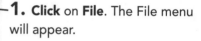

1. **Click** on **File**. The File menu will appear.

2. **Click** on **Page Setup**. The Page Setup dialog box will open.

Options have been grouped together by tabs in the dialog box. In this example, you can select from these groups: Margins, Paper, or Layout. You click on a tab to bring it to the front.

Depending on the dialog box, several types of selections will appear.

3. **Click** on the **Margins tab**. The Margins tab will display on top.

● **Spin Boxes.** Adjust numbers by clicking on the up and down arrows.

● **Drop-Down Lists.** You can select from drop-down lists by clicking on the down arrow and then clicking on a desired choice.

● **Option Buttons (not shown).** Select one of the available options by clicking on the small circle (or the words next to it). The selected option will display a small back dot in the circle.

4. **Click** on the **Layout tab**. The Layout tab will come to the top of the stack.

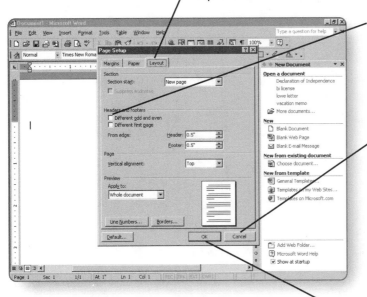

● **Check Boxes.** Turn features on or off by clicking on a box to insert or delete a check mark. Multiple check box options can be selected at once.

● **Command Buttons.** Usually indicated by an OK or Cancel button. Selecting OK tells Word to accept the choices you have made and close the dialog box. Selecting Cancel tells Word to ignore any changes you have made and close the dialog box.

5. Click on OK. The dialog box will close.

Working with Toolbars

As a wonderful time-saver, the Office applications include toolbars that include buttons to launch commonly used features. Any toolbar button function can be accessed through a menu, but may take a number of steps to get the feature. Using the toolbar button reduces the number of steps to 1.

Separating Toolbars

Most Office applications include two main toolbars, Standard and Formatting. By default, these two toolbars are displayed on the same line and unless you have an extremely large monitor screen, you can't see all the tools. I recommend you separate them into two toolbars.

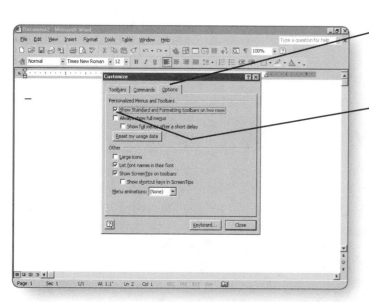

1. Open an **Office application**, for example Word.

2. Click on **Tools**. The Tools menu will appear.

3. Click on **Customize**. The Customize dialog box will open.

4. Click on the **Options tab**. The Options tab will appear in front.

5. Click on **Show Standard and Formatting toolbars on two rows**. A check mark will appear in the box.

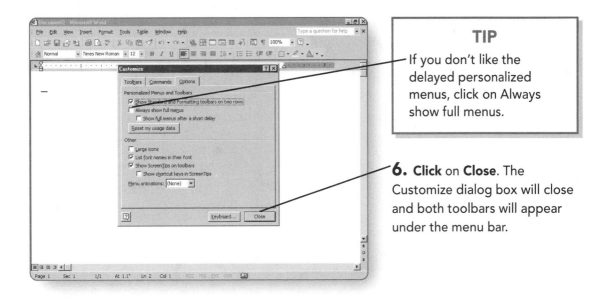

TIP

If you don't like the delayed personalized menus, click on Always show full menus.

6. Click on **Close**. The Customize dialog box will close and both toolbars will appear under the menu bar.

TIP

Pause the mouse pointer over a button to get a description of the tool.

Using the Standard Toolbar

There are several buttons on the Standard toolbar that are common to most Office applications. The following list describes these common buttons and their functions:

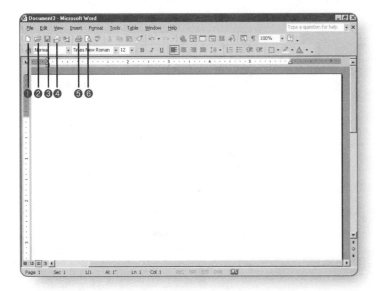

❶ **New.** Delivers a new blank document

❷ **Open.** Opens a previously created document

❸ **Save.** Saves a document

❹ **E-Mail.** E-mails a document. (Provided you have e-mail capability on your computer)

❺ **Print.** Prints a document

❻ **Print Preview.** Shows a document in full page

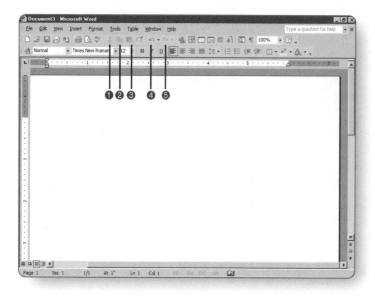

❶ **Cut.** Removes selected information to the Windows Clipboard

❷ **Copy.** Duplicates selected information to the Windows Clipboard

❸ **Paste.** Copies information on the Windows Clipboard to the current document

❹ **Undo.** Reverses the last action taken

❺ **Redo.** Reverses the most recent Undo step

Displaying Other Toolbars

There are a number of other toolbars with buttons appropriate to various tasks. You can display as many toolbars as you want, but each additional toolbar you display takes room away from your display for seeing your document.

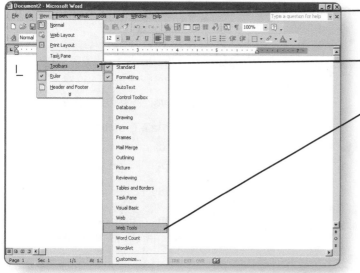

1. Click on **View**. The View menu will appear.

2. Click on **Toolbars**. The Toolbars submenu will appear.

3. Click on a **toolbar**. The toolbar will appear.

Some toolbars will appear at the top of your screen, some at the bottom of your screen, or some right in the middle of your screen. You'll learn how to move toolbars in the next section.

Moving Toolbars

Other toolbars will appear as you use certain features in Office applications. As toolbars appear on the screen, they might appear in an unsuitable location and you'll want to move them.

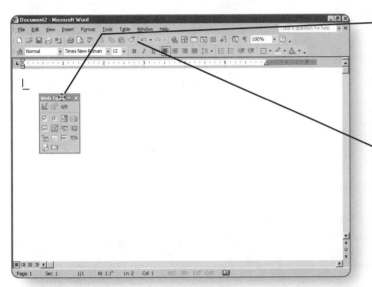

1. Press and hold the **mouse pointer** over the title bar of the toolbar. The mouse pointer turns into a four headed arrow.

TIP

If the toolbar you want to move doesn't have a title bar, for example, it is along the top or bottom of the screen, press and hold the mouse pointer along one of the light gray separation lines that appear in the toolbar.

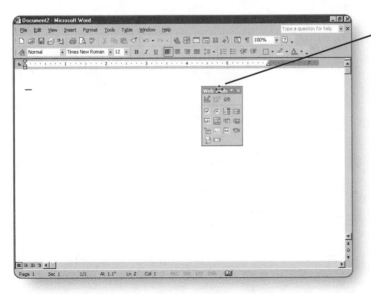

2. Press and drag the **title bar** to a new location. The toolbar will move along with the mouse.

3. Release the **mouse button**. The toolbar will remain in the new location.

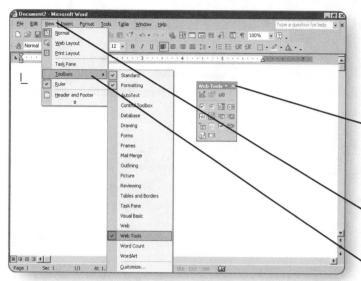

Closing Toolbars

If a toolbar is displayed and you no longer need it, you can easily close it.

1a. Click on the toolbar **close box**. The toolbar will close.

OR

1b. Click on **View**. The View menu will appear.

2. Click on **Toolbars**. The Toolbars submenu will appear.

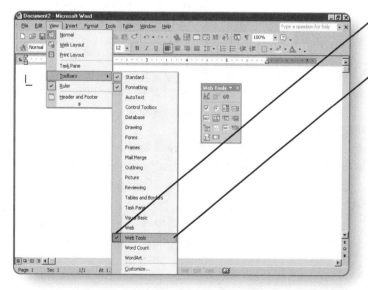

Currently displayed toolbars have a check mark next to them.

3. Click on the **toolbar** you want to close. The toolbar will close.

Understanding SmartTags

SmartTags are new to Office XP. *SmartTags* are small icons that appear throughout your document as you perform various tasks or enter certain types of text. SmartTags perform actions in Office applications that would normally require you to open other programs.

SmartTag functions range from quickly adding a name or address from your document to an Outlook contact folder to offering options when pasting data from the Clipboard.

The appearance of SmartTags will vary depending on the function, but all of them appear as small icons near the area in question.

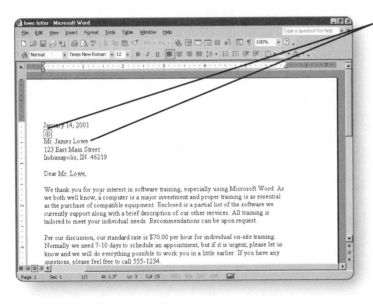

You might see text with purple dotted lines under it; Office recognizes that text as SmartTag text. As you move your mouse over the text, an indicator in the form of an icon will appear. Other times, the SmartTag will automatically appear depending on the function you used last.

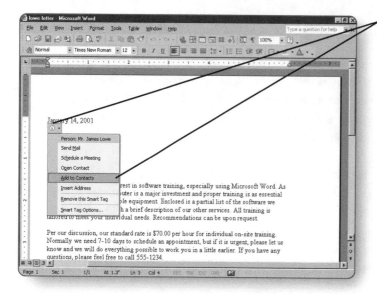

Clicking on the SmartTag icon will make a menu appear from which you can make additional choices. In this example, if you click on Add to Contacts, a contact card from Microsoft Outlook will appear with the name and possibly the address already entered. You'll learn about Outlook contacts in Chapter 19, "Working with the Address Book."

3

Finding Common Ways to Work

Microsoft Office applications let you perform tasks in the same way, regardless of the program in which you are working. In this chapter, you'll learn how to:

- Use the Task pane
- Preview a document before printing
- Print, save, and close a document
- Open an existing document
- Start a new document

Working with the Task Pane

New to Office XP is the Task pane. Most Office applications include the Task pane, with the exception of Outlook. Actually each application includes several different Task panes, each of which appears as you attempt various tasks. One feature of the Task pane assists you in creating new documents, whereas another function enables you to format your document more quickly.

Changing Task Panes

By default, Office displays the New Document Task pane. The New Document Task pane lists common features associated with creating a new document. As you select various functions of the application, the Task pane will change automatically.

See "Starting a Program" in Chapter 1 to refresh yourself on starting the Word application used in this chapter.

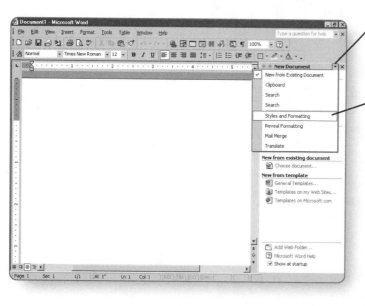

1. **Click** on the **Task pane drop-down arrow**. A list of other Task panes will appear.

2. **Click** on a **Task pane name**. The selected Task pane will appear.

Closing the Task Pane

You can close the Task pane during the current session of your current application, which will then redisplay the next time you start the program.

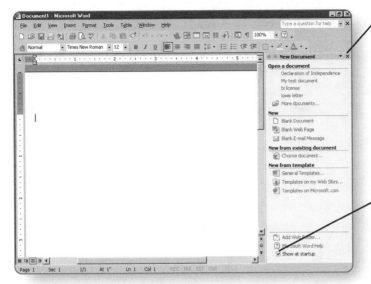

1. Click on the **Close button**. The Task pane will close.

If you choose a feature (such as mail merge in Word) that uses the Task pane, the Task pane will reappear.

Redisplaying the Task Pane

As previously mentioned, if you choose an Office feature that used the Task pane, it automatically reappears. You can, however, redisplay the Task pane whenever you want it.

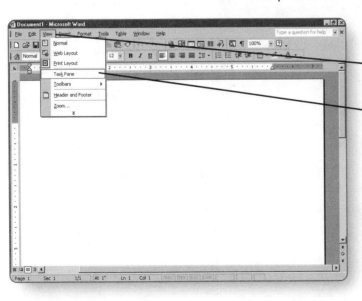

1. Click on **View**. The View menu will appear.

2. Click on **Task Pane**. The Task pane will reopen.

Adding Random Text

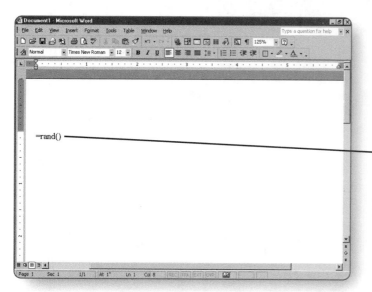

What you see (and the rest of the tasks covered in this chapter) is more meaningful when you have some text on-screen, so you'll start by letting Word add some random text.

1. Type =Rand() in the Word working area. The insertion point will move to the right as you type.

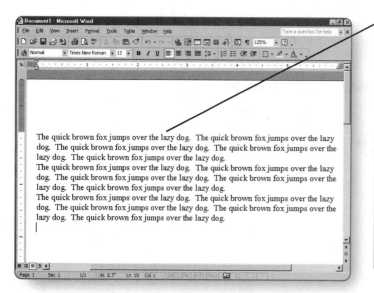

2. Press the **Enter key**. The text you typed will be replaced with several copies of the sentence "The quick brown fox jumps over the lazy dog."

NOTE

The text you typed was actually a formula that Word recognizes as meaning "Enter some sample text."

Previewing a Document

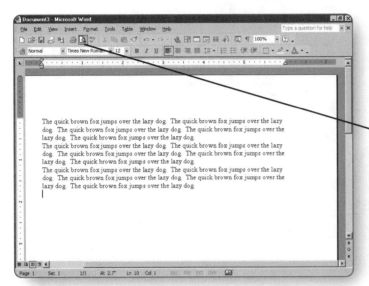

Print Preview is available in Word and Excel and is most helpful when you're trying to make sure information is aligned as you want it.

1. Click on the **Print Preview button**. Word and Excel will switch to Print Preview mode, in which you can see the layout and appearance of your document as it will appear when printed.

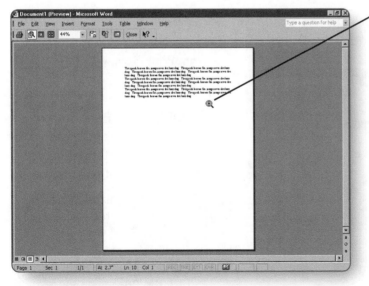

2. Move the **mouse pointer** over the document on-screen. The pointer will change to a magnifying glass.

3. Click on the **document**. It will enlarge (zoom in) so you can actually read the text.

NOTE
You must click on the portion of the document you want to enlarge.

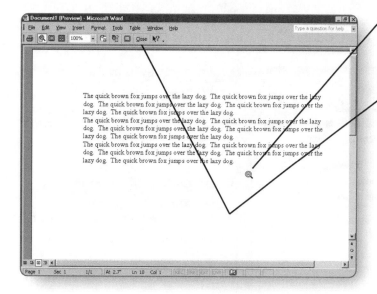

4. Click on the **document** again. The document will return to regular size.

5. Click on **Close**. The document will return to its previous view.

Printing a Document

When your document is complete, you'll probably want to print it. You can send it to your printer for a hard copy of the document.

Printing from the Toolbar

Each Office program contains a Print button on the standard toolbar that makes printing easy. In addition, you can print from Print Preview in both Word and Excel.

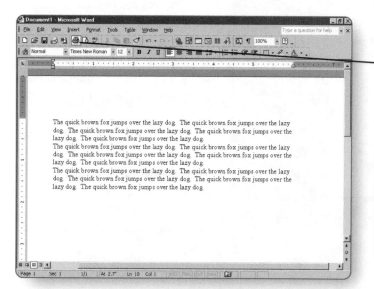

1. Click on the **Print button**. One copy of the entire document will be printed, without showing the Print dialog box.

NOTE

Clicking on the Print button in Outlook will display the Print dialog box.

Printing from the Menu

When electing to print from the menu, a dialog box will appear in which you can determine exactly what portion of the document to print, which printer to use, how many copies to print, and other printing options.

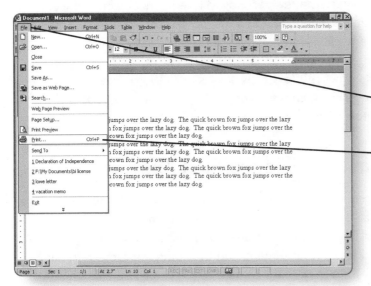

1. Click on **File**. The File menu will appear.

2. Click on **Print**. The Print dialog box will open.

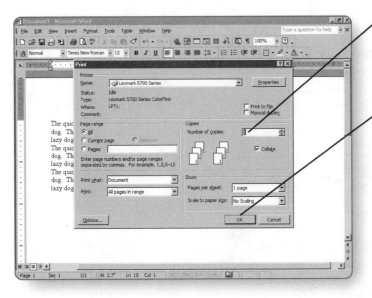

3. Make any desired **changes** in the Print dialog box. The dialog box will change to match your selections.

4. Click on **OK**. The document will be printed.

Saving Your Document

Anyone who uses a computer has probably lost data at one time or another. If you haven't been saving to disk regularly, it only takes a few seconds to lose hours of work. Office includes built-in features to help protect you against this eventuality. However, you still need to save on your own.

The process of saving is necessary in Word, Excel, and PowerPoint. Office saves Outlook and Access files automatically.

Saving a File the First Time

When you first create a file, it has no name. If you want to use that document later, it must have a name so the application can find it. The Office program asks for a name the first time you save the document, and then puts the name in the title bar at the top of the screen.

1. Click on **File**. The File menu will appear.

2. Click on **Save As.** The Save As dialog box will open.

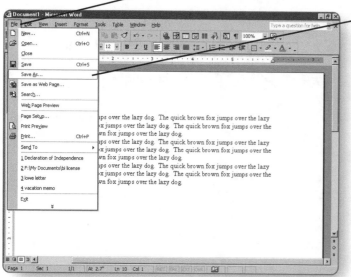

3. Type a **name** for your file in the File Name text box. The file name will be displayed.

File names can be up to 256 characters in length and can include spaces, dashes, and some other special characters, but cannot include the asterisk (*), slash (/), backslash (\) or question mark (?) characters.

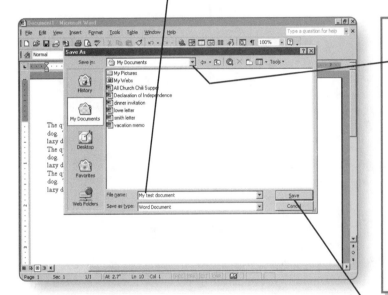

NOTE

The Save In drop-down list box lists folder options where you can save the file. The default folder that appears is "My Documents." If you don't want to save the file to this folder, or if you want to save your file to another disk, you can select another one. Click on the down arrow to browse your hard drive.

4. Click on **Save**. Your file will be saved and the name you specified will appear in the title bar.

Resaving a Document

As you continue to work on your document, resave it every 10 minutes or so to help ensure that you do not lose any changes.

1. Click on the **Save button**. The file will be resaved with any changes. No dialog box will appear because the file is resaved with the same name and in the same folder as previously specified.

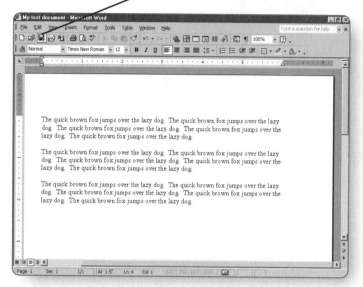

TIP

If you want to save the file with a different name or in a different folder, click on File, and then choose Save As. The Save As dialog box will prompt you for the new name or folder. You will have the original file as well as the new one.

Closing a Document

When you are finished working on a file, you should close it. *Closing* is the equivalent of putting it away for later use. When you close a file, you are only putting the document away—not the program. The application, Word for example, is still active and ready to work for you.

1a. Click on **File**. The File menu will appear.

2a. Click on **Close**. The file will be put away.

OR

1b. Click on the **document's Close button**. The file will be closed. By choosing this method, you combine steps 1 and 2.

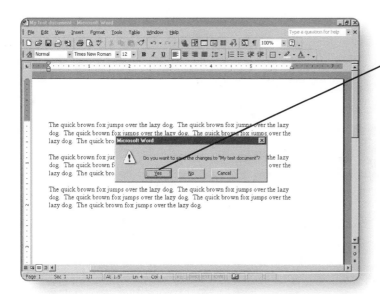

NOTE

If you close a file with changes that have not been saved, the application will prompt you with a dialog box. Choose Yes to save the changes or No to close the file without saving the changes.

Opening an Existing File

Opening a file is putting a copy of that file into the computer's memory and onto your screen so that you can work on it. If you make any changes, be sure to save the file again. Office provides several ways to open an existing file.

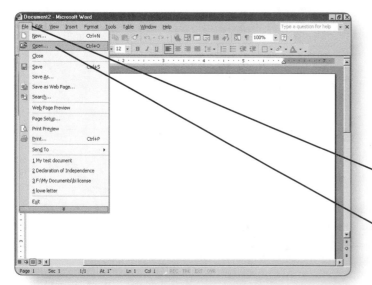

Displaying the Open Dialog Box

Office applications include an Open dialog box that lists all previously saved files located in a particular folder.

1. Click on **File**. The File menu will appear.

2. Click on **Open**. The Open dialog box will appear.

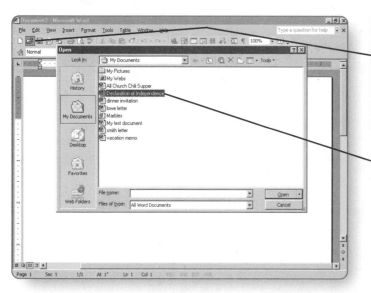

TIP

Optionally, click on the toolbar Open button to display the Open dialog box.

---

3. Click on the **file name** you want to open. The file name will be highlighted.

NOTE

If your file is located in a different folder than the one displayed in the Look In list box, click on the drop-down arrow to navigate to the proper folder.

4. Click on **Open**. The file will be placed on your screen, ready for you to edit.

TIP

Optionally, double-click on a file name to open the document.

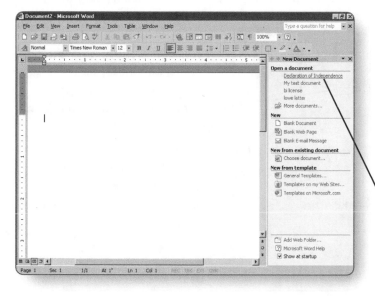

Opening a Recently Used Document

The Task pane lists several of the files you've recently used with the current Office application. You can quickly open a file using the Task pane.

1. From the Task pane, **click** on the **file name** you want to open. The file will appear on your screen.

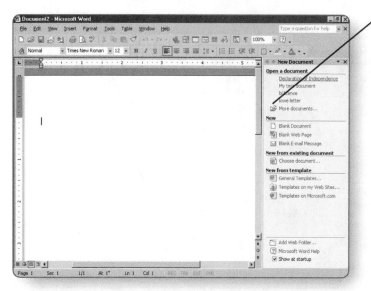

If the file you want isn't listed, click on More Documents to display the Open dialog box, from which you can select additional files.

TIP

Recently used files are also listed under the File menu.

Starting a New Document

When a Word, Excel, PowerPoint, or FrontPage session first begins, a new empty blank document appears ready for you to use. However, during the course of using one of these applications you might need to begin another new file.

1. Click on the **New button**. A new screen will appear.

If you are using Access, a blank screen doesn't automatically appear. Instead, the Task screen appears to assist you in selecting options. You'll learn more about Access in Part VI "Using Access".

4

Getting Help
with Office

Although you'll find many answers to your questions in this book, sometimes you need additional information. Microsoft supplies you with several types of assistance. In this chapter, you'll learn how to:

- Work with the Office Assistant
- Use the Help menu
- Get help on the Web

Using the Office Assistant

When you opened an Office application for the first time, what you probably noticed first was that cute little paper clip trying to get your attention. That's *Clippit* the Office Assistant, Office's Help feature. You can use Clippit to assist you with common tasks or help you understand a topic.

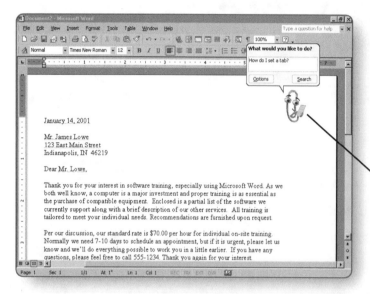

Asking the Assistant for Help

What sets Office Assistant apart from other help features is that you can use simple, everyday language to ask for assistance.

1. **Click anywhere** on the Office Assistant. A balloon will appear asking, "What would you like to do?" with an insertion point flashing in the white text box.

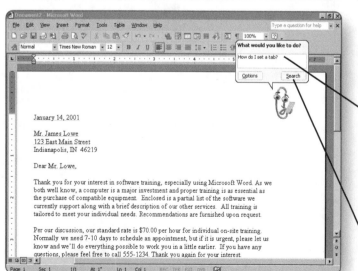

> ### TIP
> Pressing F1 also brings up the Assistant query window.

2. **Type** a **question** or just a word or two about what you need assistance with. An example might be: "How do I set a tab?" The text will appear in the white text box.

3. **Click** on **Search**. A new window will appear with more choices related to your topic.

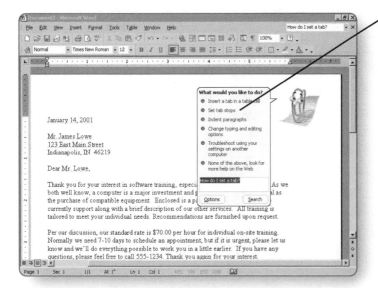

4. Click on a **topic**. The help information window will appear on your screen.

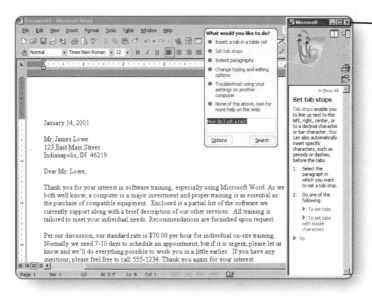

5. Click on the help **Close box** when you are finished reading the help topic. The help window will close and the original window will return to full size.

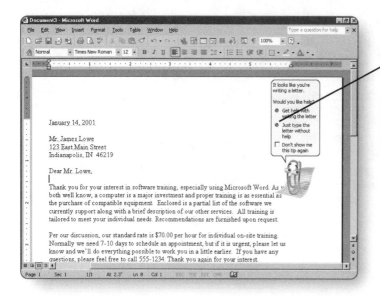

NOTE
Sometimes the Assistant will try to guess what you are doing and offer assistance. Click on an option when this happens.

Choosing a Different Assistant

Is Clippit, the helpful little piece of metal, getting a little dull or just not your style? There is a way to select a different icon for Office Assistant.

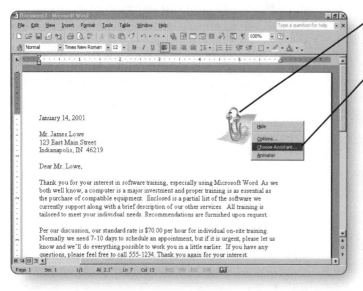

1. Right-click on the Assistant. A shortcut menu will appear.

2. Click on **Choose Assistant**. The Office Assistant dialog box will appear with the Gallery tab displayed.

3. Click on **Back** or **Next** to view other Assistants. A picture and description of the available assistants will appear.

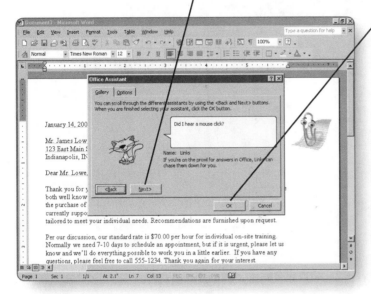

4. Click on **OK** when you see the one you want. The Office Assistant dialog box will close and you'll have a new helper!

NOTE

Depending upon the options selected when Office was installed, you might be prompted to insert your Office CD in order to install the new Assistant.

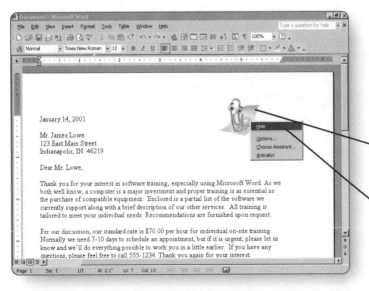

Hiding the Assistant

The Office Assistant is cute, but sometimes it's just in your way. You can hide the assistant and recall it whenever you need it.

1. Right-click on the Assistant. A shortcut menu will appear.

2. Click on **Hide**. The Office Assistant will disappear.

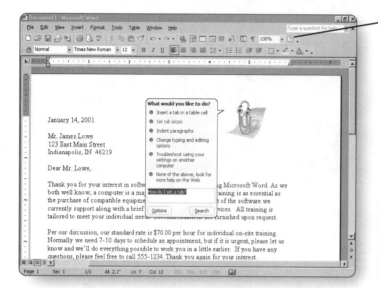

3. Click on the **Help button**. The Assistant will reappear.

NOTE

If the Assistant is in the way when you are typing text in your document, it will automatically move as your insertion point gets close to it. You can also move it manually by clicking on it and dragging it to a new location.

Turning Off the Assistant

If you find that you don't use the Assistant and don't want to see it, you can turn it off.

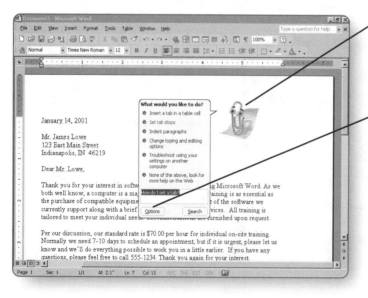

1. Click anywhere on the Office Assistant. The "What would you like to do?" balloon will appear.

2. Click on **Options**. The Office Assistant dialog box will open.

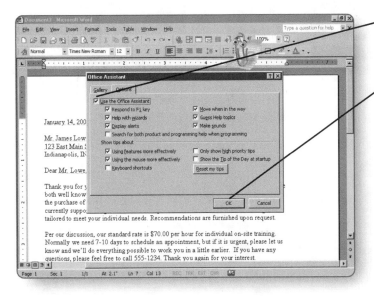

3. Click on **Use the Office Assistant**. The check mark will be removed from the box.

4. Click on **OK**. The Office Assistant will be turned off until you manually choose to use it again.

> **TIP**
>
> Click on Help and choose Use Office Assistant to return the Assistant to an active status.

Using What's This?

There are so many items on an Office application screen, it's hard to remember what each item is or does. You can use the *What's This?* feature to identify the various buttons and components:

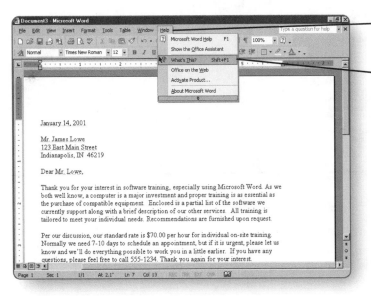

1. Click on **Help**. The Help menu will appear.

2. Click on **What's This?** The mouse pointer will change to a black pointer with a question mark.

> **TIP**
>
> Pressing Shift+F1 is another way to access the What's This? feature. You can also cancel the What's This? feature by pressing the Esc key.

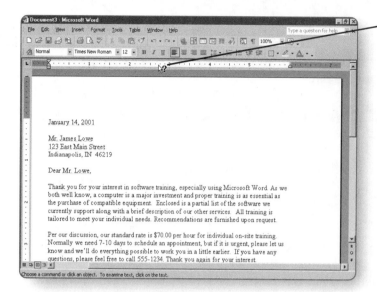

3. Click the **mouse pointer** over any button or item on the screen. A detailed information screen will appear and explain the item's function.

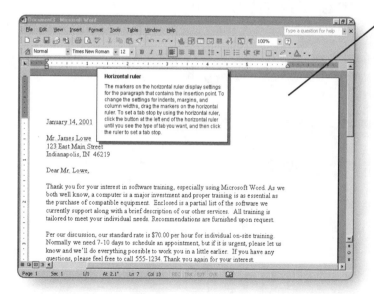

4. Click anywhere on the document window. The *What's This?* box will close.

Searching the Web for Help

If you have access to the Internet, Microsoft includes some wonderful assistance from its Web site.

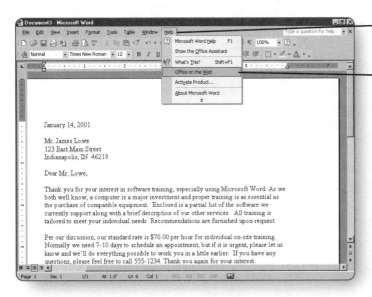

1. Click on the **Help command**. The Help menu will appear.

2. Click on **Office on the Web**. If you are not already connected to the Internet, you will be prompted to connect. Your Web browser will launch and a Microsoft Office Web page will display.

NOTE

Web pages change frequently. The Web page that you see might not be the same one displayed in this book.

3. Follow the **instructions** on the screen to access various help topics.

When you have completed accessing the Web help, you'll want to close the Internet Explorer window.

4. Click on the **Close button**. The Internet Explorer window will close.

You might be prompted to disconnect from your Internet Service Provider (ISP).

Part I Review Questions

1. How do you start an Office XP program? *See "Starting a Program" in Chapter 1*

2. Why should you follow proper procedures when exiting an Office XP program? *See "Exiting a Program" in Chapter 1*

3. What are personalized menus? *See "Discovering Personalized Menus" in Chapter 2*

4. How do you display a shortcut menu? *See "Using Shortcut Menus" in Chapter 2*

5. What must you do to access a drop-down list in a dialog box? *See "Working with Dialog Boxes" in Chapter 2*

6. Name three toolbar buttons that are common to the Office applications. *See "Using the Standard Toolbar" in Chapter 2*

7. What must you specify when saving a document? *See "Saving a File the First Time" in Chapter 3*

8. What happens when you try to close a document with changes that have not been saved? *See "Closing a Document" in Chapter 3*

9. What is the Office Assistant? *See "Using the Office Assistant" in Chapter 4*

10. What happens to the mouse pointer when you click on "What's This?" from the Help menu? *See "Using What's This?" in Chapter 4*

PART II

Using Word

5

Learning Word Basics

When you first start any Office program, including Word, you need to learn how to enter and manipulate information. If you don't have Word open on your screen, follow the steps in Chapter 1, "Welcome to Office XP," to open Word. In this chapter, you'll learn how to:

- Type, delete, and select text
- Insert special characters
- Use Undo and Redo
- Move around in a document
- Use Click and Type

Typing Text

Notice that there is a flashing vertical bar on your screen when you're in Word. This is called the *insertion point*. It marks the location where text will appear when you type.

If you type a few lines of text, you'll notice that you don't need to press the Enter key at the end of each line. The program automatically moves down or wraps to the next line for you. This feature is called *word wrap*. You only press the Enter key to start a new paragraph.

1. Type some **text**. The text will display on the screen.

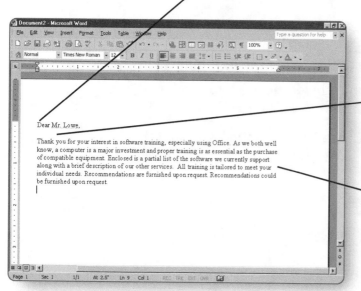

2. Press Enter. The insertion point will move down to the next line.

3. Press Enter again. The insertion point will move down another line, creating a blank line between your paragraphs.

4. Type a **paragraph** of text. Don't press Enter, just keep typing until you have several lines of text. The word wrap feature will take care of moving the insertion point down to the next line when necessary.

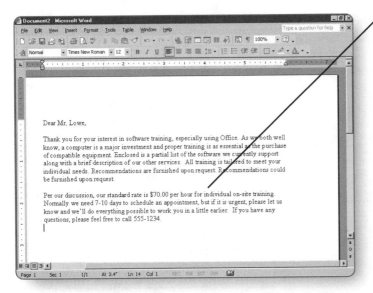

5. Continue typing text until your document is complete. The text you type will display on the screen.

TIP

Press the Enter key twice to end a paragraph and insert a blank line between the previous paragraph and the new paragraph.

Inserting, Selecting, and Deleting Text

Editing text with Word is a breeze. Need extra words? Just type them in. Need to delete words? Just highlight them and press the Delete key.

Inserting Text

Word begins in *insert* mode. This means that when you want to add new text to a document, simply place the insertion point where you want the new text to be and start typing.

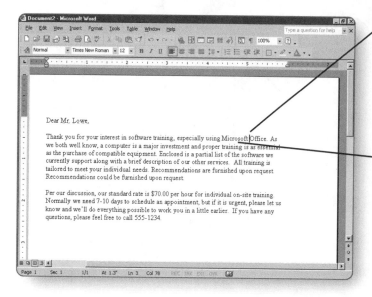

1. Click the **mouse pointer** directly in front of the word within the body of the document where you want new text to appear. The blinking insertion point will appear.

2. Type any **new word** or **phrase**, adding a space before or after as necessary. The new text is inserted into the document. Word will push the existing text to the right and keep moving it over or down to make room for the new text.

Selecting Text

To move, copy, delete, or change the formatting of text, select the text you want to edit. When text is selected, it will appear as light type on a dark background on your screen, the reverse of non-selected text. In previous versions of Microsoft Word, you could only select a sequential block of text at a time, not bits of text in different places. New to Word XP is the capability to select non-sequential blocks of text.

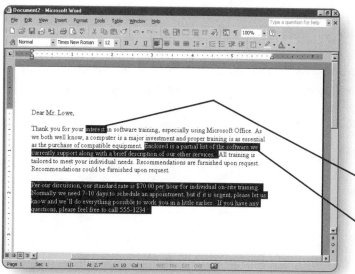

The following list shows different selection techniques:

- To select one word, double-click on the word.

- To select a sentence, hold down the Ctrl key and click anywhere on the sentence.

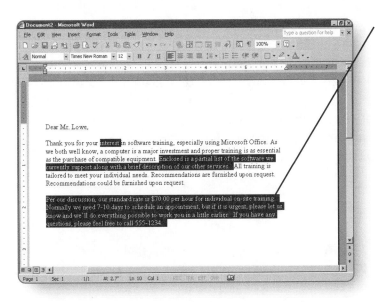

- To select an entire paragraph, click three times (triple-click) anywhere in the paragraph.

TIP

To select the entire document, press Ctrl+A or choose Edit, Select All.

To select a single line of text, move the mouse pointer to the left margin next to the line. The mouse pointer will change to an arrow. Click once.

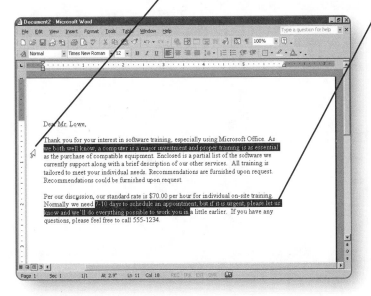

- To select a block of text, click at the beginning of the text, hold the mouse button down, and drag across the balance of the text to be selected.

- To select non-sequential blocks of text, hold down the Ctrl key and use the previous selection techniques for each additional text block you want to include.

TIP

To deselect text, click any-where in the document where the text is not highlighted.

Deleting Text

You can delete unwanted text one character, one word, and one paragraph at a time; or any combination of these. Two common keys used to delete text are the Backspace and the Delete keys. Pressing the Backspace key will delete one character at a time to the left of the insertion point, whereas pressing the Delete key will delete one character at a time to the right of the insertion point.

TIP

An easy way to remember which direction the Backspace key will delete is to look at the arrow printed on the Backspace key (most keyboards). The arrow points to the left, indicating this is the direction the characters are deleted.

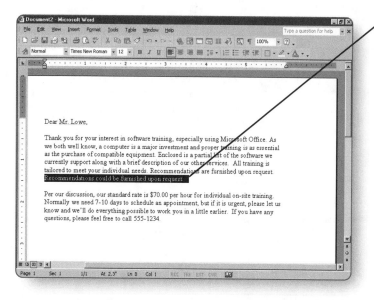

1. **Select** the **text** to be deleted. The text will be highlighted.

2. **Press** the **Delete key**. The text will be deleted.

Using Undo and Redo

If you want to restore text that you deleted, or reverse an action recently taken, use the Undo feature of Word. You're one click away from reversing your previous action.

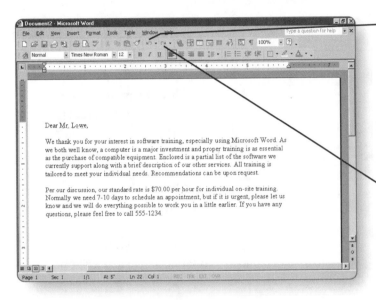

1. **Click** on the **Undo button**. The last action taken will be reversed.

If you chose to undo an action and then decided that you liked it better the way you had it, choose the Redo feature.

2. **Click** on the **Redo button**. The Undo action will be reversed.

Word keeps track of several steps that you have recently taken. When you undo a previous step, you'll also undo any actions taken after that step. For example, you changed the case of some text, and then you bolded and underlined the text. If you choose to undo the Change Case action, the bolding and underlining will also be reversed.

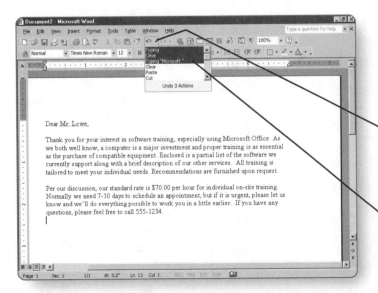

3. **Click** on the **arrow** next to the Undo button. A list of the most recent actions will be displayed.

4. **Click** on the **action** that you want to undo. The action will be undone as well as all actions above it on the list.

Inserting Special Characters or Symbols

Word includes hundreds of special characters and symbols for you to include in your document. Symbols include items like copyright or trademark symbols, stars, check marks, or small graphics.

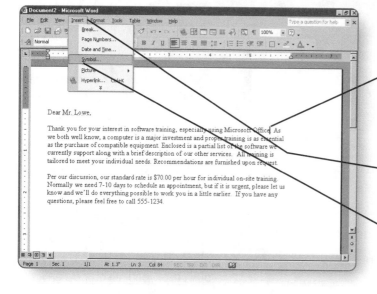

1. Click the **mouse** where you want the special character to appear. The blinking insertion point will appear.

2. Click on **Insert**. The Insert menu will appear.

3. Click on **Symbol**. The Symbol dialog box will open.

4. Click on the **down arrow** next to the Font list box. A list of fonts will appear.

5. Click on a **font**. The symbols available for that font will display.

TIP

For a large variety of unusual characters, look at the Monotype Sorts or the Wingdings fonts.

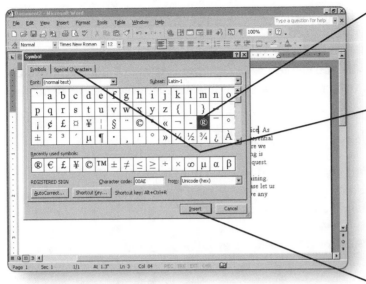

6. **Click** on a **character**. The character will appear selected.

7. **Click** on the **Insert button**. The symbol or character will be inserted into your document.

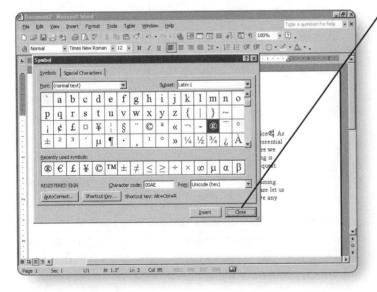

8. **Click** on the **Close button**. The symbol dialog box will close.

Moving Around the Screen

To work with your document, you'll need to place the insertion point. You can use several methods to move around the Word screen, and Word includes a feature called *Click and Type*.

Using Click and Type

With Click and Type, you can quickly position the insertion point anywhere on a page using the mouse and double-click where you want to enter text.

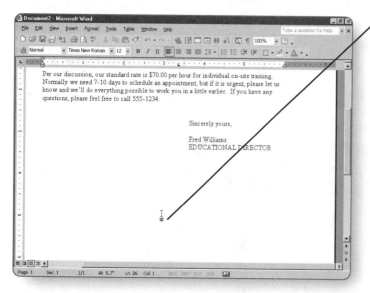

Before double-clicking the mouse, pay close attention to the position of the lines surrounding the pointer. If the lines are to the right of the I-beam, the text you type will be flow to the right of the insertion point. If the lines are to the left, the text will flow to the left of the insertion point. If the lines are under the I-beam, the text will be centered at the insertion point.

NOTE

If your mouse pointer doesn't appear with the little lines next to or below the mouse similar to the mouse in this figure, (make sure it's in the same position) the Click and Type feature might not be enabled. Click on Options from the Tools menu. On the Edit tab, check the Enable click and type box.

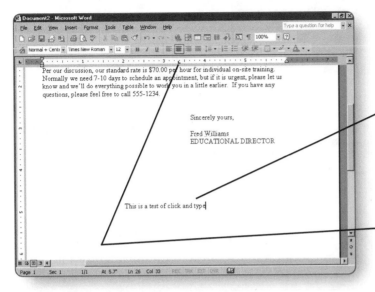

1. Double-click the **mouse pointer** anywhere on the white text area of the screen. A blinking insertion point will appear.

2. Type some **text**. The text will appear at the insertion point you clicked.

NOTE

Word is actually placing a tab stop at the position of the double-click. Tabs are covered in Chapter 6, "Formatting a Word Document."

Using the Scroll Bars

Two scroll bars are in the document window—a vertical scroll bar and a horizontal scroll bar. You can scroll through a document by clicking on the scroll bar's arrows. Scrolling through text using the scroll bars does not, however, move the insertion point. You need to click the mouse wherever you want the insertion point to be located.

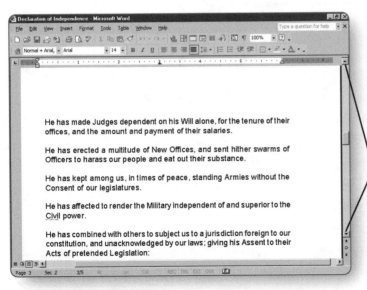

1a. Click on the **arrow** at either end of the vertical scroll bar. This will move the document up or down in the window.

OR

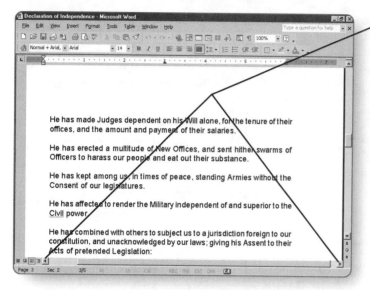

1b. **Click** on the **arrow** at either end of the horizontal scroll bar. This will move the document left or right.

Using the Keyboard to Move Around

As you've seen, you can work on any part of the document that shows on your screen simply by clicking the mouse pointer where you want to be. You can also move around in a Word document by pressing the Up, Down, Right, or Left Arrow keys on the keyboard. There are several additional shortcut keys designed to speed up the process of moving around in a Word document. The following table illustrates these shortcut keys.

To Move	Press
A word at a time	Ctrl+Right Arrow or Ctrl+Left Arrow
A paragraph at a time	Ctrl+Up Arrow or Ctrl+Down Arrow
A full screen up at a time	The PageUp key
A full screen down at a time	The PageDown key
To the beginning of a line	The Home key
To the end of a line	The End key
To the top of the document	Ctrl+Home
To the bottom of the document	Ctrl+End
To a specified page number	Ctrl+G; then enter the page number

Using the Go To Command

If you have a rather lengthy document, use the Go To command to jump to a specific location in the document.

1. Click on **Edit**. The Edit menu will appear.

2. Click on **Go To**. The Go To page of the Find and Replace dialog box will appear.

NOTE

Go To is one of those commands that might not appear immediately upon choosing the Edit menu. Hold the mouse over the Edit menu for a few seconds to display the full Edit menu.

TIP

Press Ctrl+G to quickly display the Go To page of the Find and Replace dialog box.

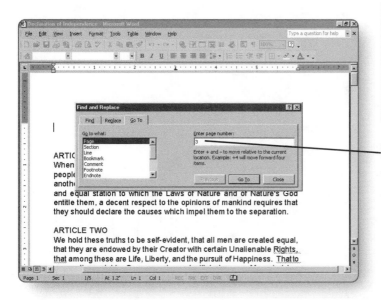

3. Type the **page number** you want to display. The number will appear in the Enter Page Number text box.

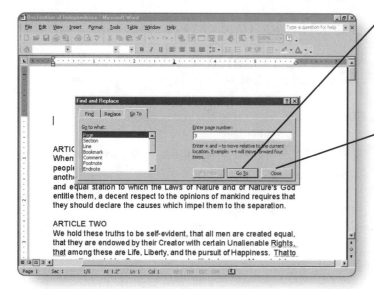

4. Click on the **Go To button**. The specified page will be displayed. The insertion point will be located at the beginning of the specified page.

5. Click on the **Close button**. The Go To dialog box will close.

6

Formatting a Word Document

Word includes several features to assist you in making your text look just the way you want it to. You can change fonts and sizes, align text on a page, or even create bulleted or numbered lists. In this chapter, you'll learn how to:

- Change fonts, font sizes, and font appearances
- Arrange text on a page
- Move and copy text and formatting
- Create bulleted and numbered lists

Enhancing Text

Enhancing text is the process of changing its appearance. For example, you can change fonts or point sizes or add embellishments, such as boldface, italic, or underline.

Changing the Font

The *font* is the typeface of the text. Windows comes with a variety of fonts, and Office adds some additional fonts. Other programs installed on your computer might also install fonts.

1. Select some **text** in the document. The text will be highlighted.

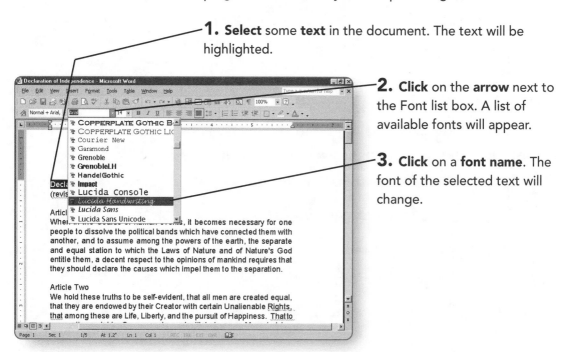

2. Click on the **arrow** next to the Font list box. A list of available fonts will appear.

3. Click on a **font name**. The font of the selected text will change.

Changing the Font Size

The *font size* controls how large the font appears. Each font can be used in a number of sizes. Font sizes are measured in *points*, and a point is $1/72$ of an inch.

1. Select some **text** in the document. The text will be highlighted.

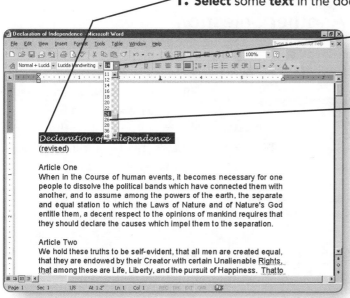

2. Click on the **arrow** next to the Font Size list box. A list of available font sizes will appear.

3. Click on a **font size**. The size of the selected text will change.

Applying Bold, Italic, or Underline

Applying formatting attributes such as **bold**, *italic*, or <u>underline</u> will call attention to particular parts of your text. You can easily access these choices with the Word toolbar.

1. Select the **text** to be formatted. The text will be highlighted.

2. Click on the appropriate **toolbar button**: either **B** for bold, *I* for italic, or <u>U</u> for underline, or any combination of the three. The formatting will be applied. You can repeat the previous steps to remove the attribute.

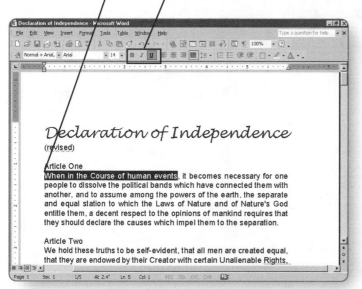

TIP

Shortcut keys include Ctrl+B for bold, Ctrl+I for italic, and Ctrl+U for underline. Pressing these key combinations once activates the formatting and pressing them again removes the formatting.

Copying Formatting to Another Selection

If you spend several minutes setting up just the right formatting for a heading that will appear multiple times in a long document, you don't have to try to remember your selections and repeat them each time. Instead, you can use the Format Painter tool.

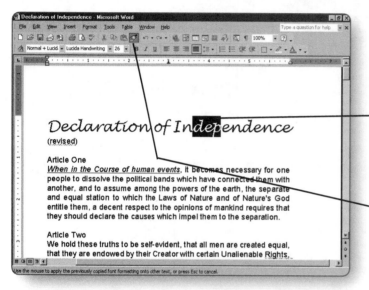

1. **Select** any of the **text** that has the formatting you want to use elsewhere. The text will be highlighted.

2. **Click** on the **Format Painter button**. The mouse pointer will change to a paintbrush.

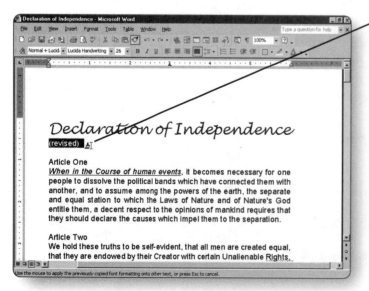

3. **Press** and **hold** the **mouse button** and **drag** over the text to be formatted. The new text becomes highlighted. (If you want to apply the formatting to just one word, you can simply click anywhere in that word.)

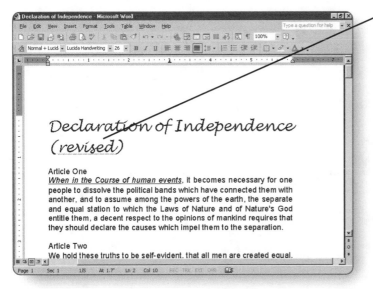

4. Release the **mouse button**. The new text take on the attributes of the original text

---

TIP

To use the Format Painter function repeatedly, double-click on the Format Painter button. When you're finished using the Format Painter function, click on the button again to turn it off.

Changing Text Case

When you need to change the capitalization of text, Word provides an easy way to change it without retyping.

1. Select the **text** to be changed. The text will be highlighted.

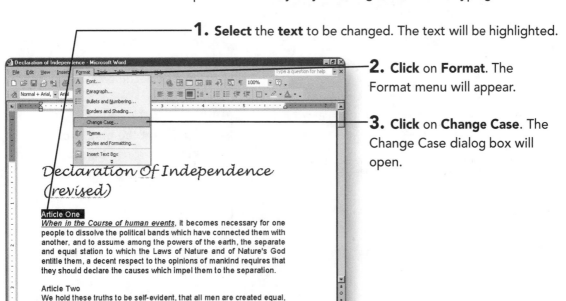

2. Click on **Format**. The Format menu will appear.

3. Click on **Change Case**. The Change Case dialog box will open.

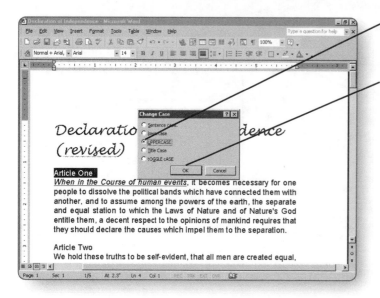

4. Click on a **case option**. The option will be selected.

5. Click on **OK**. The text will be modified.

Working with Bulleted or Numbered Lists

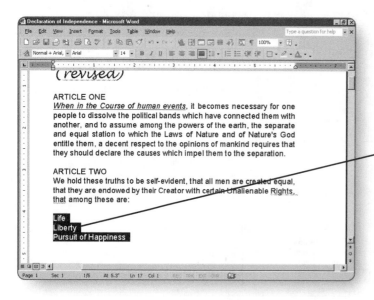

Everyone uses lists—from shopping lists and check lists to meeting agendas and outlines. Word can help you format lists in your documents automatically.

1. Select the **text** to be bulleted or numbered. The text will be highlighted.

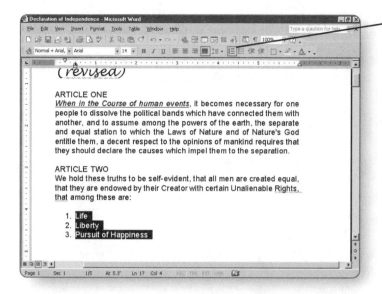

2a. **Click** on the **Numbering button** on the toolbar. The list will have numbers applied to it.

OR

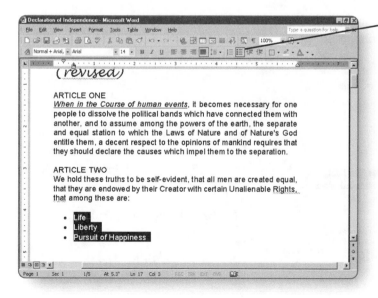

2b. **Click** on the **Bullets button** on the toolbar. The list will have bullets applied to it.

TIP

Repeat the previous steps to remove the bullets or numbering.

Arranging Text on a Page

Arranging text includes indenting text and modifying line spacing as well as aligning text horizontally.

Aligning Text

Alignment arranges the text to line up at one or both margins, or centers it across the page. Like line spacing, alignment is usually applied to an entire paragraph or document.

You can align paragraphs of text to the left, right, or in the center. You can also *justify* your text, which means that the text will be evenly spaced across the page from the left edge to the right edge.

1. **Select** the **text** that you want to align. The text will be highlighted.

2. **Click** on the appropriate **alignment button**:

❶ **Align Left**. The text will be aligned at the left margin. This is the default choice in Word.

❷ **Center**. The text will be centered.

❸ **Align Right**. The text will be aligned at the right margin.

❹ **Justify**. The text will be evenly spaced across the page.

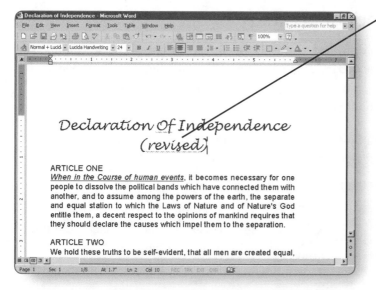

The selected text will realign according to the option you selected (centered in this example).

Changing Line Spacing

Line spacing is the amount of vertical space between each line of text. You might want to change line spacing when you want to make a document easier to read, for example, or for a draft so that the reader has room to make changes.

1. Select the **text** in which you want to change the line spacing. The text will be highlighted.

2. Click on the **Line Spacing button**. Line spacing options will appear.

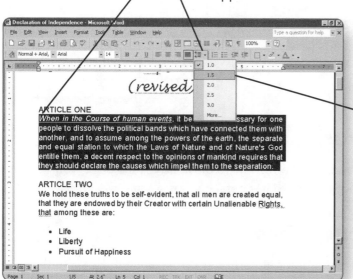

You can select from single spacing (1.0), one and one-half line spacing (1.5), or double spacing (2.0).

3. Click on an **option.** The new spacing selection is applied to the highlighted text.

TIP

Shortcut keys to set line spacing are: Ctrl+1 for single spacing, Ctrl+2 for double spacing, and Ctrl+5 for 1.5 line spacing.

Indenting Text

To draw the reader's attention to certain text, you sometimes want to indent that text so it doesn't line up with the left margin. Word includes a toolbar button to help you quickly indent your text.

1. **Select** the **text** to be indented. The text will be highlighted.

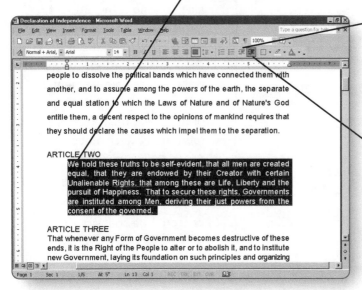

2a. **Click** on the **Increase Indent button**. The selected text will move ½ inch from the left margin.

OR

2b. **Click** on the **Decrease Indent button**. The selected text will move ½ inch closer to the left margin.

TIP

Each time you click on an indent button, the text will indent an additional ½ inch.

Working with Tabs

If you press the Tab key to move across the page, you'll notice that Word has default stops set at every ½ inch.

Setting Tabs

You can set tabs at particular points along the ruler so that when you press the Tab key, the cursor moves to that point automatically, instead of stopping every five spaces.

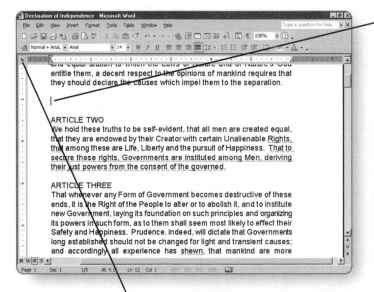

1. Click the **mouse pointer** at the location you want to create a tabbed paragraph. The blinking insertion point will appear.

2. Click the **mouse pointer** on the Tab button at the left end of the ruler to select from the following alignments:

- **Left**. The Tab button is already set to the left tab symbol, an "L." Text will appear with the left edge of the text at the tab.

- **Center**. Click one time to display the center tab symbol. An upside down "T" will appear. Text will center around a center tab.

- **Right**. Click two times to display the right tab symbol. A backward "L" will appear. Text will appear with the right edge of the text at the tab.

- **Decimal**. Click three times to display the decimal tab symbol. An upside-down "T" with a dot on the right will appear. Decimal points, such as dollars and cents, align to the tab. The decimal tab is selected in this example.

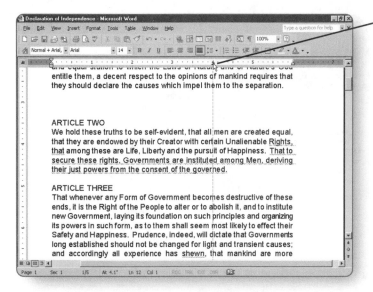

3. **Click** on the **ruler** to set the tab for the current paragraph or any currently selected text. A left, right, center, or decimal tab symbol will appear in the ruler at the spot you selected.

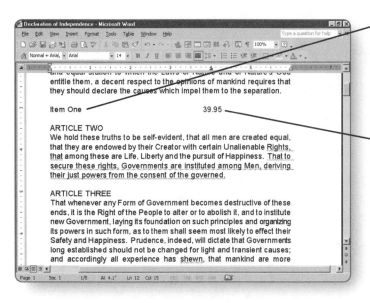

4. **Click** in the **paragraph** and **press** the **Tab key.** This moves the insertion point to the tab where you want the text to appear.

5. **Type** some **text**. The text will conform to the chosen tab. This example shows the decimal tab alignment.

Moving Tabs

If you don't like the position of a tab stop, you can easily move it!

1. Select the **paragraphs** that have a tab that needs to be moved. The text will be highlighted.

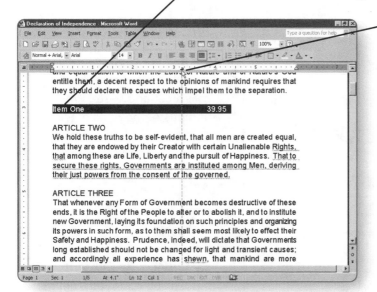

2. Drag the **current tab setting** to the desired location on the ruler bar. A vertical dotted line helps you visualize the new tab position.

3. Release the **mouse button**. The tab will be reset and any text will be moved.

Deleting Tabs

Deleting an unwanted tab stop is an easy process when using Words' ruler.

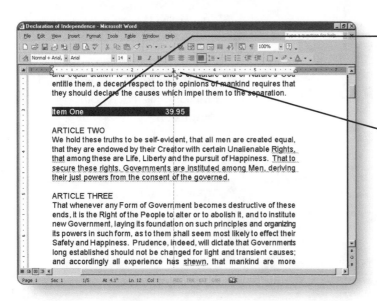

1. Select the **paragraphs** that have a tab that you want to delete. The text will be highlighted.

2. Drag the **current tab setting** off the ruler, into the body of the document. As you are dragging across the ruler, a vertical dotted line will appear.

3. Release the **mouse button**. The tab will be deleted.

Moving or Copying Text

Windows includes a feature called the *Clipboard*, which lets you hold information temporarily. Microsoft Word, as well as the other Office applications, uses the Clipboard feature to move or copy text from one place to another.

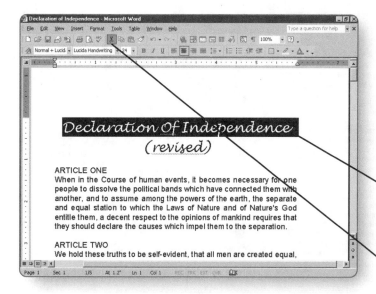

Moving Text

The feature used to move text from one place to another is called *cut and paste*. With cut and paste, the original text is deleted and placed in the new location.

1. **Select** the **text** to be moved. The text will be highlighted.

2. **Click** on the **Cut button**. The text will be removed from the document, and will be stored on the Windows Clipboard.

3. **Click** the **mouse** where you want the text to be located. The blinking insertion point will appear.

4. **Click** on the **Paste button**. The text will be placed at the new location.

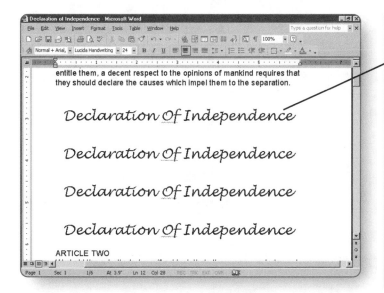

Copying Text

The process of copying text will leave the text in its original location while a copy of it is placed on the Windows Clipboard.

1. **Select** the **text** to be copied. The text will be highlighted.

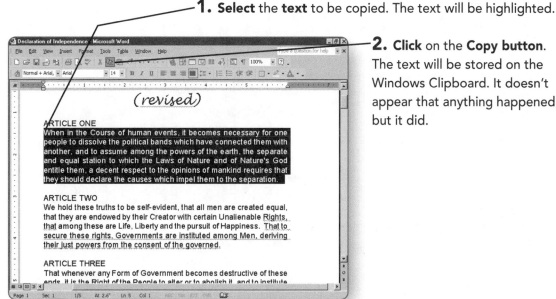

2. **Click** on the **Copy button**. The text will be stored on the Windows Clipboard. It doesn't appear that anything happened, but it did.

3. Click the **mouse** where you want the text to be located. The blinking insertion point will appear.

4. Click on the **Paste button**.

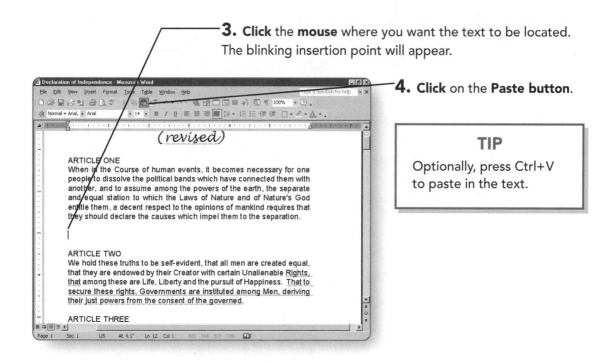

TIP

Optionally, press Ctrl+V to paste in the text.

The text will be placed at the new location, yet remains at the original location as well.

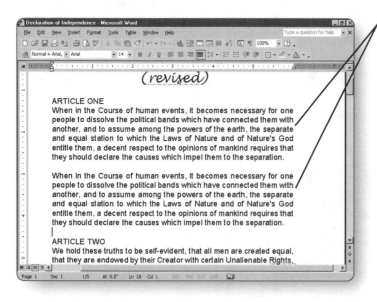

Using Drag-and-Drop

Another method of moving text from one location to another is to use the drag-and-drop method. The drag-and-drop method works best when you're moving a small amount of text a short distance:

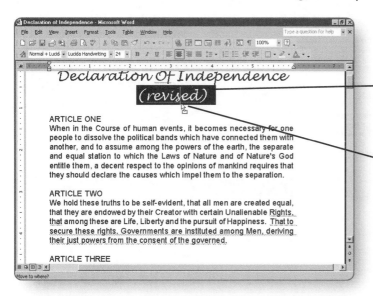

1. Select the **text** to be moved. The text will be highlighted.

2. Position the **mouse pointer** on top of the highlighted text. The white mouse arrow will point to the left.

3. Hold down the **mouse button** and **drag** the **mouse** to the desired location. A small box will appear at the bottom of the mouse arrowhead and a gray line will indicate the position of the text.

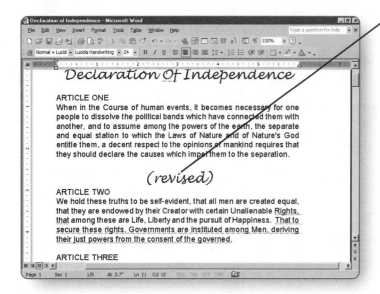

4. **Release** the **mouse button**. The text will be moved.

TIP

To copy text with drag-and-drop, hold down the Ctrl key before dragging the selected text. Release the mouse button before releasing the Ctrl key.

7

Improving Your Writing

Whatever you're writing, spelling or grammatical errors can ruin the impression that you're trying to create. Word has spelling and grammar checkers to correct these errors and several other tools to improve your writing. In this chapter, you'll learn how to:

- Use AutoCorrect and AutoFormat
- Find and replace text
- Find and correct spelling and grammatical errors
- Use the Thesaurus

Working with AutoCorrect and AutoFormat

AutoCorrect is a great feature. If you type something wrong, Word automatically corrects it. Or, if you type "(c)" and Word interprets it as a copyright symbol, it will insert ©.

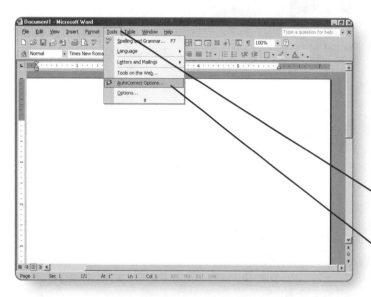

Adding AutoCorrect Entries

If you know that you commonly make the same typing mistake, such as typing "clcik" when it should be "click," you can instruct Word to fix it for you.

1. Click on **Tools**. The Tools menu will appear.

2. Click on **AutoCorrect Options**. The AutoCorrect dialog box will open with the AutoCorrect tab in front.

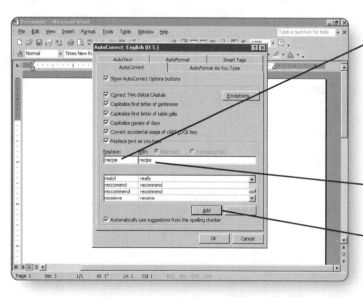

3. Type your **common mistake** in the Replace text box. The text will display.

4. Click in the **With text box**. A blinking insertion point will display.

5. Type the **correct word spelling.** The text will display.

6. Click on **Add.** The word will be added to your permanent AutoCorrect list.

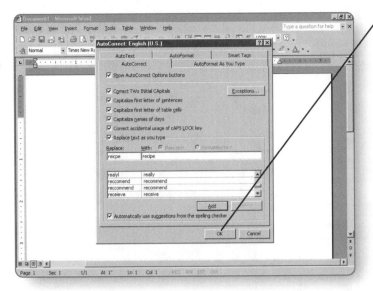

7. Click on **OK**. The dialog box will close.

Now, Word will automatically correct your mistake each time you type it and press the spacebar or a punctuation mark.

Deleting AutoCorrect Entries

What if you're typing an article about common misspellings and you *want* to type the word "teh" or you want to use "(c)" to indicate a heading in a report, but Word keeps changing them?

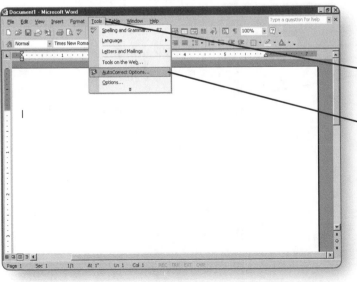

1. Click on **Tools**. The Tools menu will appear.

2. Click on **AutoCorrect Options**. The AutoCorrect dialog box will appear with the AutoCorrect tab in front.

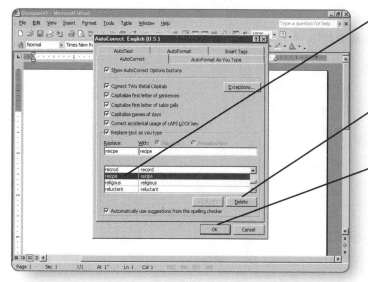

3. Click on an **entry** from the AutoCorrect list. The entry will appear in the Replace and With text boxes.

4. Click on **Delete**. The entry will be deleted.

5. Click on **OK.** The AutoCorrect dialog box will close.

Exploring AutoFormat As You Type

Word can also format text as you are typing it. This can include automatically creating bulleted and numbered lists or replacing fractions with fraction characters.

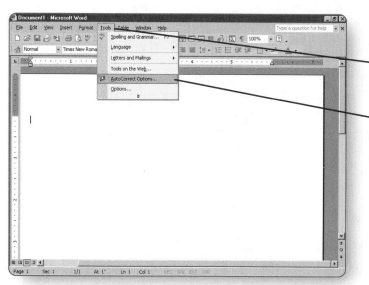

1. Click on **Tools**. The Tools menu will appear.

2. Click on **AutoCorrect Options**. The AutoCorrect dialog box will open.

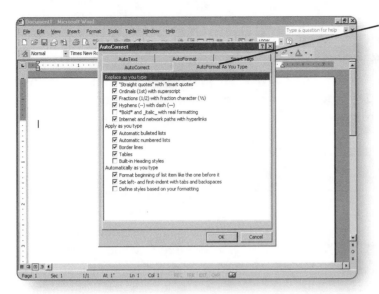

3. Click on the **AutoFormat As You Type tab.** The AutoFormat As You Type tab will come to the front. More automatic features are available from this tab.

4. Click on any **option** that you want to apply. A selected option will have a check mark in the box next to it. You'll notice options such as the following:

- Word can apply "smart quotes," change 1st to 1st, make 1/2 into ½, and more!

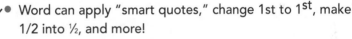

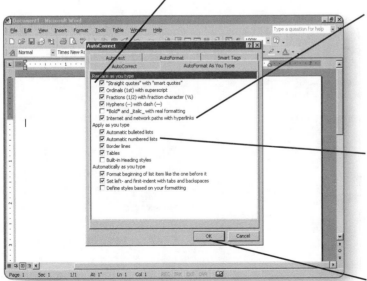

- When you type a Web or e-mail address in a document, Word can automatically turn the address into a hyperlink. You can then click on the link to launch your Web browser or e-mail program.

- Word can generate automatic bulleted or numbered lists. For example, type a 1. and then some text and press Enter. Word automatically starts the next line with 2.

5. Click on **OK.** The Auto-Correct dialog box will close.

Using Find and Replace

Word's Find and Replace features are real time savers. You can quickly find out whether you covered a topic in a lengthy report, and you can change names, dates, and prices throughout documents with just a few keystrokes.

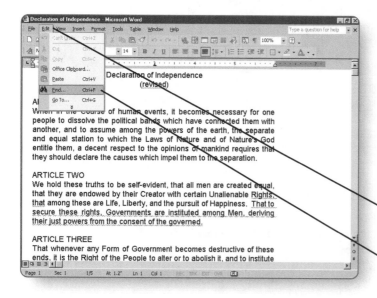

Using Find

Word's Find command is useful to seek out text in a document that you have trouble visually locating. The Find command does not change any text, it simply locates and highlights it for you.

1. Click on **Edit**. The Edit menu will appear.

2. Click on **Find**. The Find and Replace dialog box will open.

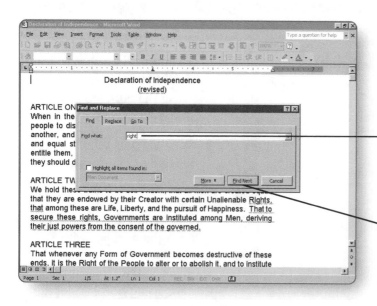

TIP

Optionally, press Ctrl+F to open the Find and Replace dialog box.

3. Type the **word** or **phrase** you want to locate. The typed text will appear in the Find What text box.

4. Click on **Find Next.** Word will take you to the first occurrence of the search word or phrase.

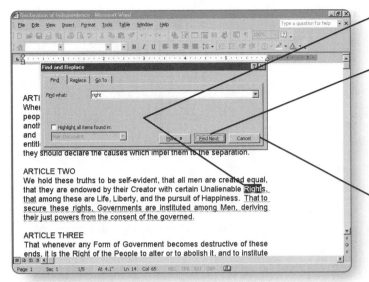

The first occurrence of the word or phrase is highlighted.

5. Click on **Find Next** again. Word will take you to the next occurrence of the word or phrase that you're looking for.

TIP

Click on Cancel if you want to discontinue the search.

Word will notify you when there are no more occurrences of the search text.

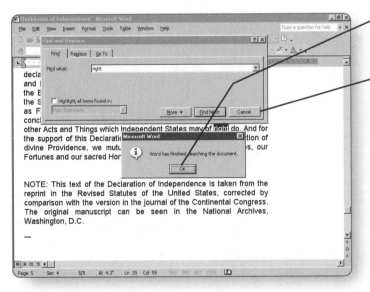

6. Click on **OK**. The message box will close.

7. Click on **Cancel**. The Find and Replace dialog box will close.

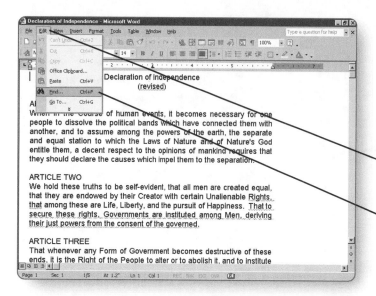

Finding All Occurrences

New to Word 2002 is the ability to find and highlight all occurrences of your search text.

1. Click on **Edit**. The Edit menu will appear.

2. Click on **Find**. The Find and Replace dialog box will open.

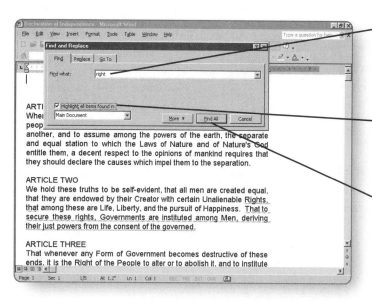

3. Type the **word** or **phrase** you want to locate. The typed text will appear in the Find What text box.

4. Click on the **Highlight all items found in check box.** The option will be selected.

5. Click on **Find All.** Word highlights all occurrences of the search word or phrase.

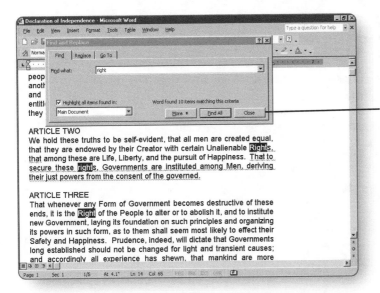

After you've examined the found occurrences, you'll need to close the Find and Replace dialog box.

6. Click on **Close**. The Find and Replace dialog box will close.

Using Replace

If you want to locate text and change it to something else, let Word do it for you with the Replace feature.

1. Click on **Edit**. The Edit menu will appear.

2. Click on **Replace**. The Find and Replace dialog box will open.

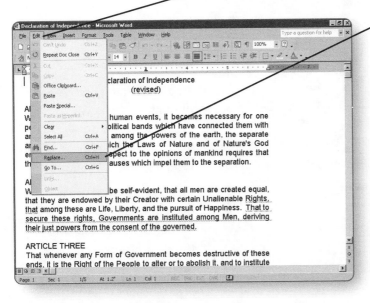

3. **Type** the **text** for the search. The text will appear in the Find What text box.

4. **Click** in the **Replace With text box**. The blinking insertion point will appear.

5. **Type** a **replacement word or phrase**. The text will appear in the Replace With text box.

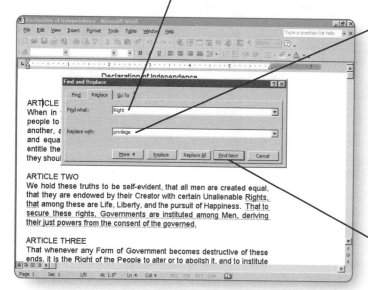

> **TIP**
>
> To delete the "found" text, leave the Replace With box empty. You'll be replacing the found text with nothing.

6. **Click** on **Find Next**. Word will highlight the first match.

7. **Choose one** of the following:

- **Replace.** The text will be replaced and Word will highlight the next match.

- **Replace All**. All occurrences of the found text will be replaced with the new text and you will be notified of the total number of replacements.

- **Find Next**. Word will not make any changes to this occurrence and will jump to the next occurrence of the text.

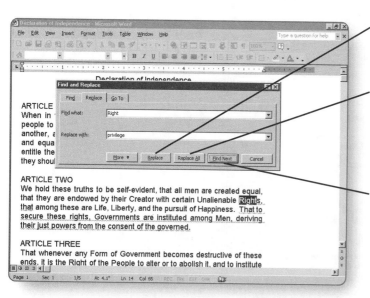

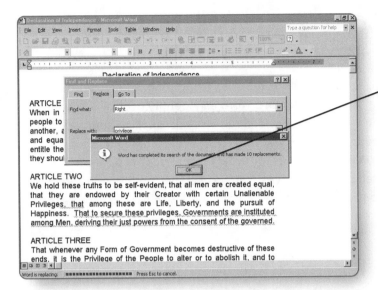

Word will notify you when there are no more occurrences of the search text.

8. Click on **OK**. The message box will close.

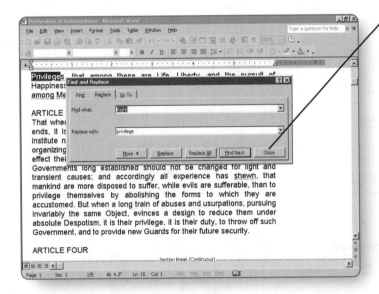

9. Click on **Close**. The Find and Replace dialog box will close.

Correcting Spelling and Grammatical Errors

Word has built-in dictionaries and grammatical-rule sets to check your document. Word can identify possible problems as you type, and it also can run a special spelling and grammar check to provide you with more information about the problems and tools for fixing them. These features aren't infallible—if you type "air" instead of "err," Word probably won't catch it. However, combined with a good proofreading, these tools can be very helpful.

Checking Spelling as You Go

By default, Word identifies problems right in your document as you type. Spelling errors have a red wavy line underneath them, whereas grammatical errors are indicated with a green wavy line.

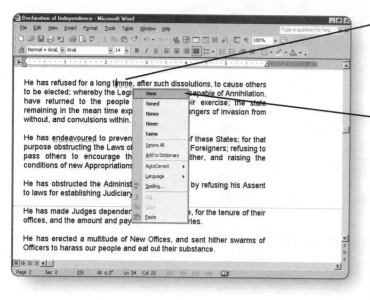

1. Right-click on the questionable **word.** The shortcut menu will appear with suggested corrections.

2. Click on the **correct spelling** or **grammatical suggestion.** The erroneous word will be replaced with your selection.

NOTE

Sometimes, Word cannot give a suggested grammatical suggestion. In those cases, you'll need to correct the error yourself.

TIP

Do *not*, repeat do *NOT*, rely on the spell check and grammar features to catch all errors. They are far from perfect and can miss many items. They can also flag errors when your text is really okay, and can suggest wrong corrections to both real problems and false error reports. You are the only one who knows what your document intends to say. Proofread it yourself!

Running a Spelling and Grammar Check

By default, Word can run both a spelling and grammar check at the same time.

1. Click on **Tools**. The Tools menu will appear.

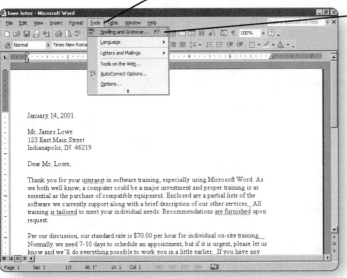

2. Click on **Spelling and Grammar**. The Spelling and Grammar dialog box will open.

The first error encountered, whether spelling or grammar, will be displayed. If it's a spelling error, it is identified in the Not in Dictionary text box. In the Suggestions text box, there are possible correct spellings for the word.

The misspelled word appears highlighted in its sentence.

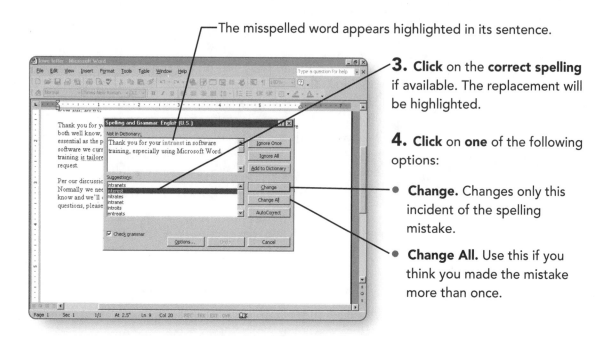

3. Click on the **correct spelling** if available. The replacement will be highlighted.

4. Click on **one** of the following options:

- **Change.** Changes only this incident of the spelling mistake.

- **Change All.** Use this if you think you made the mistake more than once.

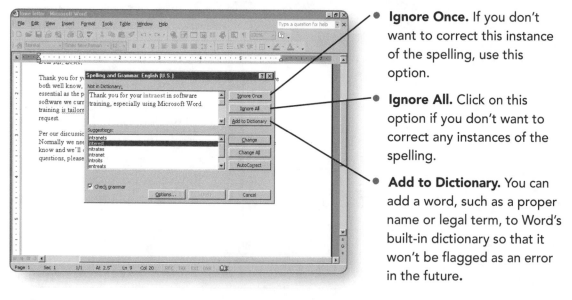

- **Ignore Once.** If you don't want to correct this instance of the spelling, use this option.

- **Ignore All.** Click on this option if you don't want to correct any instances of the spelling.

- **Add to Dictionary.** You can add a word, such as a proper name or legal term, to Word's built-in dictionary so that it won't be flagged as an error in the future.

After you choose one of these actions, the check will proceed to the next possible error.

If Word finds a grammatical error, it will display it in the top text box, with a suggested revision or explanation of the error in the Suggestions text box.

A description of the grammatical error appears above the first text box.

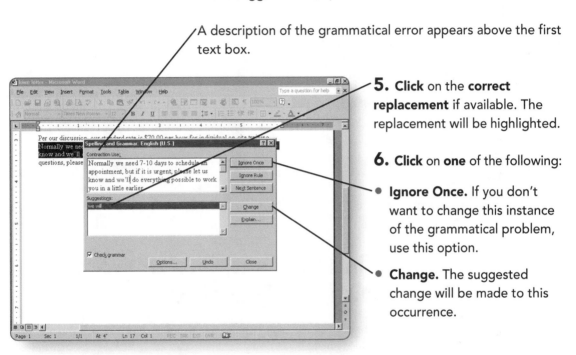

5. Click on the **correct replacement** if available. The replacement will be highlighted.

6. Click on **one** of the following:

- **Ignore Once.** If you don't want to change this instance of the grammatical problem, use this option.

- **Change.** The suggested change will be made to this occurrence.

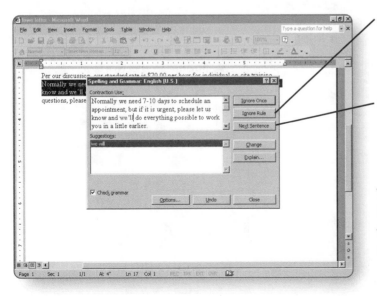

- **Ignore Rule.** Clicking on this option will ignore all instances of the grammatical problem.

- **Next Sentence.** This option moves on to the next sentence, making no changes.

When all mistakes have been identified, Word will notify you that the spelling and grammar check is complete.

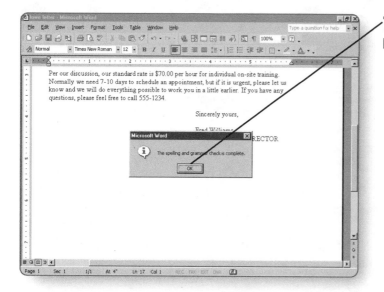

7. Click on **OK**. The message box will close.

Finding That Elusive Word with the Thesaurus

When you just can't remember the word you need, the Thesaurus is invaluable.

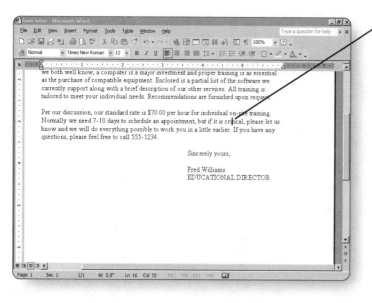

1. Click on the **word** that you want to replace with a better one. The insertion point will appear in the word.

2. Click on **Tools**. The Tools menu will appear.

3. Click on **Language**. A submenu will appear.

4. Click on **Thesaurus**. The Thesaurus dialog box will open.

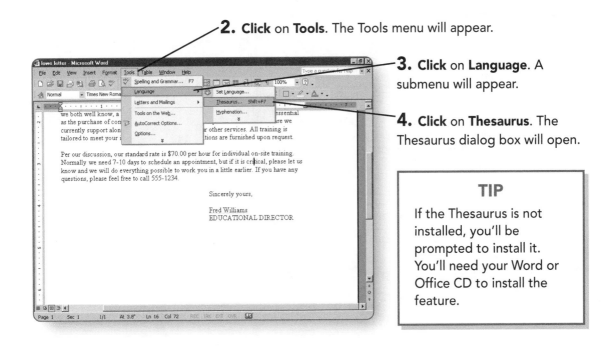

TIP

If the Thesaurus is not installed, you'll be prompted to install it. You'll need your Word or Office CD to install the feature.

Many words have multiple meanings. Word frequently lists many of the possible meanings of your word.

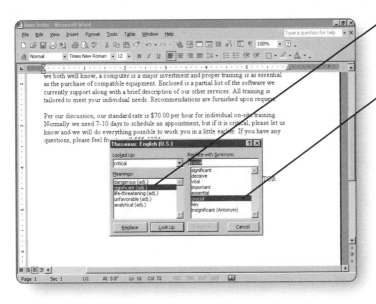

5. Click on a **meaning**. A selection of synonyms will appear on the right.

6. Click on a **word** in the Replace with Synonym text box that fits your document better than the original. The word will be highlighted.

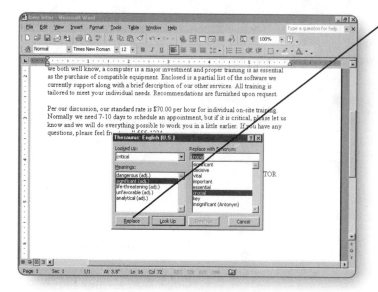

7. **Click** on **Replace**. The word will be replaced with the suggestion.

8

Working with Longer Documents

Much of the time that you spend word processing is spent making documents look a certain way. When working with longer documents, you'll find some of the Word features wonderful time-savers for you. In this chapter, you'll learn how to:

- Set document margins
- Set paper size and orientation
- Manage page breaks
- Work with headers and footers
- Display non-printing characters

Setting Page Options

Page options that you can modify include the margins, the orientation (direction the paper prints), and the size of the paper.

Changing Margins and Orientation

Margins encompass the amount of space between the edges of the paper and where the text actually begins to appear. Word allows you to set margins for any of the four sides of the document and also allows you to mix and match margins for different pages. The default margins are 1" on the top and bottom and 1.25" for the left and right margins.

Setting your document to landscape orientation will print along the long edge of the paper. The default setting is portrait, which will print along the short edge of the paper.

1. Click on **File**. The File menu will appear.

2. Click on **Page Setup**. The Page Setup dialog box will open.

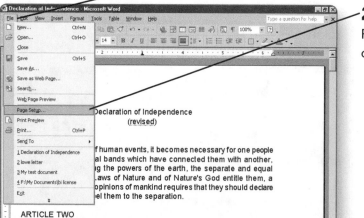

3. If necessary, **click** on the **Margins tab**. The Margins tab will be displayed.

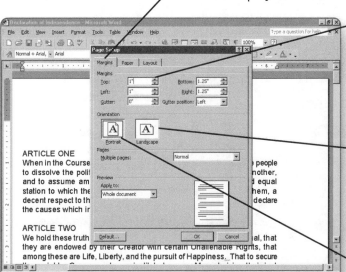

4. Click on the **up or down arrows** to the right of the Top, Bottom, Left, and Right list boxes to increase or decrease the top, bottom, left, or right margin settings, respectively.

5a. Click on **Landscape**. The option will be selected and the document will print along the long edge of the paper.

OR

5b. Click on **Portrait**. The option will be selected and the document will print along the short edge of the paper.

Selecting a Paper Size

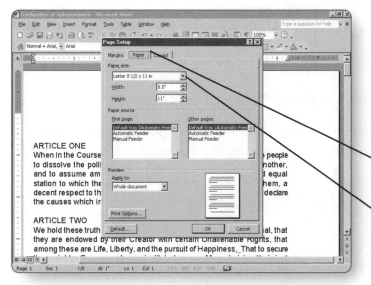

Although Word can work with many sizes of paper, the available selections will depend on the type of printer you use. You change paper size from the Page Setup box you discovered in the previous section.

1. Click on the **Paper tab**. The Paper tab will come to the front.

2. Click on the **down arrow** to the right of the Paper Size list box. A list of available paper sizes will appear.

3. Click on a **paper size**. The selected paper size will be highlighted.

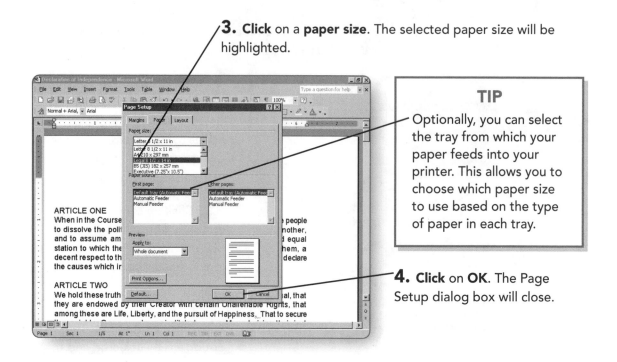

TIP

Optionally, you can select the tray from which your paper feeds into your printer. This allows you to choose which paper size to use based on the type of paper in each tray.

4. Click on **OK**. The Page Setup dialog box will close.

Managing Page Breaks

Word automatically inserts a page break when text fills the page. If you want the page break to be in a different place, you can override the automatic page break by creating your own.

Inserting a Page Break

You can break the page at a shorter position than Word chooses, but you cannot make a page longer.

1. Click the **mouse** in front of the text where you want the new page to begin. The blinking insertion point will appear.

2. Click on **Insert**. The Insert menu will appear.

3. Click on **Break**. The Break dialog box will open.

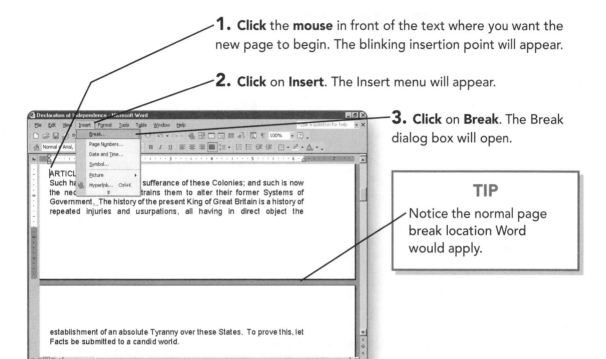

TIP

Notice the normal page break location Word would apply.

4. Click on **Page break**. The option will be selected.

5. Click on **OK**. The page break will be inserted.

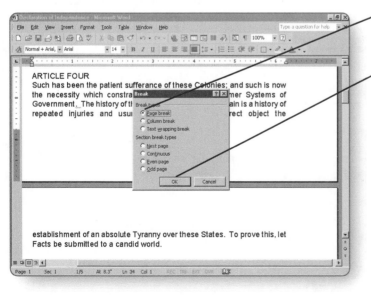

TIP

A faster way to insert a page break is to follow step 1 and then press Ctrl+Enter.

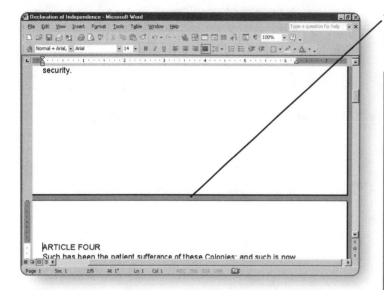

The text page breaks in the new location.

NOTE

Manual page breaks are called *hard page breaks* because, unlike the page breaks that Word inserts, hard page breaks will not move if you delete text above them, adjust the margins, or otherwise change the amount of text on the page.

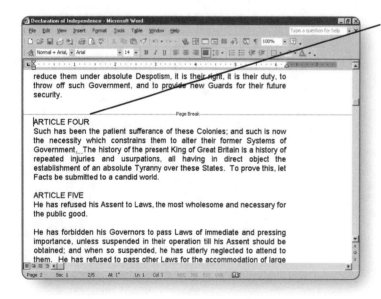

If you are using Word's "Normal" view instead of the default "Print Layout" view, you might see the words "Page Break" along with a dotted line where the new page begins.

Deleting a Page Break

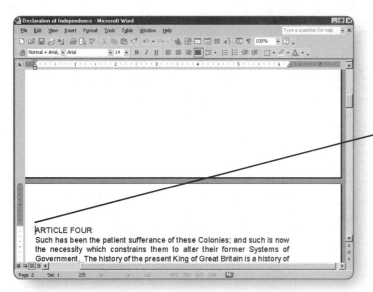

Word's automatic page breaks cannot be deleted, but the hard page breaks that you have inserted manually can be deleted at any time.

1. Click the **mouse pointer** at the beginning of the text after the page break indication. The blinking insertion point will appear.

2. Press the **Backspace key**. The page break will be deleted.

The text will automatically readjust to fit on the pages correctly.

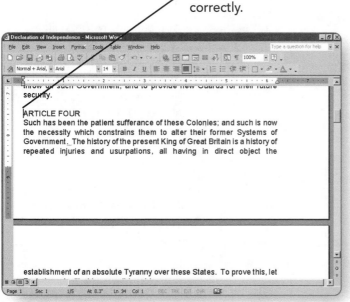

Working with Headers and Footers

Headers and footers are features used for placing information at the top or bottom of every page of a document. You can place any information in headers and footers: the author of the document, the date of last revision, or a company logo. It's a good idea to include dates and page numbers as well.

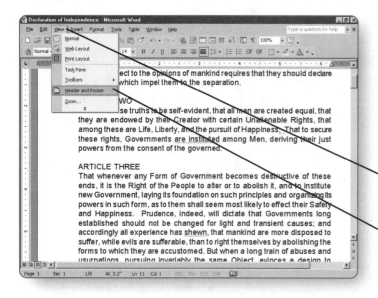

Creating a Header or Footer

As you might expect, a header prints at the top of every page, and a footer prints at the bottom.

1. **Click** on **View**. The View menu will appear.

2. **Click** on **Header and Footer**. The Header box will appear along with the Header and Footer toolbar.

3. **Type** your **text**. The text will appear in the Header box.

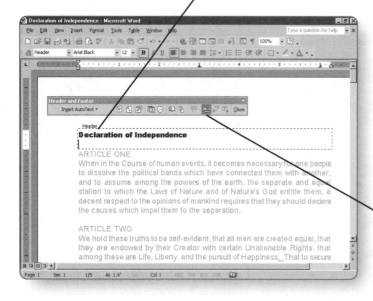

TIP

You can apply fonts, sizes, alignments choices, and most other attributes to header or footer text. See Chapter 6, "Formatting a Word Document," for more information.

---

4. **Click** on the **Switch Between Header and Footer button**. The Footer box will appear.

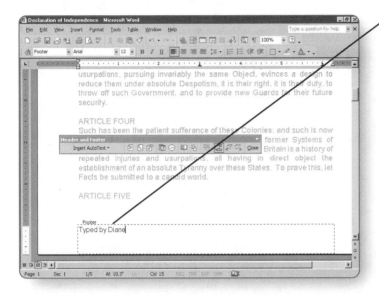

5. **Type** your **text**. The text will appear in the Footer text.

Adding the Date, Time, or Page Numbering

When either the header or footer box is open, you can add a field for the date and time. Word inserts the current date and time in that field based on the computer's clock and calendar settings when you print the document.

The Insert Page Number feature places the correct page number on each page.

1. **Press** the **Tab key**. The insertion point will jump to the center of the page.

2. **Click** on the **Insert Date button**. The current date will be inserted.

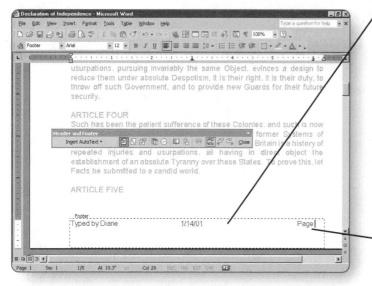

3. Press the **Tab key**. This will right align the next text you insert.

When adding page numbering, Word uses a code that correctly adjusts the page count as your document shrinks or grows. Don't type in a number instead.

TIP

Optionally, precede insertion of the page numbering with any desired text such as "Page".

4. Click on the **Insert Page Number button**. The page number will be inserted.

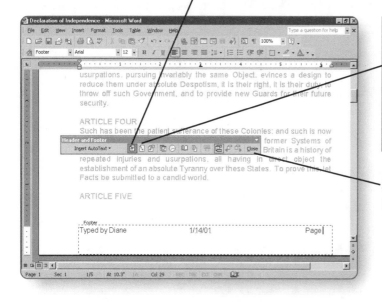

TIP

Optionally, click on the Insert Number of Pages button to insert the total number of pages in the document.

5. Click on **Close**. The Header/Footer bar will close.

Displaying Non-Printing Characters

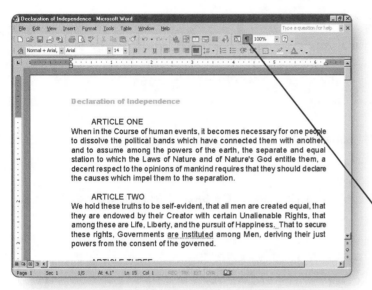

To assist you in editing a document, Word can display some hidden symbols it uses to indicate spaces, tabs, and hard returns (created when you press the Enter key). These symbols do not print, but can be displayed on your screen for your convenience.

1. **Click** the **Show/Hide ¶ button**. The hidden characters will be displayed.

Tabs are indicated by arrows.

Paragraph hard returns are displayed with the paragraph symbol.

Spaces are indicated by a dot.

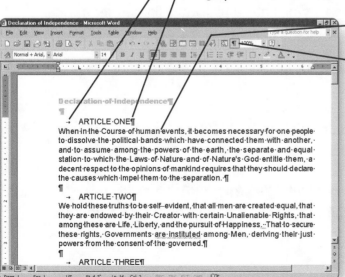

2. **Click** the **Show/Hide ¶ button**. The displayed special characters will be hidden again.

Part II Review Questions

1. What must you do to text in order to move, copy, delete, or change the formatting of it? *See "Selecting Text" in Chapter 5*

2. Name three examples of symbols. *See "Inserting Special Characters or Symbols" in Chapter 5*

3. How do you change the font of your text? *See "Changing the Font" in Chapter 6*

4. What happens to text when it is indented? *See "Indenting Text" in Chapter 6*

5. Which feature of Word automatically corrects your typing? *See "Working with AutoCorrect and AutoFormat" in Chapter 7*

6. Which feature of Word locates text and changes it to different text? *See "Using Replace" in Chapter 7*

7. What does it mean when a word has a red wavy line under it? *See "Checking Spelling As You Go" in Chapter 7*

8. What are the default margins in a Word document? *See "Changing Margins and Orientation" in Chapter 8*

9. How do you create a manual page break? *See "Inserting a Page Break" in Chapter 8*

10. How can Word inform you when you've entered spaces, tabs, or pressed the Enter key? *See "Displaying Non-Printing Characters" in Chapter 8*

PART III

Using Excel

9

Creating a Simple Spreadsheet

Office has a full-featured spreadsheet program called Excel that you can use to make calculations, create charts, and even sort data! In this chapter, you'll learn how to:

- Create a spreadsheet
- Explore and move around in the spreadsheet screen
- Enter and edit labels and values
- Edit the contents of a cell

Exploring the Spreadsheet Screen

In Chapter 1, "Welcome to Office XP," you learned several ways to launch an Office application. Use any of those methods to open Excel.

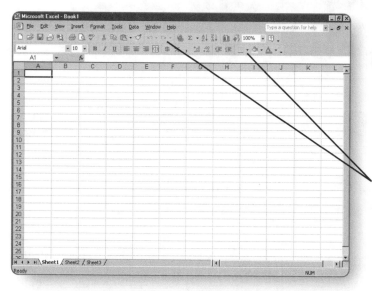

Many items that you see when you open a new spreadsheet are standard to most Windows programs. However, the following list illustrates a few elements that are specific to a spreadsheet program. These include:

- **Toolbars.** Customizable toolbars with a series of commonly used Excel features.

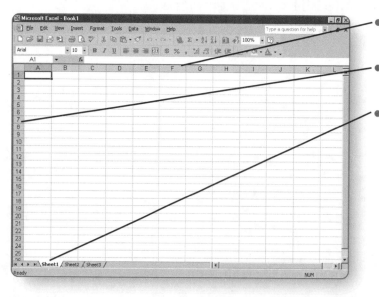

- **Column Headings.** Each spreadsheet has 256 columns.

- **Row Headings.** Each spreadsheet has 65,536 rows.

- **Sheet Tabs.** Each Excel file can contain 256 worksheets.

- **Edit Line.** This line consists of two parts:

  - **Selection Indicator.** This shows the address or name of the current selection.

  - **Contents box.** This area displays the entry you are typing or editing, or the contents of the current cell.

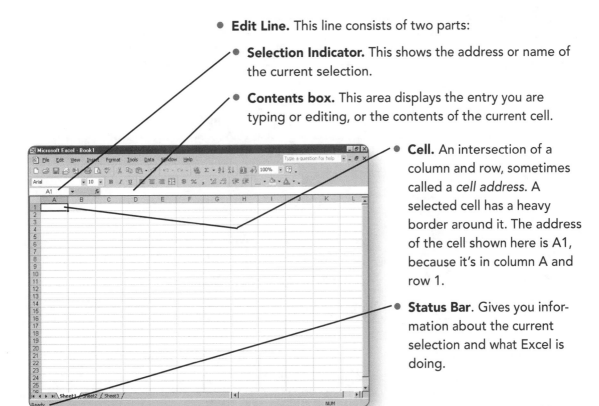

- **Cell.** An intersection of a column and row, sometimes called a *cell address*. A selected cell has a heavy border around it. The address of the cell shown here is A1, because it's in column A and row 1.

- **Status Bar**. Gives you information about the current selection and what Excel is doing.

Moving Around the Spreadsheet Screen

You can use your mouse or keyboard to move around in a spreadsheet. Because of the large size of an Excel worksheet, you need ways to move around quickly.

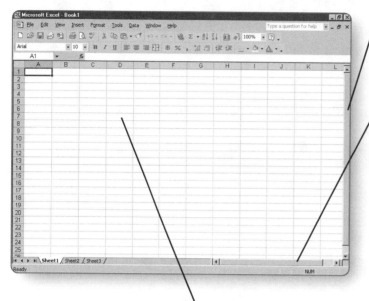

1. **Click and drag** the **vertical scroll bar** until the row you are looking for is visible.

2. **Click and drag** the **horizontal scroll bar** until the column you are looking for is visible.

3. **Click** on the **desired cell**. It will become the current cell.

The following table describes keyboard methods for moving around in your spreadsheet.

Keystroke	Result
Arrow keys	Moves one cell at a time up, down, left, or right
Page Down	Moves one screen down
Page Up	Moves one screen up
Home	Moves to column A of the current row
Ctrl+Home	Moves to cell A1
Ctrl+Arrow key	Moves to the beginning or end of a row or column
F5	Displays the GoTo dialog box, which enables you to specify a cell address

Entering Data

Spreadsheet data is made up of three components: labels, values, and formulas. This section discusses entering labels and values, and you'll learn about formulas in Chapter 11 "Working with Functions and Formulas".

Entering Labels

Labels are traditionally descriptive pieces of information, such as names, months, or types of products. Excel identifies a cell as a label if it begins with a letter or contains any letters.

1. Click on the **cell** where you want to place the label. A border will appear around the selected cell.

2. Type some **text**. A blinking insertion point will appear.

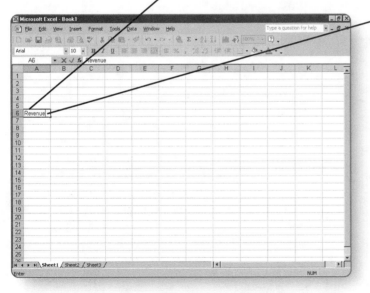

TIP

If you make a mistake and you have not yet pressed Enter, press the Backspace key to delete characters and type a correction, or press the Escape key to cancel the typing.

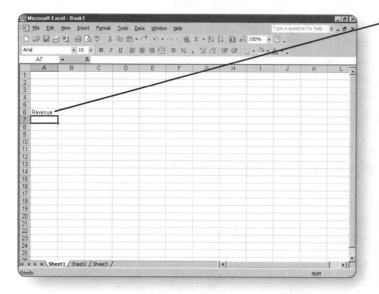

3. **Press** the **Enter key** to accept the label. The text will be entered and will align along the left edge of the cell. The cell below the one where you just entered data will then be selected.

TIP

Optionally, press the Tab key and the cell to the right of the current cell will be selected.

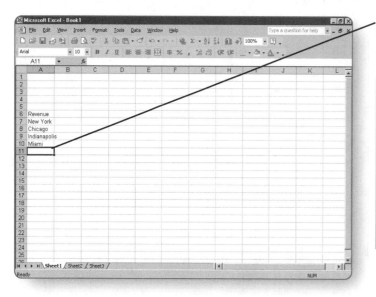

4. **Repeat steps 1–3** for each label you want to enter.

NOTE

Optionally, you can press an arrow key instead of the Enter key. This will accept the cell you were typing in and move to the next cell in the direction of the arrow key.

Entering Values

Values are the raw numbers that you track in a spreadsheet. There is no need to enter commas or dollar signs. In Chapter 12 "Formatting Worksheets", you'll let Excel do that for you.

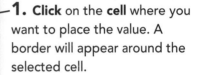

1. **Click** on the **cell** where you want to place the value. A border will appear around the selected cell.

2. **Type** the numerical **value**. A blinking insertion point will appear.

3. **Press Enter** to accept the value. The number will be entered into the cell.

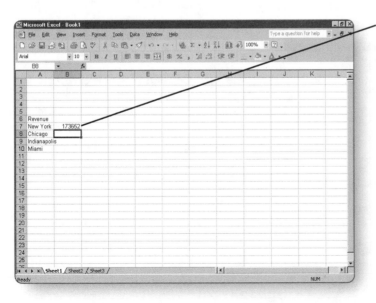

Notice how values are aligned along the right edge of the cell.

4. **Repeat steps 1–3** for each value you want to enter.

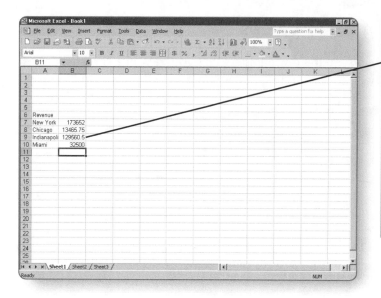

Editing Data

You can edit your data in a variety of ways. You might need to change the contents of a cell, or you might want to move the data to another part of the spreadsheet.

Replacing the Contents of a Cell

You can make changes to the contents of a cell in two ways. One is by typing over the contents of a cell.

1. Click on an occupied **cell**. The cell and its contents will be selected.

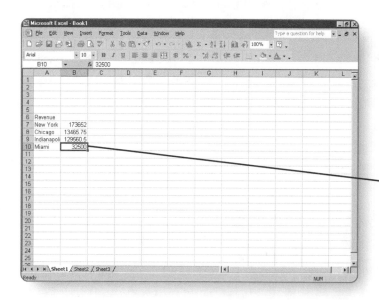

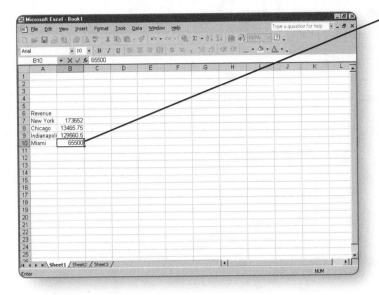

2. Type a new **label** or **value**. The new data will appear in the cell.

3. Press the **Enter key**. The text will be entered in the selected cell.

Editing the Contents of a Cell

The other way to make changes to the contents of a cell is by using the Edit feature.

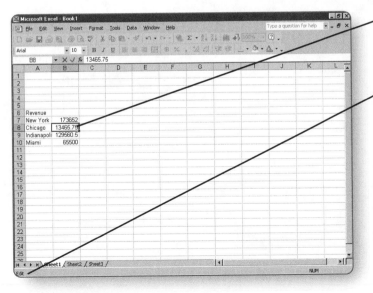

1. Double-click on the **cell** to be edited. The insertion point will blink within the cell.

Notice how the status bar indicates that you are in Edit mode.

TIP

You can also press the F2 key to edit the contents of a cell.

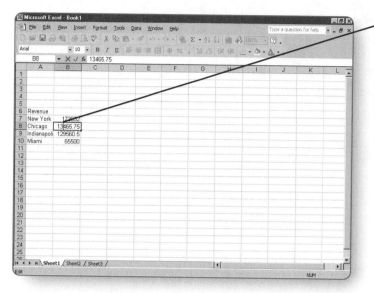

2. **Press** the **left arrow key**. The insertion point will be relocated within the current cell.

3. **Type** the **changes**. The changes will appear in the current cell.

4. **Press** the **Enter key**. The changes will be entered into the current cell.

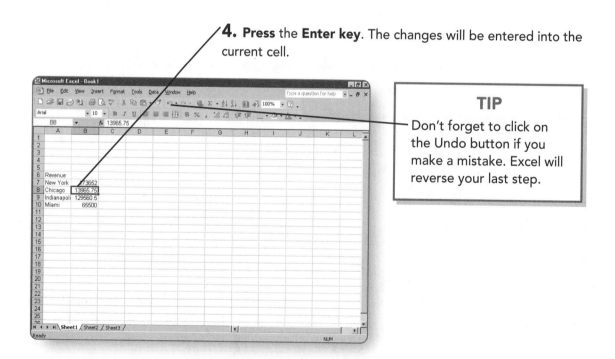

TIP

Don't forget to click on the Undo button if you make a mistake. Excel will reverse your last step.

10

Editing a Spreadsheet

Frequently after data is entered into a spreadsheet, you'll need to change the location of the data. You can insert or delete rows or columns as needed or just move the data to a new location. In this chapter, you'll learn how to:

- Select cells, rows, and columns
- Insert and delete rows and columns
- Move data
- Use the Fill feature

Learning Selection Techniques

To move, copy, delete, or change the formatting of data in the spreadsheet, the cells to be modified must first be selected. When cells are selected, they appear darker on screen—just the reverse of unselected text. However, if a block of cells is selected, the first cell will not have the darker shading around it.

The following table describes some of the different selection techniques.

To Select	Do This
❶ A cell	Click on the desired cell.
❷ A row	Click on the row number on the left side of the screen.
❸ A column	Click on the column letter at the top of the screen.
❹ A sequential block of cells	Click on the first cell and drag to highlight the rest of the cells.
❺ A nonsequential block of cells	Click on the first cell, then hold down the Ctrl key and click on any additional cells.

TIP

Make sure the mouse pointer is a white cross before attempting to select cells.

TIP

To deselect a block of cells, click the mouse in any other cell.

Inserting Rows and Columns

Occasionally you need a column or a row to be inserted into the middle of information that you have already entered. Inserting a row or column moves existing data to make room for blank rows or columns.

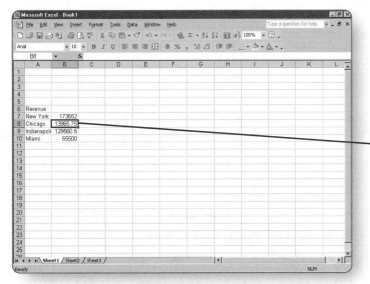

Inserting Columns

You can insert a column anywhere you need it. Excel will move the existing columns to make room for the new one.

1. Click anywhere in the column after which you want to insert the new column. (The new column will be inserted in front of the old one.) A cell in that column will be selected.

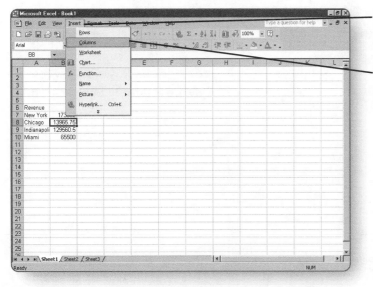

2. Click on **Insert.** The Insert menu will appear.

3. Click on **Columns**. A new column will be inserted.

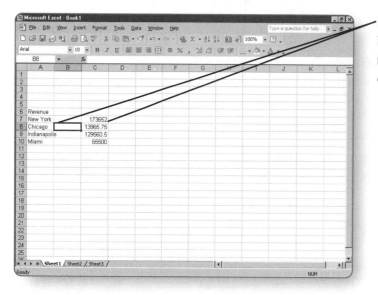

In this example, the information in the existing column B was moved to column C. The empty column B is the new column.

Inserting Rows

You also can insert a row anywhere you need it. Excel will move the existing rows down to make room for the new one.

1. Click anywhere in the row above the place you want to insert the new row. A cell in the row will be selected.

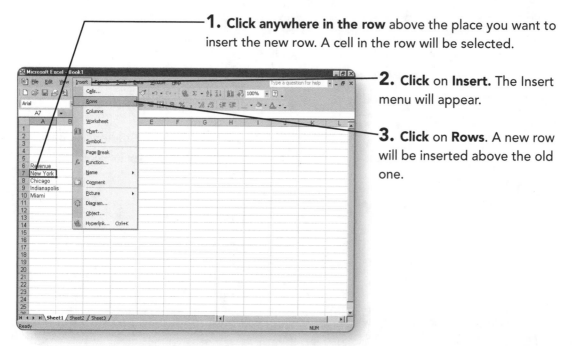

2. Click on **Insert.** The Insert menu will appear.

3. Click on **Rows**. A new row will be inserted above the old one.

Deleting Rows and Columns

Use caution when deleting a row or column. Deleting a row will delete it across all 256 columns; deleting a column will delete it down all 65,536 rows.

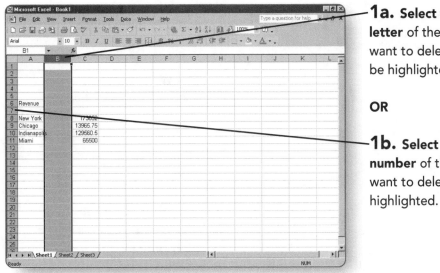

1a. Select the **column heading letter** of the column that you want to delete. The column will be highlighted.

OR

1b. Select the **row heading number** of the row that you want to delete. The row will be highlighted.

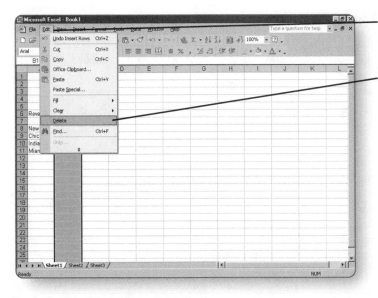

2. Click on **Edit**. The Edit menu will appear.

3. Click on **Delete**. The highlighted column or row will be deleted.

Remaining columns will move to the left; remaining rows will move up.

Moving Data Around

If you're not happy with the placement of data, you don't have to delete it and retype it. Excel makes it easy for you to move it around.

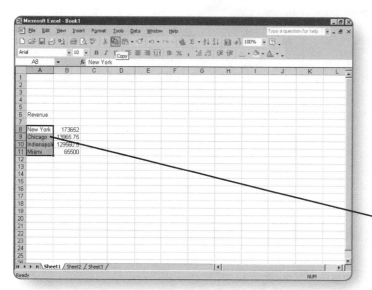

Copying and Pasting Cells

The Windows Clipboard is extremely helpful if you want to transfer information from one place to another. To copy information, Excel uses the Copy and Paste features.

1. Select some **cells** to be duplicated. The cells will be highlighted.

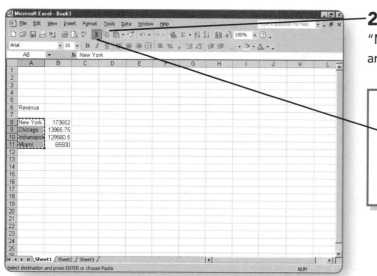

2. Click on the **Copy button**. "Marching ants" will appear around the copied cells.

TIP

If you want to move the information from one cell to another, click on the Cut button instead.

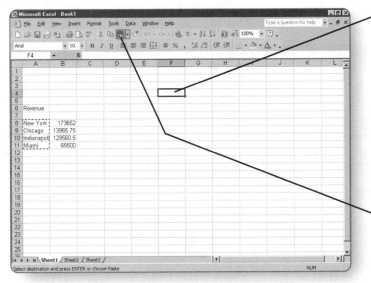

3. Click on the **beginning cell** where you want to place the duplicated information. The cell will be highlighted.

4. Press the **Enter key**. The information will be copied to the new location.

TIP

Optionally, click on the Paste button, and then press the Enter key to remove the "marching ants."

If you had elected to cut the information, the original cells in this figure would be blank and only the pasted cells would contain the data.

Using Drag-and-Drop to Move Cells

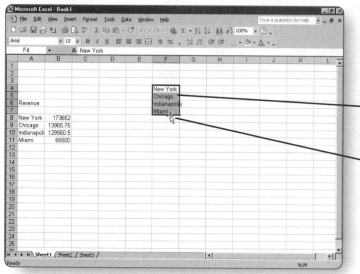

Another method that you can use to move information from one location to another is the drag-and-drop method.

1. Select some **cells** to move. The cells will be highlighted.

2. Position the **mouse pointer** around one of the outside edges of the selection. The mouse pointer will become a small white arrow with a black cross in front of it.

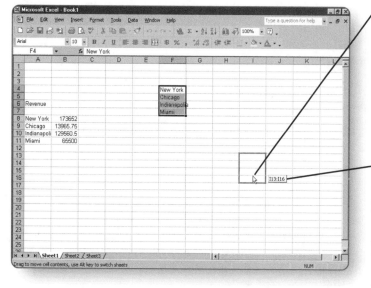

3. Keeping the mouse pointed around the outside edge, press and hold the mouse button and drag the cells to a new location. The second box represents where the moved cells will be located.

Notice that the new cells' address range is also listed for your information.

4. Release the **mouse button**. The cells will be moved.

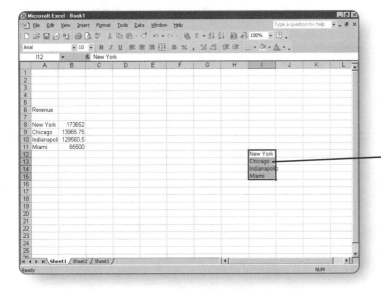

Clearing Cell Contents

If you have data in cells that you no longer want, you can easily delete the data.

1. Select some **cells** to be cleared. The cells will be highlighted.

2. Press the **Delete key**. The contents of the cells will be removed.

Using the Fill Feature

Excel has a great built-in, time-saving feature called *Fill*. If you give Excel the beginning Month, Day, or numbers, it can fill in the rest of the pattern for you. For example, if you type January, Excel fills in February, March, April, and so on.

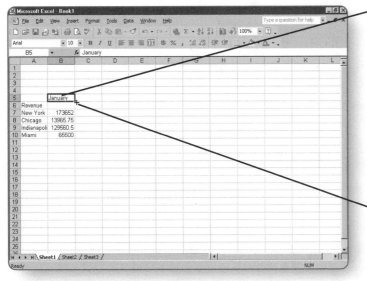

1. Type the **beginning Month, Day, or Number** in the beginning cell. The text will be displayed in the cell.

If you want Excel to fill in numbers, you must first give it a pattern. For example, enter the value of **1** in the first cell, and then enter **2** in the second cell.

2. Position the **mouse pointer** on the lower-right corner of the beginning cell. The mouse pointer will become a small black cross.

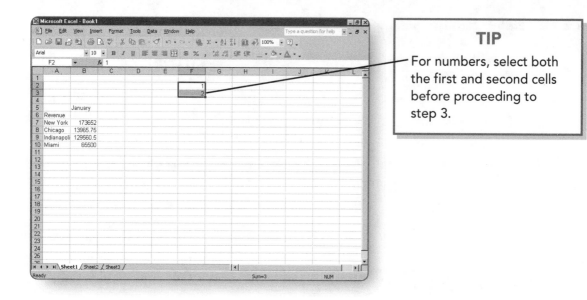

TIP

For numbers, select both the first and second cells before proceeding to step 3.

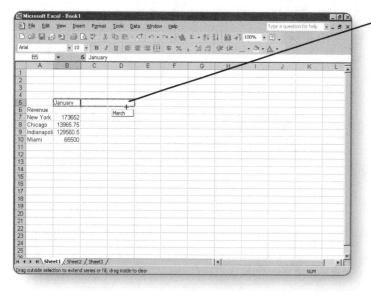

3. Press and **hold** the **mouse button** and **drag** to select the next cells to be filled in. The cells will have a gray border surrounding them.

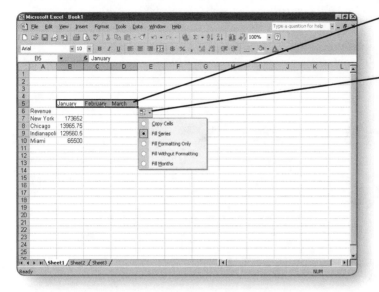

4. Release the **mouse button**. The pattern will be repeated.

A SmartTag also appears. If you click on the arrow next to the SmartTag, you can choose from additional Fill options. (For more information about SmartTags, see Chapter 2, "Choosing Commands".)

11

Working with Functions and Formulas

Formulas in an Excel spreadsheet will do the calculations for you. For example, by referencing cell addresses in a formula, if the data changes, so will the formula answer. In this chapter, you'll learn how to:

- Create simple and compound formulas
- Copy formulas
- Edit a cell
- Create an absolute reference
- Use Excel's built-in functions

Creating Formulas

All formulas must begin with the equals (=) sign, regardless of whether the formula consists of adding, subtracting, multiplying, or dividing.

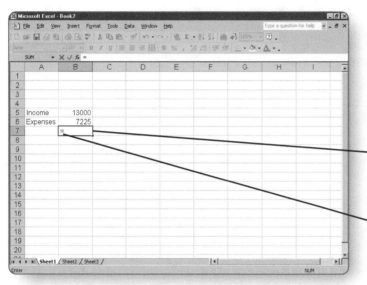

Creating a Simple Formula

An example of a simple formula is =B5+B6, which adds the contents of cells B5 and B6.

1. **Click** on the **cell** in which you want to place the formula's result. The cell will be selected.

2. **Type** an **equals sign (=)** to begin the formula. The symbol will display in the cell.

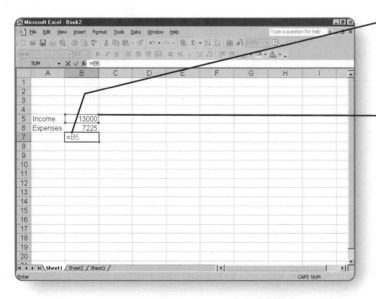

3. **Type** the **cell address** of the first cell to be included in the formula. This is called the cell *reference*.

Excel references the cell address in color and places a matching color box around the referenced address.

NOTE

Spreadsheet formulas are not case sensitive. For example, B5 is the same as b5.

A formula needs an *operator* to suggest the next action to be performed.

4. Type the **operator**: plus (+), minus (−), multiply (*), or divide (/). The operator will display in the formula.

5. Type the **reference** to the second cell of the formula. The reference will display in the cell.

Excel references the second cell address in a different color and places a matching color box around the referenced address.

6. Press the **Enter key**. The result of the calculation will appear in the cell.

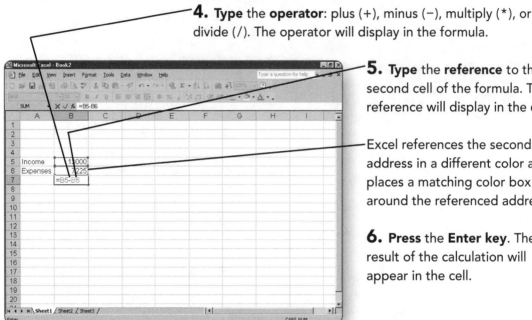

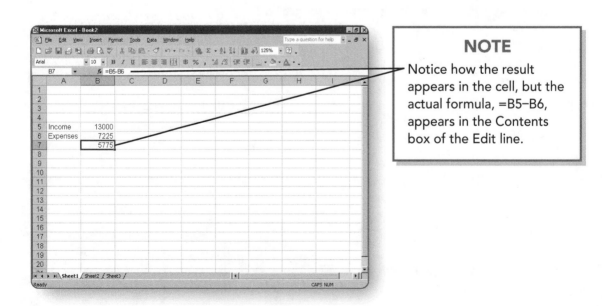

NOTE

Notice how the result appears in the cell, but the actual formula, =B5−B6, appears in the Contents box of the Edit line.

Creating a Compound Formula

You use compound formulas when you need more than one operator. Examples of a compound formula include =B7+B8+B9+B10 or =B11−B19*A23.

> ## NOTE
>
> When you have a compound formula, Excel will perform the multiplication and division first, and then the addition and subtraction. If you want a certain portion of the formula to be calculated first, put it in parentheses. Excel will perform whatever is in the parentheses before the rest of the formula. Such a formula as =B11−B19*A23 will give a totally different answer than =(B11−B19)*A23.

1. Click on the **cell** in which you want to place the formula's result. The cell will be selected.

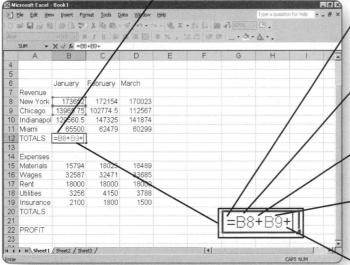

2. Type an **equals sign (=)** to begin the formula. The symbol will display in the cell.

3. Type the **reference to the first cell** of the formula. The reference will display in the cell.

4. Type the **operator**. The operator will display in the cell.

5. Type the **reference to the second cell** of the formula. The reference will display in the cell.

6. Type the **next operator**. The operator will display in the cell.

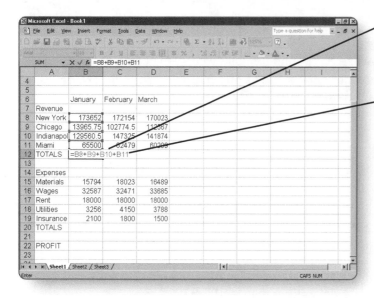

7. **Type** the **reference to the third cell** of the formula. The reference will display in the cell.

8. Repeat steps 6 and 7 until the formula is complete, adding the parentheses wherever necessary.

Excel color codes each set of parentheses to indicate how they match up. This is nice if the formula is complex so you can tell which sets go together.

9. **Press** the **Enter key** to accept the formula. The answer will be displayed in the cell and the formula will be displayed in the content bar.

Try changing one of the values you originally typed in the spreadsheet and watch the answer to the formula change.

Editing Entries

Excel provides several methods of editing an incorrect cell, whether it's a label, a value, or a formula. One method involves simply retyping the desired data in the correct cell. When you press Enter, the new data replaces the old data. If however, the data is complex or lengthy, you might want to edit only a portion of the existing information.

Editing from the Cell

You can make changes to a cell entry directly in the cell.

1. Double-click on the **cell** you want to modify. The blinking insertion point will appear in the cell.

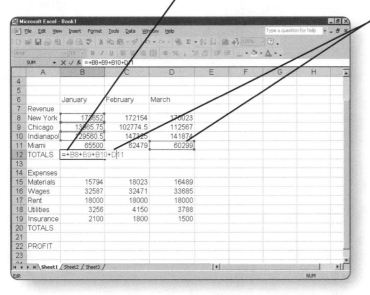

When editing formulas, Excel color codes each cell address to its corresponding cell.

2. Type any corrections. You may need to use the keyboard arrow keys to move the insertion point to the position of the incorrect data. The correction will appear in the cell and on the Formula line.

3. Press the **Enter** key. The correction will be accepted and if the data was a formula, the answer will be recalculated.

Editing from the Contents Line

Earlier in this chapter you discovered, if a cell contains a formula, the result of the formula calculation displays in the cell, however, the actual formula is displayed in the Formula line. Cell contents can be edited from the Formula line.

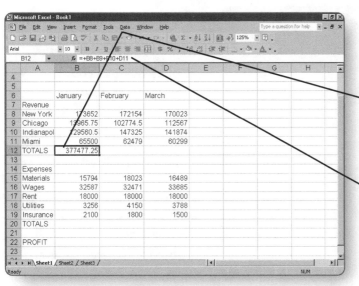

1. Click on the **cell** you want to edit. The cell will be selected and the cell contents (or formula) will appear in the Formula line.

2. Click in the **Formula line**. A blinking insertion point will appear.

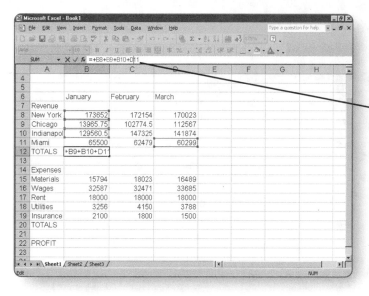

When editing formulas, Excel color codes each element in the formula to the referenced cell address.

3. **Type** any **corrections**. You might need to use the keyboard arrow keys to move the insertion point to the position of the incorrect data. The correction will appear in the Contents box.

4. **Press** the **Enter** key. The correction will be accepted and if the data was a formula, the answer will be recalculated.

Copying Formulas

Now that you've created a formula, there's no reason to type it over and over for subsequent cells. Let Excel copy the formula for you!

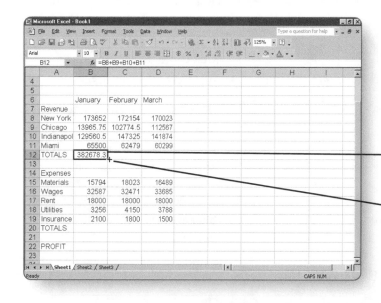

Copying Using the Fill Feature

If you're going to copy a formula to a surrounding cell, you can use the Fill method.

1. **Click** on the **cell** that has the formula. The cell will be selected.

2. **Position** the **mouse pointer** on the lower-right corner of the beginning cell. The mouse pointer will become a black cross.

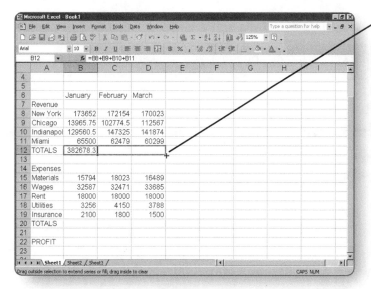

3. **Press** and **hold** the **mouse button** and **drag** to select the next cells (up, down, left, or right) to be filled in. The cells will be selected.

4. **Release** the **mouse button**. The formula will be copied.

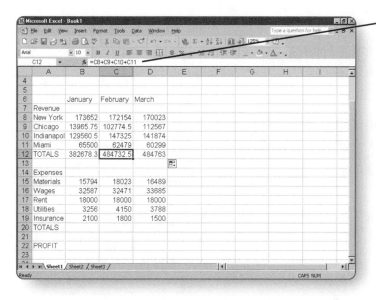

When Excel copies a formula, the references change as the formula is copied. If the original formula was =B11−B19 and you copied it to the next cell to the right, the formula would read =C11−C19. Then, if you copied it to the next cell to the right, it would be =D11−D19, and so on. Excel calls this a *relative reference*.

Copying with Copy and Paste

If the cells are not sequential, you can use Copy and Paste. Fill and Copy and Paste were discussed in Chapter 10, "Editing a Spreadsheet".

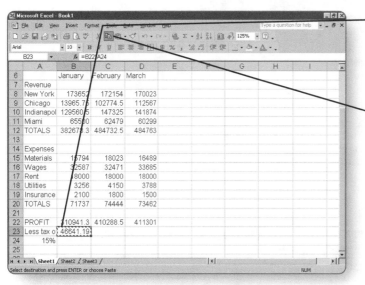

1. Select the **cell** containing the formula that you want to duplicate. The cell will be selected.

2. Click on the **Copy button**. Marching ants will appear around the copied cells.

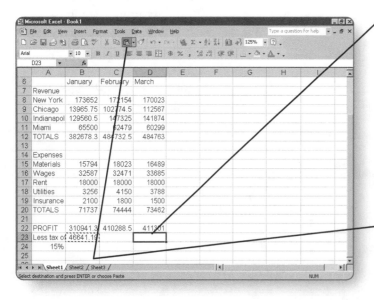

3. Highlight the **cells** in which you want to place the duplicated formula. The cells will be selected.

4. Press the **Enter key**. The formula will be copied to the new location.

TIP

Optionally, click on the Paste button and then press Esc to cancel the marching ants.

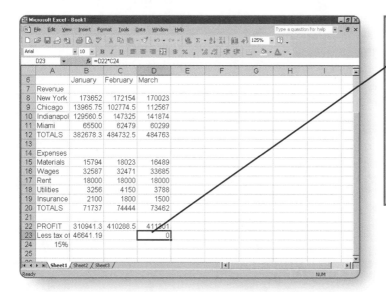

NOTE

If you are following the examples in the book, don't be alarmed by the answer you see in the exercise. You'll discover why the answer appears incorrect in the next section.

Creating an Absolute Reference in a Formula

Occasionally when you copy a formula, you do not want one of the cell references to change. For example, when you have a fixed amount in cell A1 that you want to multiply to each entry in row B, you need to create an absolute reference for cell A1. To indicate an absolute reference, you use the dollar sign ($).

It's called an *absolute reference* because when you copy it, it absolutely and positively stays that cell reference and never changes. An example of a formula with an absolute reference might be =B22*B24. The reference to cell B24 will not change when copied.

If you are following the examples in this book, for this exercise, you need to delete the original formulas and start again.

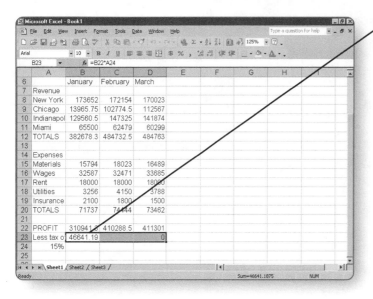

1. Highlight the **cells** in which the original formulas exist. The cells will be selected.

2. Press the **Delete key**. The information in these cells will be deleted.

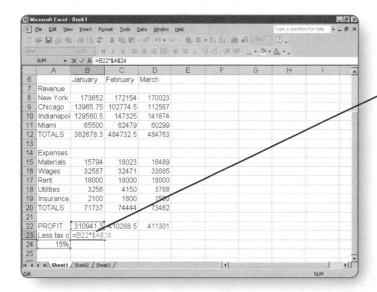

3. Click on the **cell** in which you want to place the formula answer. The cell will be selected.

4. Type the **formula** again, except this time, if any references are to be an absolute reference, add dollar signs ($) in front of both the column reference and the row reference, without any spaces in between.

NOTE

Compound formulas can also have absolute references.

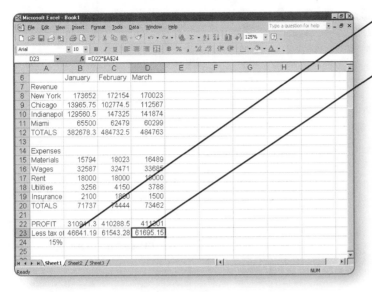

5. Press the **Enter key.** The answer will display in the cell.

6. Copy the **formula** to the adjacent cells using one of the methods in the preceding section.

Using Functions

Sometimes, formulas can be quite complex and time consuming to build. Excel has hundreds of different functions to assist you with your calculations. All Excel built-in functions begin with the equals (=) sign and have the basis (arguments) for the formula in parentheses.

Using the SUM Function

The SUM function totals a range of values. The syntax for this function is =SUM(*range of values to total*). An example is =SUM(B8:D8).

NOTE

There are two ways to reference a range of values. If the cells to be included are sequential, they are separated by a colon (:). If the range is nonsequential, the cells are separated by a comma (,). For example, the range (B8:D8) includes cells B8, C8, and D8; the range (B8:D8,F4) includes cells B8, C8, D8, and F4.

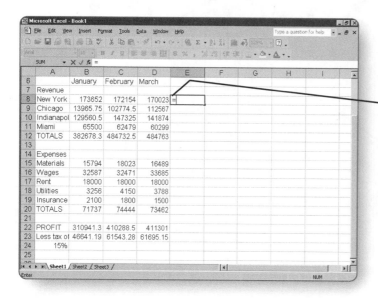

1. **Click** on the **cell** in which you want to place the sum of values. The cell will be selected.

2. **Type** the **equals (=) sign**. The symbol will display in the cell.

NOTE

Remember that functions are complex formulas and all formulas must begin with the equals (=) sign.

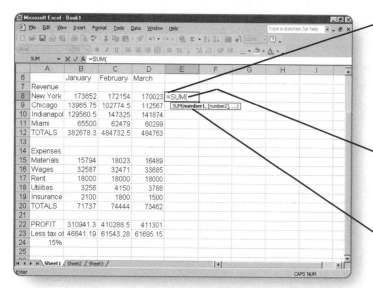

3. **Type** the function name **SUM**. The characters will display in the cell. Function names are not case sensitive, therefore typing "SUM" is the same as typing "sum".

4. **Type** the **open parenthesis** symbol. The symbol will display in the cell.

Excel tries to assist you with the rest of the formula by displaying a yellow tip box.

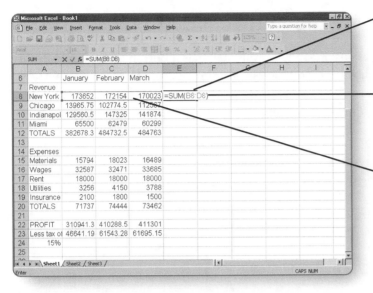

5. Type the **range** to be totaled. The range will display in the cell.

6. Type the **close parenthesis** symbol. The symbol will display in the cell.

Excel places a color box around the range to be totaled.

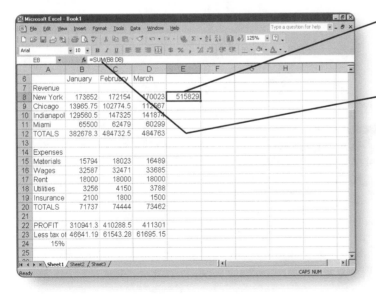

7. Press the **Enter key**. The total of the range will be displayed in the selected cell.

Again, although the result displays in the selected cell, the formula is displayed in the contents box.

Using the AutoSum Button

Excel includes the SUM function as a button on the toolbar. This makes creating a simple addition formula a mouse click away!

1. Click on the **cell** below or to the right of the values to be totaled. The cell will be selected.

2. Click on the **AutoSum button**. The cells to be totaled are highlighted.

NOTE

Excel will sum the values above it first. If no values are above it, Excel will look for values in the cells to the left.

If you want to total different cells than Excel has highlighted, select them with your mouse.

3. Press the **Enter key**. Excel will enter the sum of the values above it or to the left of it.

Using the AVERAGE Function

The AVERAGE function finds an average of a range of values. The syntax for this function is =AVERAGE(*range of values to average*). An example is =AVERAGE(B7:D7), which would calculate an average of the values in cells B7 through D7.

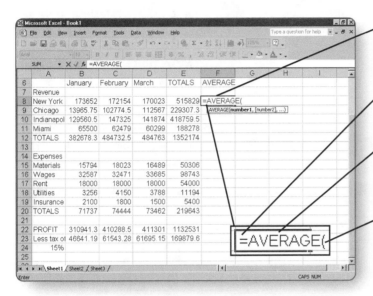

1. **Click** on the **cell** in which you want to place the average. The cell will be selected.

2. **Type** the **equals (=)** sign. The symbol will display in the cell.

3. **Type** the function name **AVERAGE**. The characters will display in the cell.

4. **Type** the **open parenthesis** symbol. The symbol will display in the cell.

TIP

Instead of typing the range as noted in step 4, you can highlight the range with the mouse. Excel will fill in the cell references for you.

5. **Type** or **highlight** the **range** to be averaged. The range will display in the cell.

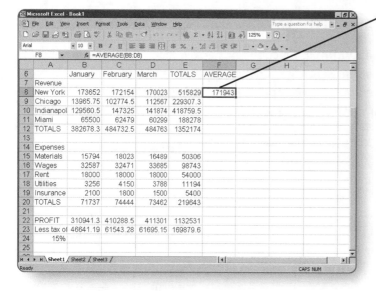

6. Press the **Enter key**. Excel will place the closing parenthesis and average the values in the selected range.

Other similar functions are MAX, MIN, and COUNT, described here:

- **MAX function.** Finds the largest value in a range of cells. Example: =MAX(B8:D8).

- **MIN function.** Finds the smallest value in a range of cells. Example: =MIN(B8:D8).

- **COUNT function.** Counts the number of non-blank cells in a range of cells. Example: =COUNT(B8:D8).

12

Formatting Worksheets

The days of the dull spreadsheet are gone. You can liven up your spreadsheet by changing its appearance. In this chapter, you'll learn how to:

- Set number formatting
- Change alignment and column width
- Select fonts
- Add borders to cells
- Adjust the view of the spreadsheet

Formatting Numbers

By default, values are displayed as general numbers. Values can be displayed as currency, percentages, fractions, dates, and many other formats.

Formatting Numbers with the Toolbar

Three popular number styles are accounting, commas, and percentages. Accounting and comma formats automatically apply two decimal points, whereas the percentage format doesn't apply any decimal points. The accounting style also applies a dollar sign to the number. Excel includes buttons on the toolbar for these formats.

1. Select some **cells** to be formatted. The cells will be highlighted.

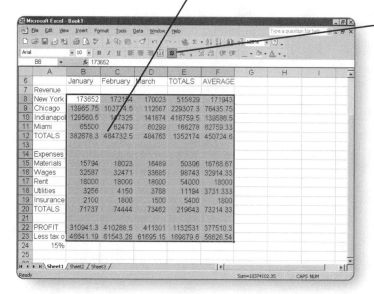

2a. Click on the **Currency button**. The cells will be formatted with a dollar sign and two decimal places.

NOTE

There's a trick here. The tooltip calls this button the "currency style," however it actually applies an accounting style. The difference is the placement of the dollar sign. In currency style, the dollar sign is right next to the numbers, whereas in accounting, the dollar sign is on the left edge of the cell.

OR

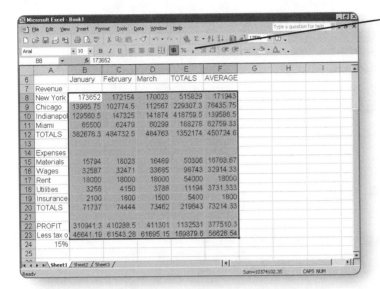

2b. **Click** on the **Comma style button**. The numbers will have two decimal points and if the number is greater than one thousand, it will also have a comma between the thousands.

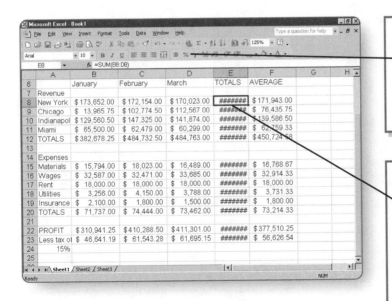

Changing the Decimal Point Places

The number of decimal places assigned to a style might not be exactly what you want. Excel includes two buttons on the toolbar to give you control over the number of decimal places. Each cell can have from 0 to 15 decimal places.

1. Select the **cells** you want to change the decimal place in. The cells will be highlighted.

2a. Click on the **Increase decimal button**. An additional decimal place will be assigned.

OR

2b. Click on the **Decrease decimal button**. The number of decimal places will be decreased.

Each additional click on these buttons will increase or decrease the decimal place one position.

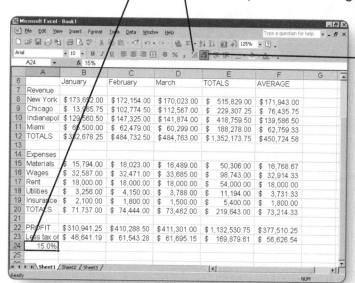

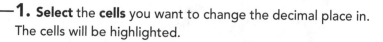

TIP

Click on Format, Cells, and then click on the Number tab, where you'll find lots of other formats for your numbers.

Adjusting Column Widths

The default width of a column is 8.43 characters, but each column can be from 1 to 240 characters wide.

A line located at the right edge of each column heading divides the columns. You will use this line to change the column width.

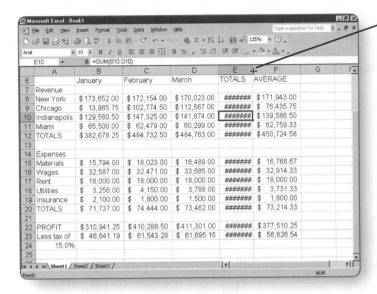

1. Position the **mouse pointer** on the right column line for the column that you want to change. The mouse pointer will become a black, double-headed arrow.

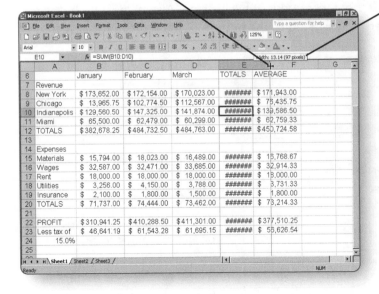

2. Press and **hold** the mouse button and **drag** the **column line**. If you drag it to the right, the column width will increase; if you drag it to the left, the column width will decrease.

A tooltip above the mouse pointer will indicate the width as you drag the column line.

TIP

Double-click on the column line to have Excel automatically adjust the column to fit all entries in that column.

3. Release the **mouse button**. The column width will be changed.

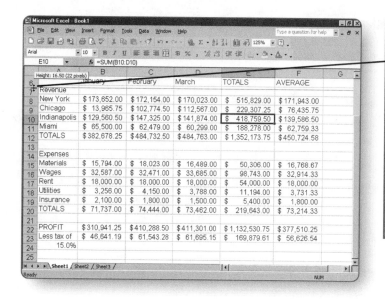

TIP

Row height can be adjusted in a similar manner. Position the mouse pointer on the bottom edge of the row heading. Again, the mouse will change to a black, double-headed arrow. Drag the line down to increase row height or up to decrease row height.

Setting Cell Alignment

Labels are left aligned and values are right aligned by default; however, you can change the alignment of either one to be left, right, centered, or full justified. Also by default, both are vertically aligned to the bottom of the cell.

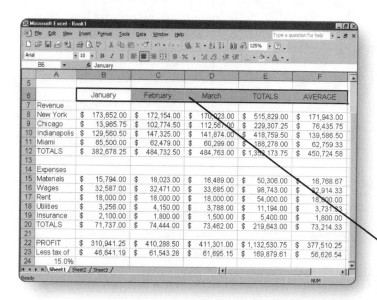

Wrapping text in cells is useful when text is too long to fit in one cell and you don't want it to overlap to the next cell.

Adjusting Cell Alignment

You can adjust cells individually or adjust a block of cells.

1. Select the **cells** to be formatted. The cells will be highlighted.

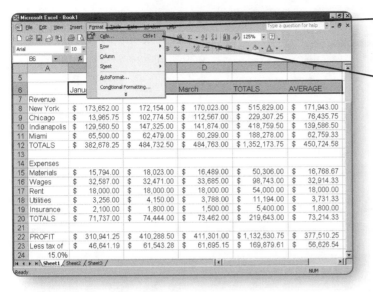

2. Click on **Format**. The Format menu will appear.

3. Click on **Cells**. The Format Cells dialog box will open.

4. If necessary, **click** on the **Alignment tab**. The Alignment tab will come to the front.

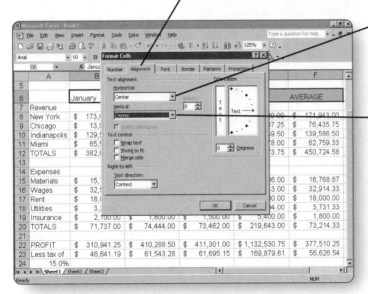

5. Click on an **option** under the Horizontal list box. The horizontal alignment of the text in the cell will change.

6. Click on an **option** under the Vertical list box. The vertical alignment of the text in the cell will change.

TIP

The Wrap text feature treats each cell like a miniature word processor, with text wrapping around in the cell.

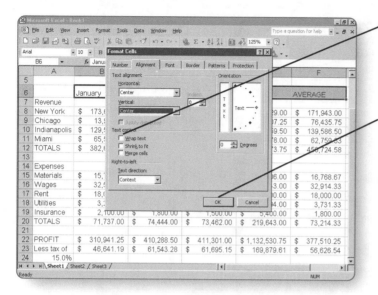

7. **Click** in a desired **check box** under Text control to make the option active. A check mark will appear in the selection box.

8. **Click** on **OK**. The selections will be applied to the highlighted cells.

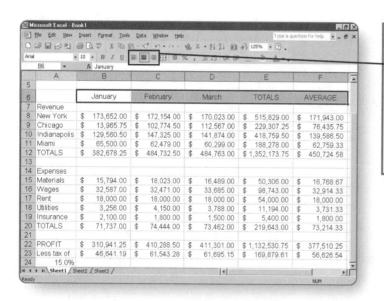

TIP

Optionally, you can select the cells to be aligned and then click on one of the three alignment buttons on the toolbar: Left, Center, or Right.

Centering Headings

Text also can be centered across a group of columns to create attractive headings.

1. **Type** the **heading text** in the first column of the worksheet body. This is usually column A.

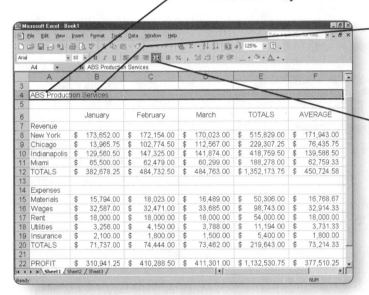

2. **Select** the **heading cell** and the **cells** to be included in the heading. The cells will be highlighted.

3. **Click** on the **Merge and Center button**. The title will be centered.

Notice the gridlines have disappeared and the cells appear to be joined together.

NOTE

In this example, it appears the heading is located in Columns C and D; however, the text is still in Column A. If you are going to make other changes, be sure to select Column A, not Column C or D.

Formatting with Fonts

The default font in a spreadsheet is Arial 10 points, but you can easily change both the typeface and size.

Selecting a Font Typeface

Your font choices will vary depending on the software installed on your computer.

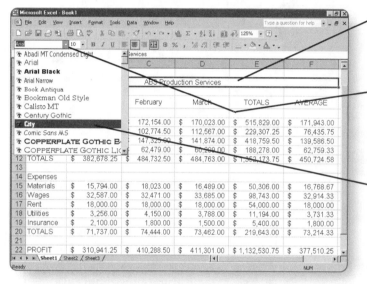

1. Select some **cells** to change the typeface. The cells will be highlighted.

2. Click on the **down arrow** to the right of the font name list box. A drop-down list of available fonts will appear.

3. Click on the **font** of your choice. The selection list will close and the new font will be applied to the selected cells. Your font selections might vary from the ones shown here.

Selecting a Font Size

The default font size in an Excel spreadsheet is 10 points. There are approximately 72 points in an inch, so a 10-point font is slightly less than one-seventh of an inch tall.

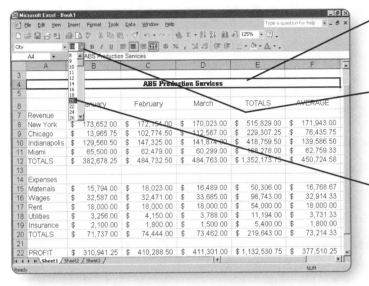

1. Select some **cells** to change the font size. The cells will be highlighted.

2. Click on the **down arrow** to the right of the font size list box. A drop-down list of available font sizes will appear.

3. Click on the **font size** of your choice. The selection list will close and the new font size will be applied to the selected cells.

Selecting a Font Style

Font styles include attributes like **bold**, *italics*, and underlining.

1. Select some **cells** to change the style. The cells will be highlighted.

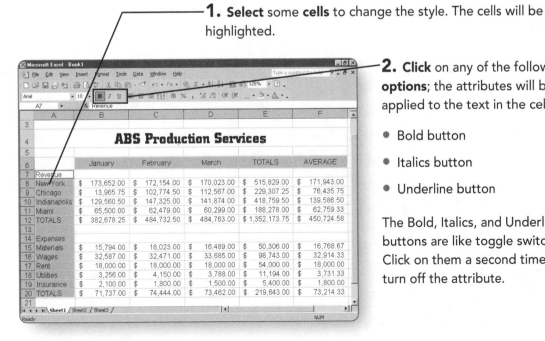

2. Click on any of the following **options**; the attributes will be applied to the text in the cell.

- Bold button
- Italics button
- Underline button

The Bold, Italics, and Underline buttons are like toggle switches. Click on them a second time to turn off the attribute.

Adding Cell Borders

You can add borders or lines to cells to emphasize important data. Borders are different from the gridlines that separate cells in the sheet. You can change the style and color of borders.

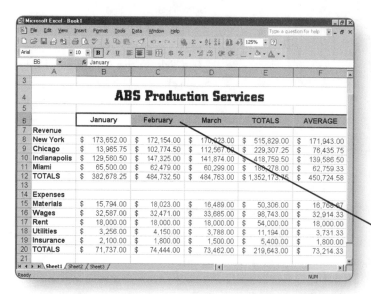

1. Select the **cells** you want to have borders or lines. The cells will be highlighted.

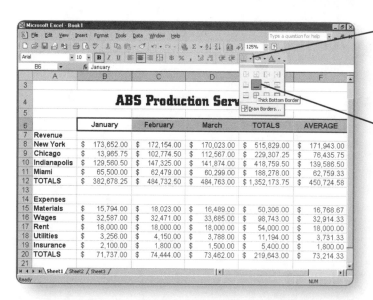

2. Click on the **down arrow** next to the Borders button. A selection of border styles will display.

3. Choose a **border line style**. The selected cells will display the border.

Changing the Spreadsheet Display

Excel includes several options to modify the display of your spreadsheet. Most display options do not affect how the spreadsheet prints, only the way you see it on the monitor. You'll learn about printing in Chapter 13, "Completing Your Spreadsheet".

Freezing Spreadsheet Titles

You can freeze columns, rows, or both so that column and row titles remain in view as you scroll through the sheet. This is particularly helpful with larger spreadsheets.

1. Click on the desired **cell**:

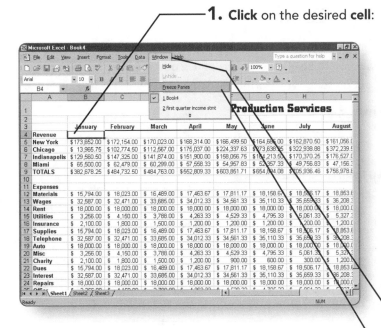

- To freeze columns, position the mouse pointer one cell to the right of the columns you want to freeze.

- To freeze rows, position the cell pointer one cell below the rows you want to freeze.

- To freeze both columns and rows, position the cell pointer in the cell below the rows and to the right of the columns you want to freeze.

2. Click on **Window**. The Window menu will appear.

3. Click on **Freeze Panes**. Lines will appear on the document indicating the frozen areas.

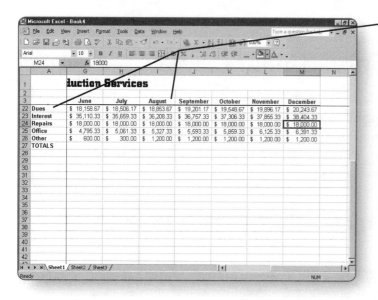

As you scroll downward or across in your document, the frozen part stays stationary on the screen while the rest of the text moves.

TIP

Repeat steps 2 and 3 to unfreeze the windows.

Using Zoom

Zoom enlarges or shrinks the display of your spreadsheet to allow you to see more or less of it. Zooming in or out does not affect printing. The normal display of your spreadsheet is 100%.

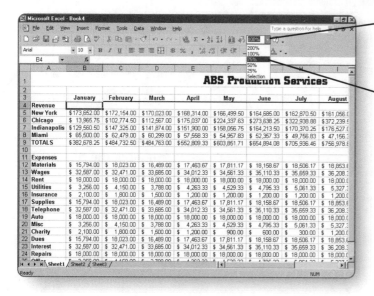

1. **Click** on the **down arrow** to the right of the Zoom button. A list of choices will display.

2. **Click** on a **magnification** (%) choice. The higher the number, the larger the cells will appear on-screen, and the less of the overall spreadsheet you'll be able to see. The display of your screen will adjust according to your selection.

TIP

Optionally, type your own magnification percentage.

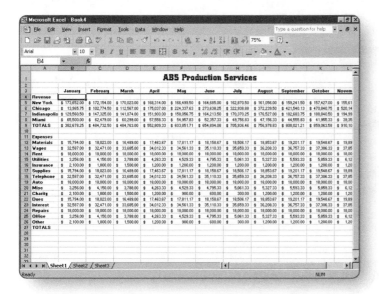

In this example, the zoom was set to 75%, which allowed more of the worksheet to display on the screen.

TIP

To reset the display to normal, change the zoom to 100%.

Viewing Formulas

When you create formulas, the result of the formula is displayed in the spreadsheet, not the formula itself. Having the formula displayed is a wonderful tool for troubleshooting formula errors in your spreadsheet.

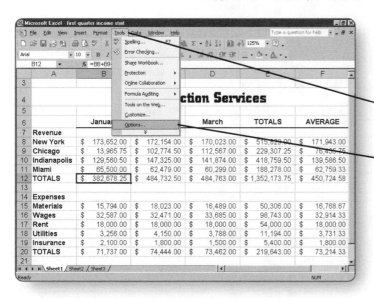

1. Click on **Tools**. The Tools menu will appear.

2. Click on **Options**. The Options dialog box will open.

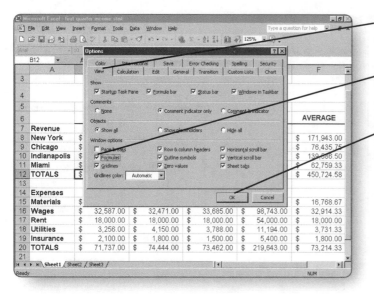

3. Click on the **View tab**. The View tab will come to the front.

4. Click on **Formulas**. A check mark will display in the option.

5. Click on **OK**. The dialog box will close.

The spreadsheet formulas will be displayed in each cell instead of the result of the formula. Each cell reference in a formula is assigned a color and a corresponding colored box surrounds the referenced cell.

The Formula Auditing toolbar will appear to assist you in tracing through formulas.

6. Repeat steps 1-5 to turn off display of the formulas.

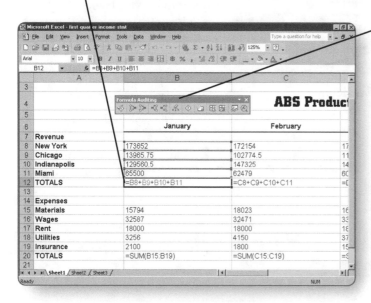

NOTE

If you print the spreadsheet while the formulas are displayed, the formulas will print, not the formula results.

13

Completing Your Spreadsheet

Now that you have created your spreadsheet with all its text, values, and formulas, you'll want to prepare it for final output. You should proof it for errors and specify what area you want to print. In this chapter, you'll learn how to:

- Prepare your sheet for printing
- Use Print Preview
- Print a spreadsheet
- E-mail a spreadsheet

Preparing to Print

Before you print your spreadsheet, you might want to tell Excel what size paper you'd like to use, how large the margins should be, and whether to print the gridlines or not. These options and others are selected from the Page Setup feature of Excel.

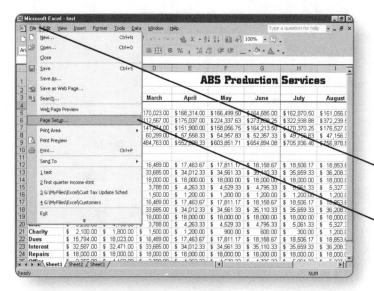

Setting Up Margins

By default, the top and bottom margins are set at 1 inch and the left and right margins are set at .75 inch. You can change these margins.

1. Click on **File**. The File menu will appear.

2. Click on **Page Setup**. The Page Setup dialog box will open.

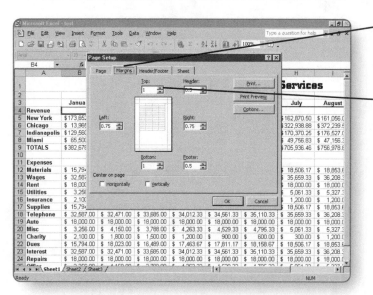

3. Click on the **Margins tab**. The Margins tab will come to the front.

4. Click on the **up/down arrows** on each margin that you want to change. A sample is displayed in the sample box.

Setting Page Orientation and Size

If your spreadsheet uses quite a few columns, you might want to change the orientation or paper size. The default size is 8½ by 11 inch paper in portrait orientation—the short side at the top. Changing to landscape orientation will print with the long edge of the paper at the top.

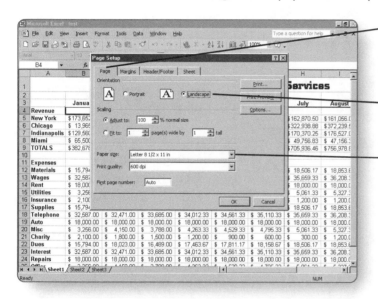

1. From the Page Setup dialog box, **click** on the **Page tab**. The Page tab will come to the front.

2. **Click** on an **Orientation**. The option will be selected.

3. **Click** on the **down arrow** at the right of the Paper Size list box. The list of available paper size options will appear.

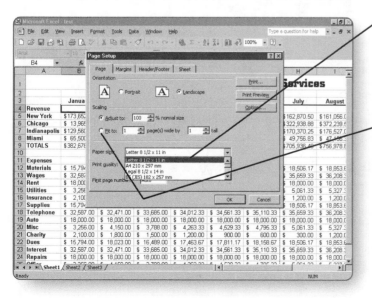

4. **Click** on a **paper size**. The paper size will be selected.

TIP

If you want to reduce the spreadsheet data when you print so that it fits on a specified number of pages, click on the Fit to option and enter the desired number of pages wide and pages tall.

Setting Other Printing Options

You might want to consider other options for your worksheet, such as whether to print the gridlines or the row and column headings.

1. From the Page Setup dialog box, **click** on the **Sheet tab**. The Sheet tab will come to the front.

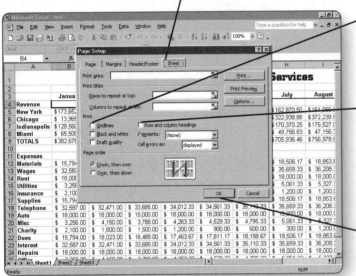

2. Click on **Gridlines** if you want to print the gridlines. A check mark will appear in the selection box.

3. Click on **Row and column headings** if you want the column headings or row headings to print on the spreadsheet. A check mark will appear in the selection box.

4. Click on **OK**. The Page Setup dialog box will close.

Printing a Spreadsheet

After you have created your spreadsheet, you can print a hard copy to send to someone else or have one for your records.

Using Print Preview

Print Preview allows you to check the overall spreadsheet on-screen prior to printing.

1. **Click** on the **Print Preview button**. The document will be sized so that an entire page is visible on the screen.

Don't strain your eyes trying to read the text in the Preview windows. You are looking at the overall perspective here, not necessarily the individual cells. The document is not editable on this screen.

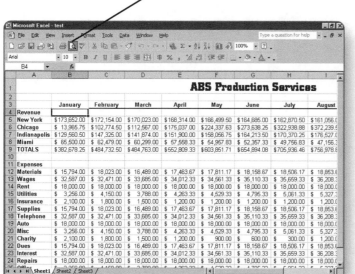

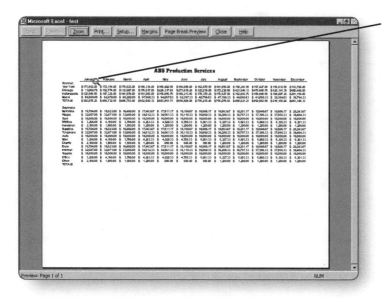

2. **Position** the **mouse pointer** over the document. The mouse pointer will turn into a magnifying glass.

3. **Click** on the **document**. The text will become larger on-screen.

4. **Click** on the **document** again. The text will become smaller on-screen.

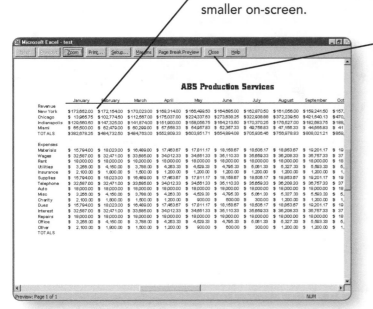

5. **Click** on **Close**. The spreadsheet will be returned to the normal view.

Printing Your Work

Typically, the end result of entering a document into Excel is to get text onto paper. Excel gives you a quick and easy way to get that result.

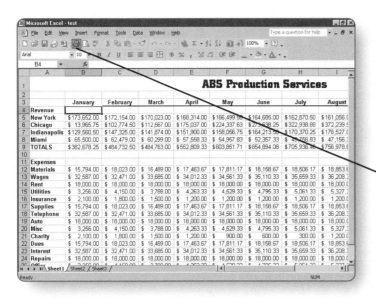

1a. **Click** on the **Print button**. The spreadsheet will print with standard options.

OR

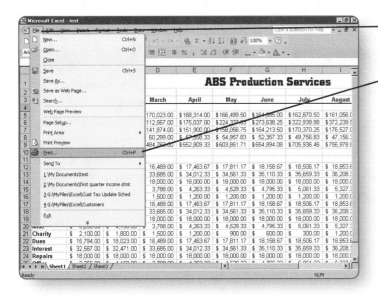

1b. Click on **File**. The File menu will appear.

2. Click on **Print**. The Print dialog box will open.

Many options are available from the Print dialog box, including:

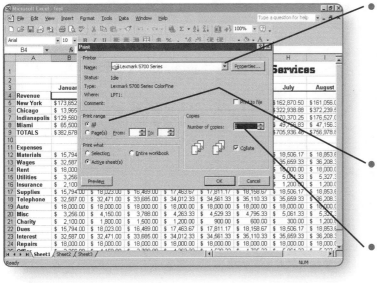

- **Printer name.** If you are connected to more than one printer, you can choose the name of the printer to use for this print job. Click on the down arrow at the right of the Name list box and make a selection.

- **Print range.** Choose which pages of your document to print with the Print range option boxes.

- **Number of copies.** Choose the number of copies to be printed by clicking on the up/down arrows in the Number of copies list box.

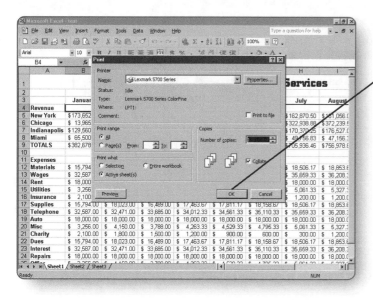

3. Click on any desired **option**. The option will be activated.

4. Click on **OK** after you have made your selections. The document will be sent to the printer. You can also click on the Preview button at this point to review the document before printing it.

E-mailing a Spreadsheet

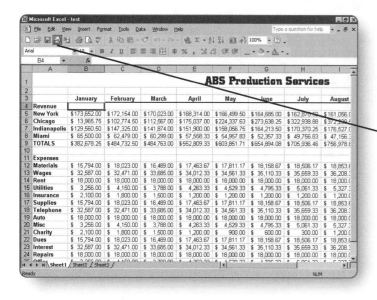

If you have e-mail access, you can send a document directly to another person. Excel copies the content of the spreadsheet into a blank e-mail message.

1. Click on the **e-mail button**. The e-mail header box will open.

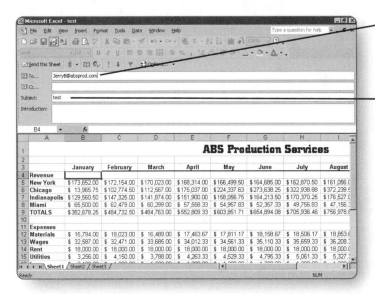

2. Type the **recipient's e-mail address**. The e-mail address will appear in the To box.

3. Click in the **Subject box and type** a **subject**. If you are using a previously saved document, Excel will automatically insert the document name as the subject of the e-mail.

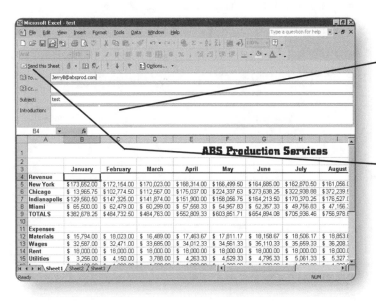

TIP

Optionally, click in the Introduction text box and type any additional introductory text.

4. Click on **Send this Sheet**. The spreadsheet text is sent to the recipient in the form of an e-mail message.

14

Creating Charts

A chart is an effective way to illustrate the data in your spreadsheet. It can make relationships between numbers easier to see because it turns numbers into shapes and the shapes can then be compared to one another. In this chapter, you'll learn how to:

- Create a chart
- Modify a chart
- Delete a chart

Creating a Chart

Creating a chart is a simple process using the Excel Chart Wizard. You first decide what you want data to chart and how you want it to look.

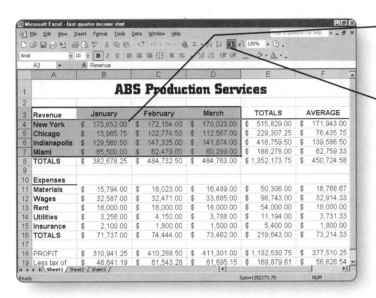

1. Select the **range** that you want to chart. The range will be highlighted.

2. Click on the **Chart Wizard button**. Step 1 of the Chart wizard will display on-screen.

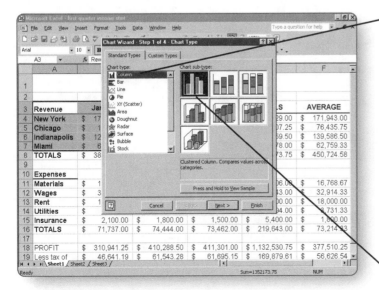

3. Click on a **Chart type**. A selection of chart subtypes will be displayed.

NOTE

Traditionally, bar charts compare item to item, pie charts compare parts of a whole item, and line charts show a trend over a period of time.

4. Click on a **Chart subtype**. The option will be selected.

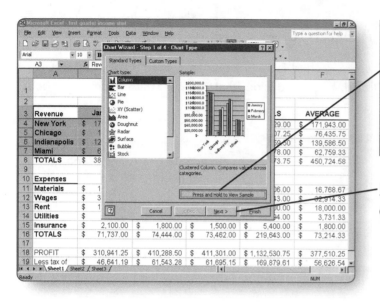

TIP

Click and hold the "Press and Hold to View Sample" button to see your highlighted data displayed as the selected chart type.

5. **Click** on **Next**. Step 2 of the Chart Wizard will display.

Excel will next try to determine the direction of the data; whether the values to be plotted are in rows or columns.

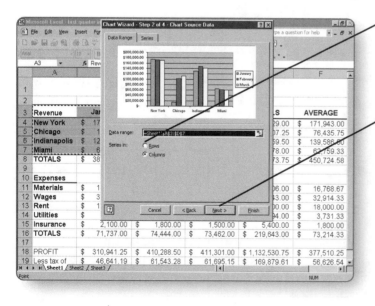

6. **Click** on **Rows** or **Columns** to display the data series in rows or columns. The option will be selected.

7. **Click** on **Next**. Step 3 of the Chart Wizard will display.

8. Click in the **Chart Title text box**. A blinking insertion point will appear.

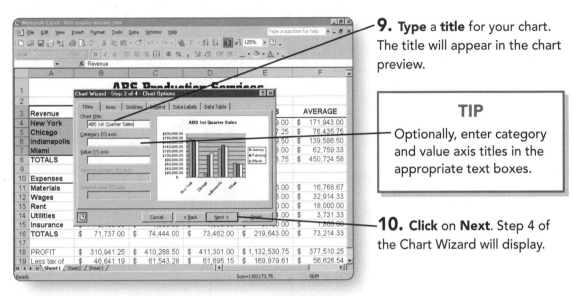

9. Type a **title** for your chart. The title will appear in the chart preview.

TIP

Optionally, enter category and value axis titles in the appropriate text boxes.

10. Click on **Next**. Step 4 of the Chart Wizard will display.

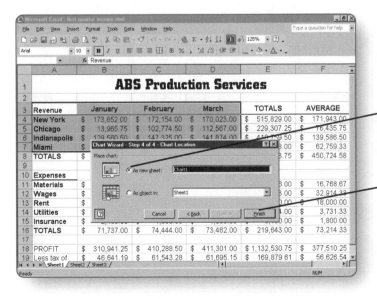

You must now choose whether you want the chart to display on its own sheet or to appear on the same sheet as the data.

11. Click on a **Place Chart option button**. The option will be selected.

12. Click on **Finish**. The Wizard will close. The chart will be displayed either as a new sheet or below the existing data.

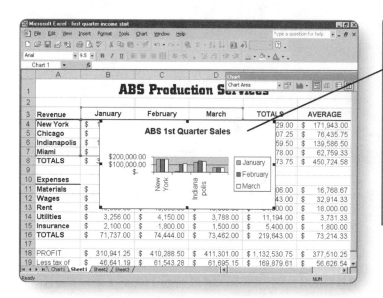

NOTE

When a chart is on the same page as the data, the chart is selected when eight black handles appear around the outer edge of a chart. Click outside of the chart to deselect it, or click on the chart to select it.

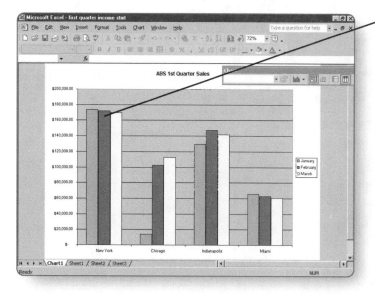

The data from the selected cells of the spreadsheet is plotted in a chart. If the data in the spreadsheet changes, the chart will also change automatically.

In the next section, you'll learn how to change the size and look of your chart.

Modifying a Chart

Creating a chart is so simple that it probably will make you want to enhance the chart to improve its appearance. Items you can change include the size, style, color, and placement.

Resizing a Chart

When a chart is inserted on the spreadsheet page, it will probably be too small to read the data correctly. You can use your mouse to resize it.

1. If necessary, **click** on the **chart** to select it. The chart will have eight small handles around it.

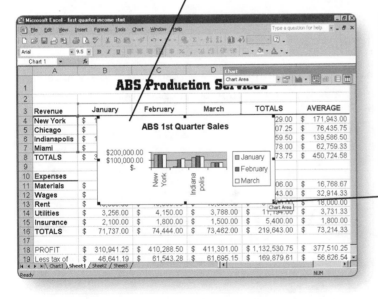

2. Position the **mouse pointer** over one of the handles. The mouse pointer will change to a double-headed arrow.

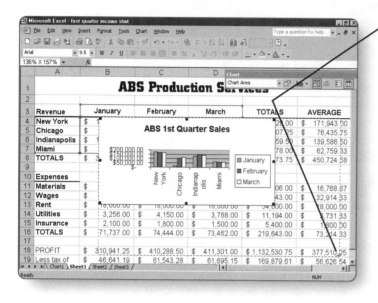

3. **Press** the **mouse button** and **drag** the black **handle**. A dotted line will indicate the new chart size.

4. **Release** the **mouse button**. The chart will be resized.

Moving a Chart

When a chart is inserted on the spreadsheet page, you can easily move it to any location on the page.

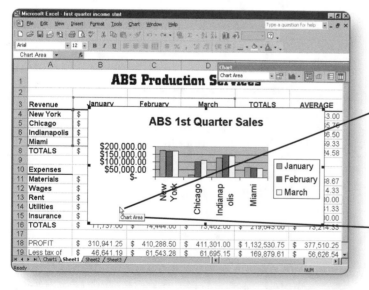

1. If necessary, **click** on the **chart** to select it. The chart will have eight small handles around it.

2. **Position** the **mouse pointer** anywhere over a blank area of the chart. The mouse pointer will be a left-pointing, white arrow.

You will also see a yellow tool tip indicating you're pointing to the chart area.

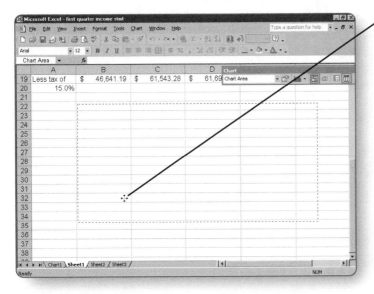

3. **Press** the **mouse button** and drag the **chart** to the new location. The mouse will turn into a four-headed arrow and a dotted line box will indicate the new position.

4. **Release** the **mouse button**. The chart will be moved.

Changing a Chart Style

If you want to change the style of the chart, you can select a bar, area, pie, line, or a number of other style charts. Most of these charts can also be 3-D.

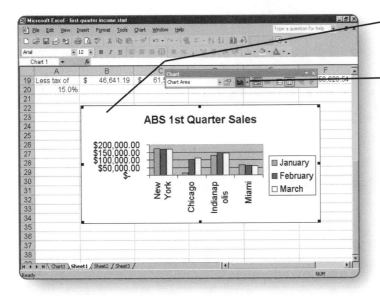

1. If necessary, **click** on the **chart**. The chart will be selected.

2. **Click** on the **down arrow** to the right of the Chart Type button on the Chart Toolbar. A list of chart types will display.

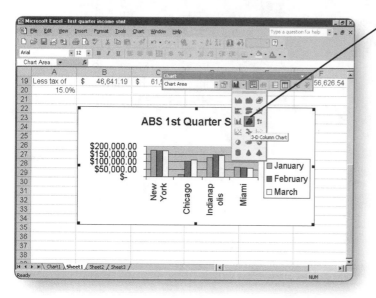

3. Click on a **chart type**. The chart will change to the selected type.

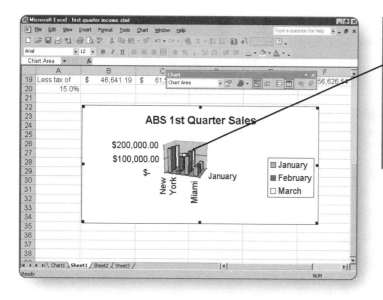

TIP

Use 3-D charts sparingly. Adding the extra dimension might make the chart look nice, but can also make the data difficult to read.

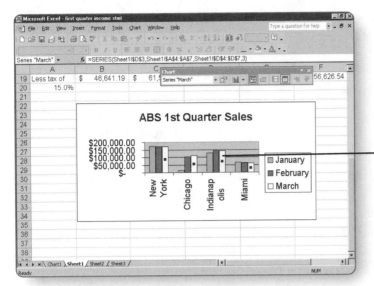

Changing the Series Appearance

If you do not like the default colors assigned to a chart, you can change them for any series.

1. Double-click on any colored **bar, line, or series** item. A small black square will appear in all items in the selected series and the Format Data Series dialog box will open.

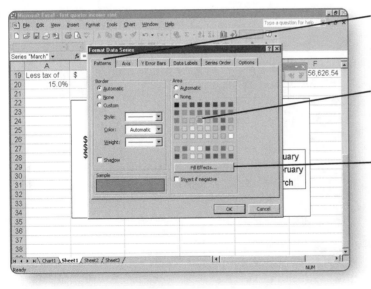

2. If necessary, **click** on **Patterns**. The Patterns tab will come to the front.

3. Click on a **color** for the selected series. The color will be highlighted.

4. Click on **Fill Effects**. The Fill Effects dialog box will open.

5. Click on the **Gradient, Texture, or Pattern tabs**. The tab will come to the front with its available options.

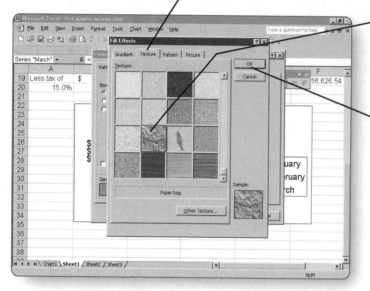

6. Click on any desired **gradient, texture, or pattern options** for the selected series. The pattern will be highlighted.

7. Click on **OK**. The Fill Effects dialog box will close.

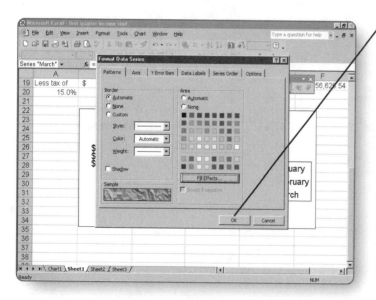

8. Click on **OK**. The Format Data Series dialog box will close and the series will change to the selected options.

9. Repeat the previous **steps** for each series to be modified.

> ### TIP
> Double-click on any section of the chart to edit options for that section.

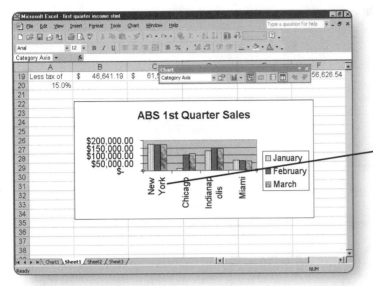

Modifying Chart Text

You can modify any text font, size, color, or border by double-clicking on the text.

1. Double-click on the **text** to be modified. The Format dialog box for that section will open. For example, here the Format Axis dialog box appeared, because the axis text was selected.

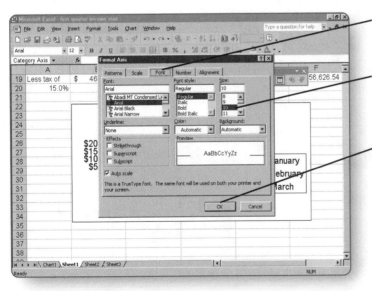

2. Click on the **Font tab**. The Font tab will come to the front.

3. Click on any desired **font changes**. The options will be selected.

4. Click on **OK**. The dialog box will close and the font changes will take affect.

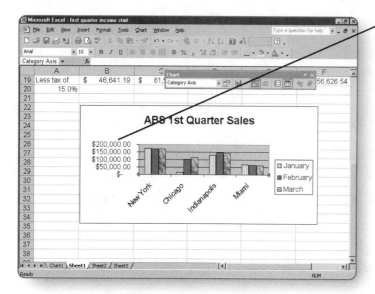

5. Repeat for any **text** to be modified.

Deleting a Chart

If you no longer want the chart created from your spreadsheet, you can delete it. The method you'll use to delete the chart depends on whether the chart is on the same sheet as the data or on a separate sheet.

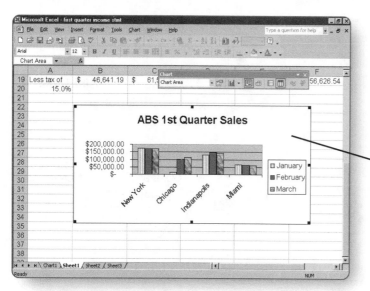

Deleting a Chart on a Data Sheet

If the chart is on the same sheet as the data, you'll delete it with the Delete key.

1. Click on the **chart**. The chart will be selected.

2. Press the **Delete key**. The chart will be deleted.

Deleting a Chart on Its Own Sheet

If the chart is on a separate sheet, you'll need to delete the entire sheet to delete the chart.

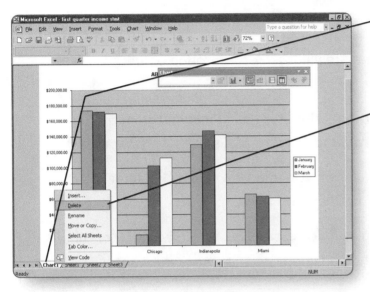

1. **Right-click** on the **sheet tab**. This tab is usually marked Chart1, Chart2, and so forth. A shortcut menu will appear.

2. **Click** on **Delete**. A confirmation message will appear.

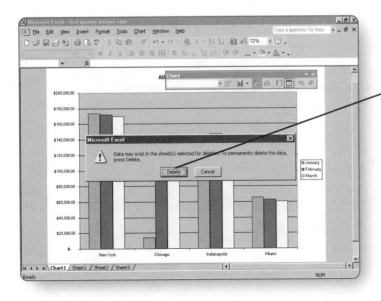

Note that deleting a chart sheet does *not* delete *any data* from the originating spreadsheet.

3. **Click** on **Delete**. The chart sheet will be deleted.

Part III Review Questions

1. What is a cell address? *See "Exploring the Spreadsheet Screen" in Chapter 9*

2. In a spreadsheet, what are values? *See "Entering Values" in Chapter 9*

3. How can you move information from one location to another in Excel? *See "Using Drag-and-Drop to Move Cells" in Chapter 10*

4. All spreadsheet formulas must begin with which character? *See "Creating Formulas" in Chapter 11*

5. In a compound formula, which is calculated first: addition or multiplication? *See "Creating a Compound Formula" in Chapter 11*

6. What does the SUM function do? *See "Using the SUM Function" in Chapter 11*

7. What is the maximum width of an Excel column? *See "Adjusting Column Widths" in Chapter 12*

8. What does freezing columns or rows do? *See "Freezing Spreadsheet Titles" in Chapter 12*

9. How do you tell Excel you want to print row and column headings? *See "Setting Other Printing Options" in Chapter 13*

10. How does the Chart Wizard assist you when creating a chart? *See "Creating a Chart" in Chapter 14*

PART IV

Using PowerPoint

15

Creating and Viewing Presentations

You can use PowerPoint to enhance your presentations. Each PowerPoint presentation file consists of *slides* that contain information that you want to convey to an audience. Think of PowerPoint slides as pages of your presentation. Don't confuse PowerPoint presentation slides with 35mm slides, which are only one of the ways you can store (and present) your presentation. You can also store your PowerPoint presentation slides on overhead transparencies, or you can simply print them on paper and give them to your audience. And, if you prefer, you can create a computer slide show in PowerPoint as well. In this chapter, you'll learn how to:

- Create a presentation using a template
- Add text to a slide
- Add slides
- Change views

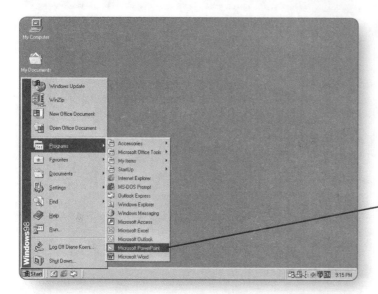

Creating a Presentation

PowerPoint creates each presentation file based on a *template*. A template contains predefined information, such as text and colors.

1. Start PowerPoint. PowerPoint will launch with a blank presentation on the screen.

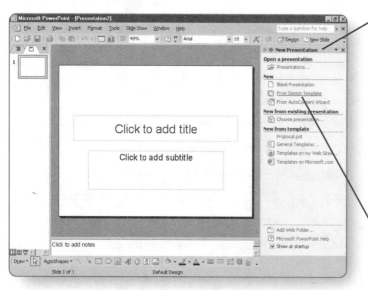

The New Presentation Task Pane will appear on the right side on the screen.

NOTE

You'll find the Task Pane helpful when working with PowerPoint.

2. Click on **From Design Template**. The Slide Design task pane will appear.

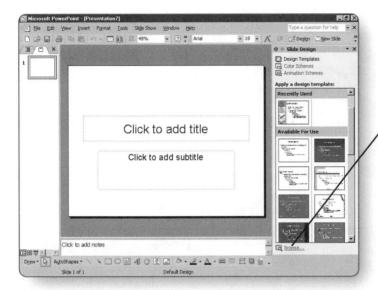

Although a selection of design templates will appear in the task pane, I personally find them hard to see, so I prefer to use the Browse dialog box.

3. **Click** on **Browse**. The Apply Design Template dialog box will open.

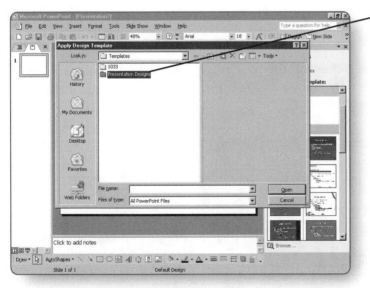

4. **Double-click** on **Presentation Designs**. A selection of design templates will appear.

5. Click on a **template** on which to base your presentation. You will see a preview of the template on the right side of the dialog box. Choose a template that most closely represents the concept you're trying to communicate.

In Chapter 16, "Editing a Presentation," you'll learn how to add or edit any sample text to match your needs.

6. Click on **Apply**. PowerPoint will display the first slide of your new presentation in tri-pane view.

The first slide created is a title slide. You'll learn about the different types of slide layouts in Chapter 16 "Editing a Presentation."

TIP

Save this presentation using the procedures you learned in Chapter 3, "Finding Common Ways to Work."

Adding Text to a Slide

All new slides contain instruction blocks or placeholders to help you organize your presentation. The text that appears on a slide is handled differently than with a standard word processor such as Word. Text is stored in objects called *text blocks*.

Placeholders only appear in the slide edit view. They do not display or print in other views. You'll learn about views later in this chapter.

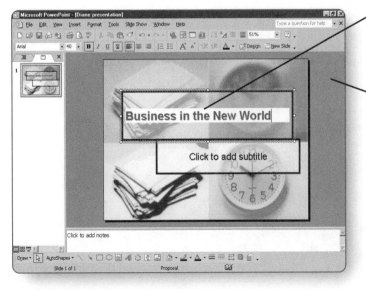

1. Click on a **text place holder**. The blinking insertion point will appear.

2. Type the desired **text**. The "Click to add" text will be replaced with your text.

3. Click on the **gray area** on-screen. The insertion point and the handles that surrounded the text object box will disappear.

NOTE

Clicking on the gray area indicates that you are done typing and ready to take some other action.

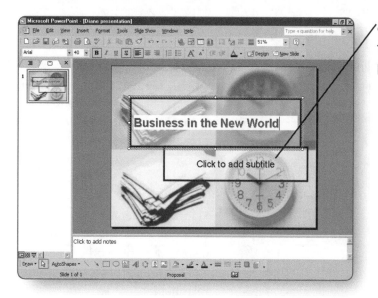

4. Optionally, **repeat steps 1–3** for any additional text placeholders.

Adding Slides

Each page in your presentation is called a slide and all the slides are saved in a single file. You can have as many slides in your presentation as you need and you can add a slide to a presentation at any time.

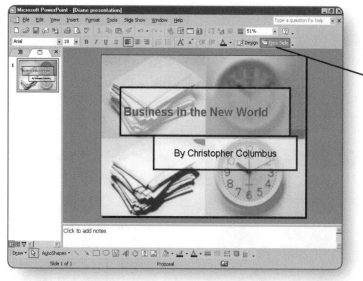

1. Click on the **New Slide button**. A new slide is added to your presentation.

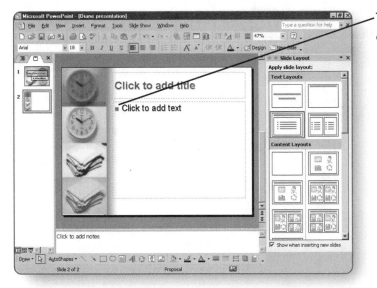

The new slide takes the layout of a bullet slide.

Adding Bullet Point Text

Bullet point slides also have a place for the slide title, but in the bottom of the slide, a text placeholder exists to add strategic bullet point text.

You add bulleted text in a similar manner as a title.

1. Click on **Click to add text**. Those words will disappear and will be replaced by a text object box containing an insertion point.

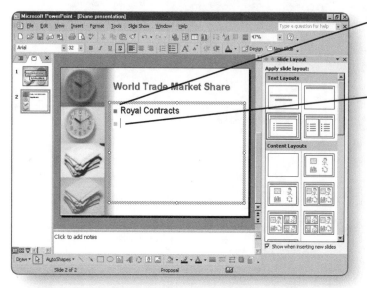

2. Type some **text**. The text will appear on the line with a bullet point in front.

3. Press the **Enter key**. PowerPoint will start a new line preceded by a bullet.

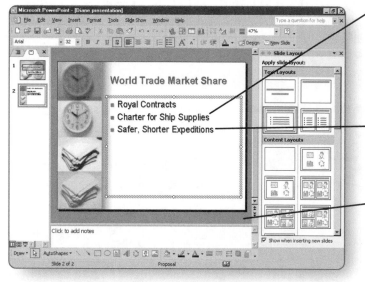

4. Type more **text**. The text will appear on the screen.

5. Press the **Enter key**. An additional bullet will appear.

6. Type text for each bullet you need until you finish typing the last bullet.

7. Click on the **gray area** on-screen. The insertion point and the handles that surrounded the text object box will disappear and you will see the bullets you typed on-screen.

Switching Views

You can display your presentation in one of several views in PowerPoint. In the following section, you will explore each of the views in PowerPoint and see how to move from slide to slide in each view.

Using Normal Tri-Pane View

Up to this point, you've been working in Normal view. Normal view is really a combination of several views. With Normal view you can see your individual slides as well as speaker notes and an overall slide view all at the same time.

Viewing Slides

The Slide pane shows you a close-up image of your slide the way it will appear when you print it.

1. Click on the **Slide you want to view**. The selected slide will appear.

The status bar tells you the number of slides in your presentation and which slide you are viewing.

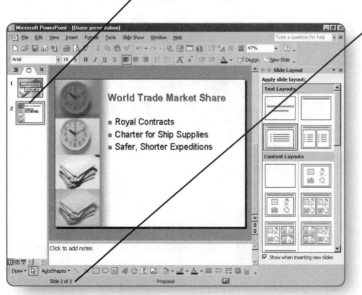

Using Slide Sorter View

Use Slide Sorter view to see a miniature view of each slide in the presentation. Slide Sorter view provides an easy way to view the overall effects of your presentation and check for variety in slide appearance —variety helps keep your audience awake. You can't edit slides in Slide Sorter view, but you can change the order in which the slides appear.

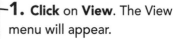

1. Click on **View**. The View menu will appear.

2. Click on **Slide Sorter**. You will see all the slides in your presentation. A dark border will appear around the selected slide.

TIP

Optionally, click on the Slide Sorter view button.

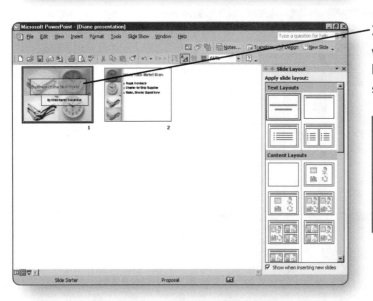

3. Click on a **slide**. PowerPoint will select the slide, and a black border will appear around the slide.

TIP

Double-click on a slide to return to Normal view in order to complete this section.

Adding and Viewing Speaker Notes

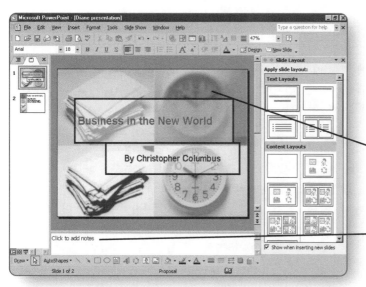

You can create *speaker notes* — notes to remind yourself of what you want to say when a slide appears. In Chapter 16, "Editing a Presentation," you'll learn how to print these notes.

1. In Normal view, **display** the **slide** to have a note attached. The slide will display in the Slide pane.

2. Click in the **Notes pane**. The blinking insertion point will appear.

3. Type the **text** that you want to store as a note for the selected slide. The text will display in the Notes pane.

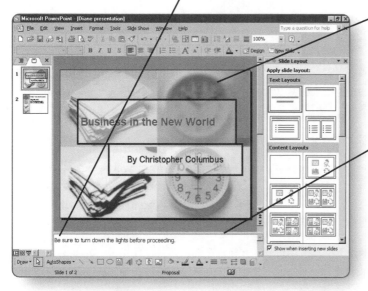

4. Click on the **slide**. PowerPoint will accept the changes to the notes box.

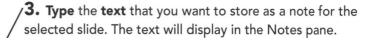

TIP

To modify the size of any window in the Normal view, position the mouse pointer over an edge of the window and drag the window to a new size.

Viewing the Outline

In the Outline pane, your presentation appears like an outline that you use when organizing your thoughts. Use the Outline view to help you organize your presentation information. In the Outline pane, you can see all the information on each slide; the title of each slide appears as a heading, and the information on the slide appears below.

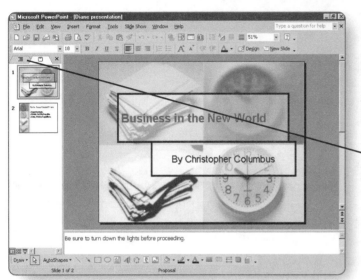

1. Click on the **Outline tab**. The Outline will display.

A number and an icon will appear to the left of each slide.

2. Position the **mouse pointer** over the slide icon. The shape of the mouse pointer will change to a four-headed arrow.

3. Click on the **icon**. PowerPoint will select all the information for that slide and display the selected slide.

4. Click on the **Slides tab**. The miniature slides will redisplay.

Viewing a Slide Show

Use Slide Show view to display your presentation on-screen. In Chapter 17, "Working with Presentation Special Effects," you'll learn how to make a livelier on-screen presentation.

1. Click on the **first slide** of the presentation. The first slide will display.

2. Click on **View**. The View menu will appear.

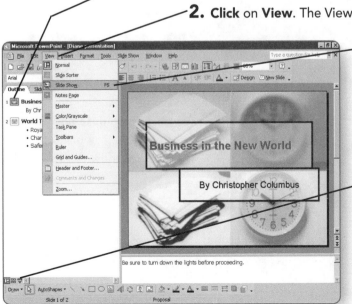

3. Click on **Slide Show**. All screen elements will disappear, and the image of the first slide will fill your screen.

TIP
Optionally, click on the Slide Show button.

4. **Click** the **mouse button** or **press** the **right arrow key**. The slide show will advance to the next slide.

TIP

Press the left arrow key to return to the previous slide.

5. **Continue clicking** the **mouse button** or **pressing** the **right arrow key**. Each subsequent slide will display.

TIP

Press the Esc key to end the slide show at any time.

At the end of the slide show a final slide message will display.

6. **Click** the **mouse** anywhere on the screen. The previous view will reappear.

16

Editing a Presentation

Although a PowerPoint template provides some rather impressive slides, you'll need to make modifications to any presentation you create. In this chapter, you'll learn how to:

- Edit and delete slides
- Rearrange the order of slides
- Change a presentation's background appearance
- Change a slide's layout
- Print a presentation

Deleting and Rearranging Slides

In Chapter 15, "Creating and Viewing Presentations," you learned about the different views provided by PowerPoint. Most editing is easiest accomplished while in the Normal tri-pane view.

Deleting Slides

Deleting unwanted slides is only a keystroke away!

1. **Click** on the **slide** you want to delete. The slide will be selected.

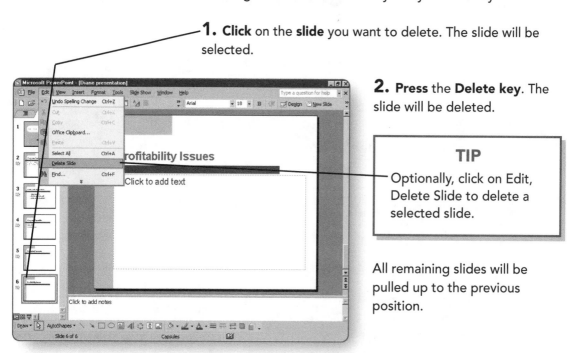

2. **Press** the **Delete key**. The slide will be deleted.

> ### TIP
> Optionally, click on Edit, Delete Slide to delete a selected slide.

All remaining slides will be pulled up to the previous position.

Rearranging Slides

You might decide that you'd rather display slides in an order other than the one you originally created.

1. Click on the **slide** you want to move. The slide will be selected.

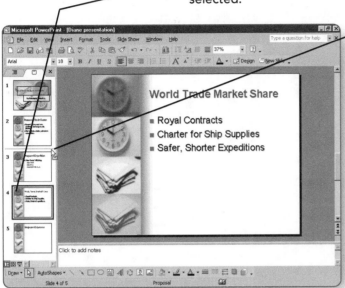

2. Drag the **selected slide** to its new location. As you drag, the mouse pointer will change to an arrow with a box at the bottom of it.

You will see a horizontal gray line as you drag. This bar represents the location where the new slide will appear when you drop the slide.

3. Release the **mouse button**. The slide will appear in its new position.

Editing Text

You might want to change text that appears on slides. You can edit the text that appears on your slides in a variety of ways. Editing text is easiest from the Normal view.

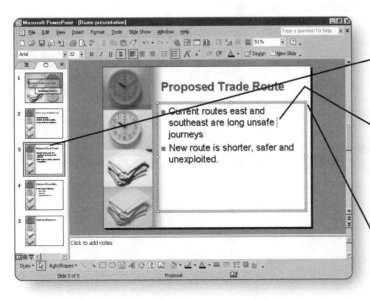

1. Click on the **slide** that contains text to be changed. The slide will display.

2. Click on the **text** you want to modify. The text will display in a text object box and a blinking insertion point will appear where you clicked.

Text object boxes appear surrounded by a border that contains small white squares called *handles*.

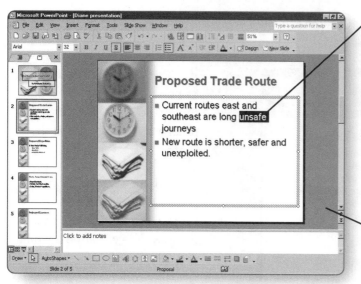

3. Optionally, **select** any **unwanted text**. Click and drag the mouse pointer across the text you want to modify. The selected text will be highlighted.

4. Type the new **text**. The new text will appear in the text object box.

5. Click on the **gray area** on-screen. Your text changes will be accepted.

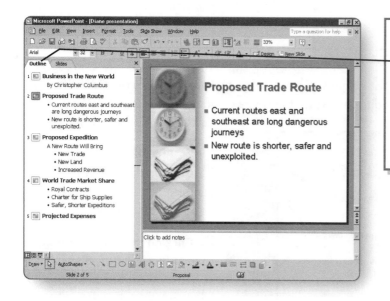

TIP

If you're more comfortable working in a word processing environment, click on the Outline tab and make your changes to text in the outline.

Changing Text Font

You might want to change the font type or size of your slide's text.

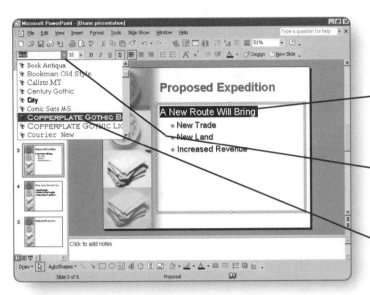

1. Display the **slide** you want to change. The slide will be in the Slide pane.

2. Select the **text** you want to change. The text will be highlighted.

3. Click on the **down arrow** next to the Font list box. A list of available fonts will appear.

4. Click on the **font** that you want to use. The selected text will reflect the new font.

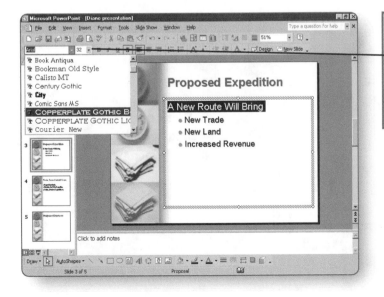

TIP

You can change font size by selecting the text and making a choice from the Font Size list box.

Deleting a Text Object

You might find that you need to delete a text object on a slide without deleting the slide.

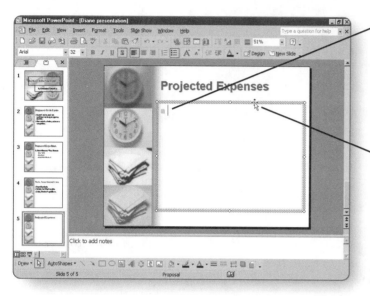

1. Click on the **text object** that you want to delete. The selected object will have eight small handles surrounding it and the border will have a striped appearance to it.

As the mouse pointer passes over the border, you will see a four-headed arrow.

If you clicked in the area of existing text, you'll need to select the outside border of the box.

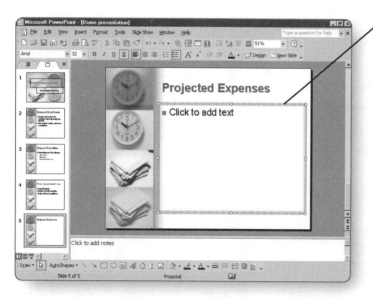

2. If necessary, **click** on the **border** of the text object. The border will change from stripes to dots.

3. Press the **Delete key**. Any existing text and the text object will disappear.

Moving a Text Object

If you have a text object that's not in the position you want, you can use your mouse to move it to a new position on the slide.

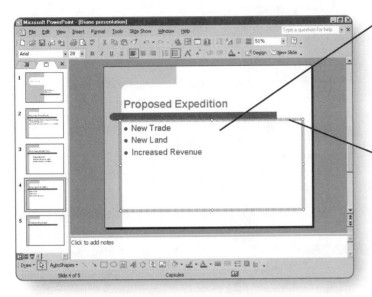

1. Click on the **text object** that you want to move. The selected object will have eight small handles surrounding it and the border will have a striped or dotted appearance to it.

2. If necessary, **click** on the **border** of the text object. The border will change from stripes to dots.

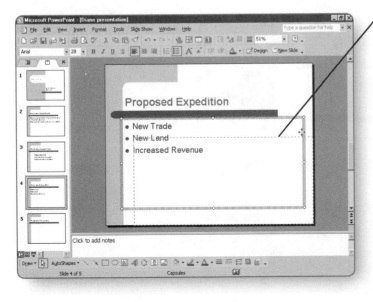

3. Drag the **border** to a new position. An outline box will indicate the new position.

4. Release the **mouse button**. The entire text object will move.

Resizing a Text Object

Any text object can be resized to make it larger or smaller.

1. Click on the **text object** that you want to resize. The selected object will have eight small handles surrounding it and the border will have a striped or dotted appearance to it.

2. If necessary, **click** on the **border** of the text object. The border will change from stripes to dots.

3. Position the **mouse** over one of the white handle boxes surrounding the text object. The mouse pointer will turn into a double-headed black arrow.

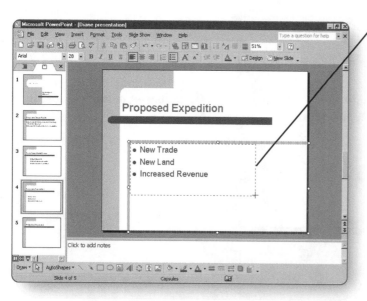

4. Click and **drag** the **handle**. The new outline of the text object will appear.

5. Release the **mouse button**. The text object will be resized.

Changing Presentation Designs

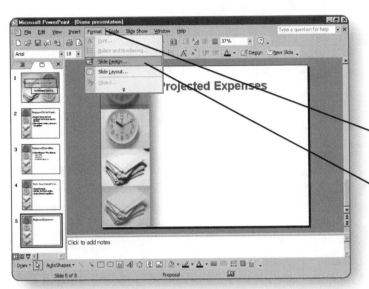

If you don't really like the background appearance of your presentation, you don't need to start over; you can simply change the presentation design.

1. Click on **Format**. The Format menu will appear.

2. Click on **Slide Design**. The Slide Design task pane will open and display available designs.

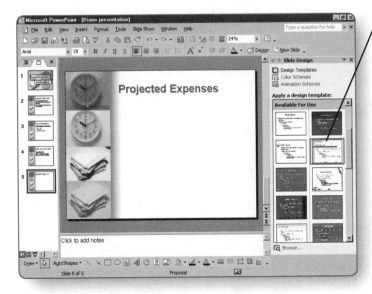

3. Click on a **design**. The design you selected will be applied to the current presentation.

TIP

To enlarge the view of the design templates, click on the arrow next to a template and choose Show Large Previews.

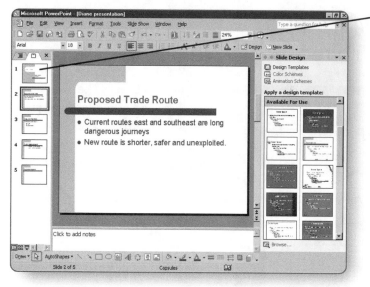

All slides will adopt the new design.

Changing Slide Layouts

You might find that you need to change the layout of a slide. For example, you might need to change a bullet layout to a table layout or a double column layout. The layout can be modified from either Normal or Slide Sorter view.

1. Click on the **slide** with the layout you want to change. The slide will be selected.

2. Click on **Format**. The Format menu will appear.

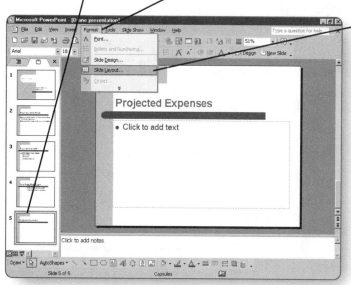

3. Click on **Slide Layout**. The Slide Layout task pane will open.

From the task pane, you will see visual representations of possible slide layout styles.

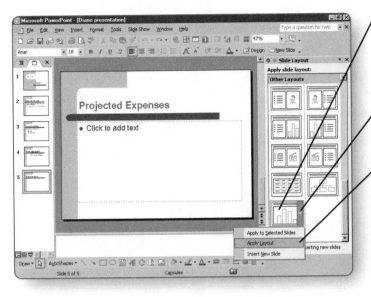

4. Click on a **layout**. The layout will be selected and an arrow will appear on the right side of the selected layout.

5. Click on the **arrow**. A menu will appear.

6. Click on **Apply Layout**. The layout of the selected slide will change to the layout you chose.

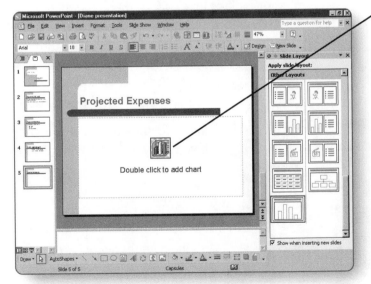

All objects on the slide are rearranged and, depending on the layout and the current view, new placeholders might appear.

Printing a Presentation

You can print your presentation on paper or on overhead transparencies (which you can use to display the presentation on an overhead projector). The steps you follow to print are the same, regardless of the medium to which you choose to print; just place the correct medium in your printer.

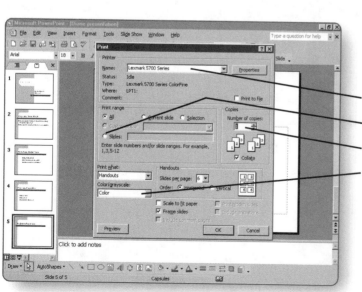

1. Click on **File**. The File menu will appear.

2. Click on **Print**. The Print dialog box will open.

TIP

Optionally, click on the Print button to automatically print one copy of each slide in your presentation to the default printer. The Print dialog box will not open.

Included among the items you can specify from the Print dialog box are:

- A printer
- A specific slide to print
- The number of copies to print
- Whether to print in color or black and white. Note: This feature is available only if you have a printer capable of printing in color.

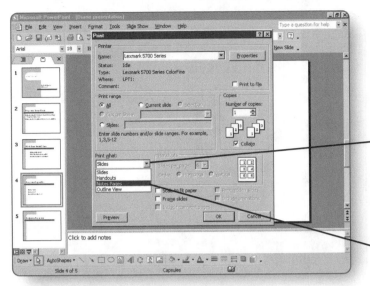

By default, the slides themselves will print, however, you can also opt to print the outline, speaker notes (called notes pages), or even handouts for your audience.

3. Click on the **down arrow** next to the Print What list box. A list of choices will appear, including slides, handouts, notes pages, and outline view.

4. Click on a **selection**. The selection will appear in the list box.

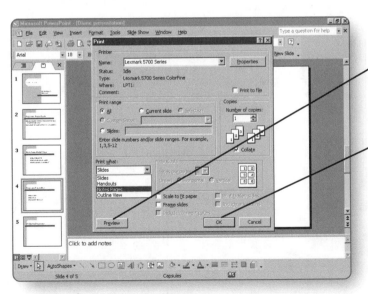

TIP

Optionally, click on Preview to preview your selections before printing.

5. Click on **OK**. The slide features you chose will print.

17

Working with Presentation Special Effects

Adding special effects to a presentation is, perhaps, the most fun part of creating a presentation. And, special effects can enhance the effectiveness of your presentation if you use them in moderation. In this chapter, you'll learn how to:

- Add tables and charts to a slide
- Work with clip art
- Add transitions between slides

Adding Tables

When you add a table to a slide in PowerPoint, you actually insert a Microsoft Word table. Creating the slide with a table layout is the easiest method.

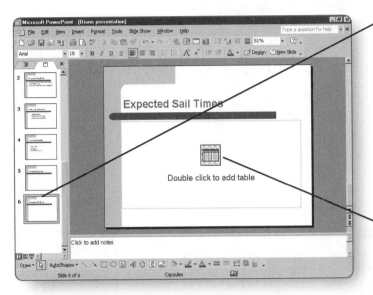

1. Display the **slide** to which you will add a table. The slide will be displayed.

> ### TIP
> If your slide doesn't have a table button in the center, click on Insert, Table.

2. Double-click on the **button** in the center of the slide. The Insert Table dialog box will open, suggesting a table of two columns and two rows.

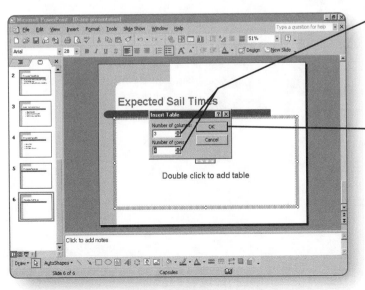

3. Click on the **up or down arrows** to increase or decrease the number of columns or rows. The new quantity will display in the box.

4. Click on **OK**. After a few moments, a table will appear on your slide.

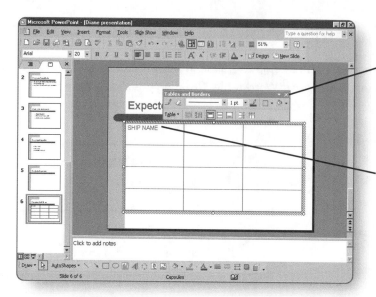

TIP

Optionally, click on the Close box to close the Tables and Borders Toolbar.

5. Type some text in the first column. The text will display in the first table cell.

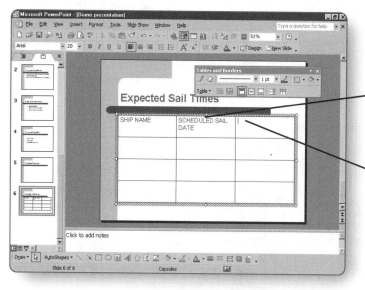

6. Press the **Tab key**. The blinking insertion point will move to the next cell.

7. Type some text in the second column. The text will display in the second table cell.

8. Press the **Tab key.** The insertion point will move to the next cell.

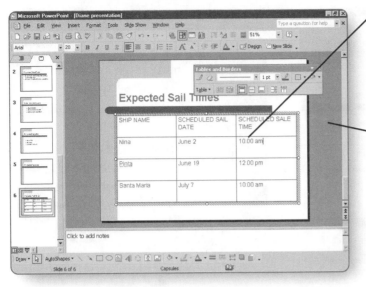

9. Type some **text** for the rest of the cells in the table, pressing the Tab key to move from cell to cell. The text will display in the table cells.

10. When you are done, **click** on the **gray area** outside the slide. The table will be deselected.

TIP

To edit the data in the table, click in the cell to be modified and type any changes.

Inserting Charts

You can insert charts in PowerPoint in two ways: you can create the chart in PowerPoint or you can copy a chart you previously created in Excel.

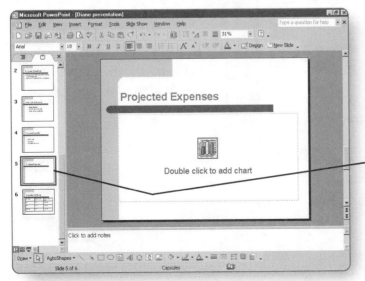

Creating a Chart in PowerPoint

You can add a slide that contains a chart created by PowerPoint.

1. Display the **slide** to contain the chart. A button in the middle of the slide will display telling you how to add a chart.

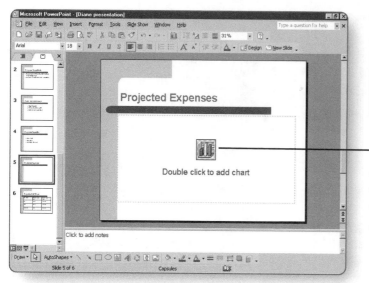

TIP

If your slide doesn't have a chart button in the center, click on Insert, Chart.

2. Double-click on the **button**. A sample chart and a datasheet window will display containing the data used in the sample chart.

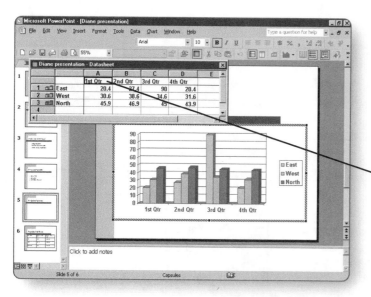

You'll make changes in the datasheet window to make changes to the chart. Make changes to the cells of a datasheet just like you learned in Chapter 9, "Creating a Simple Spreadsheet."

3. Change the **text** and **values** in the cells of the datasheet as needed. Your text and values will display.

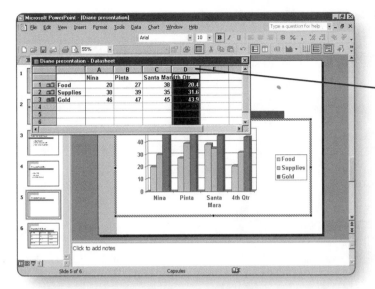

You might need to delete any extra sample column or row data.

4. Click on the **column letter or row number** you want to delete. The entire column or row will be highlighted.

5. Press the **Delete key**. All the data in the column will disappear, and the chart will adjust itself to display only the data in the remaining columns.

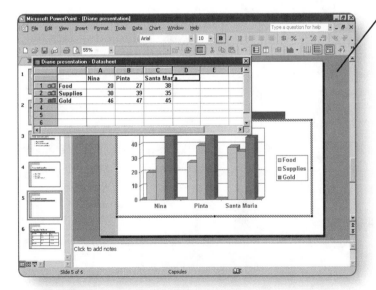

6. Click on the **gray area** outside the slide. The changes to the chart will be accepted.

The datasheet window will close.

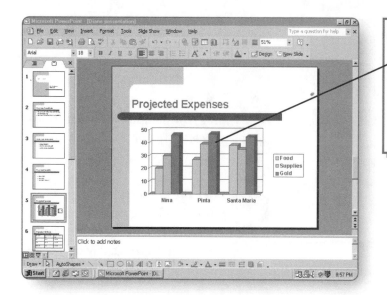

TIP

If you need to modify any information on the chart, double-click on the chart to reopen the datasheet window.

Inserting an Excel Chart

In Chapter 14, "Creating Charts," you learned how to create charts in Excel. You can insert an Excel chart into a PowerPoint slide. You'll use the Windows Copy and Paste commands to accomplish this.

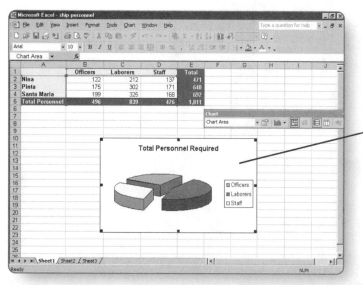

1. Start Excel and open the **worksheet** containing the chart that you want to place in PowerPoint. The chart will display on the screen.

2. Click on the **chart**. The chart will be selected.

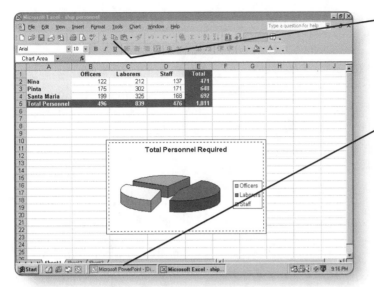

3. Click on the **Copy button.** "Marching ants" will appear around the chart and Excel will copy the chart to the Windows Clipboard.

4. Open or switch to your **PowerPoint presentation.** Your presentation will display.

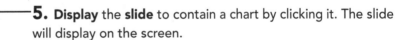

5. Display the **slide** to contain a chart by clicking it. The slide will display on the screen.

6. Click on the **Paste button.** A copy of the Excel chart will appear with handles, indicating it is selected.

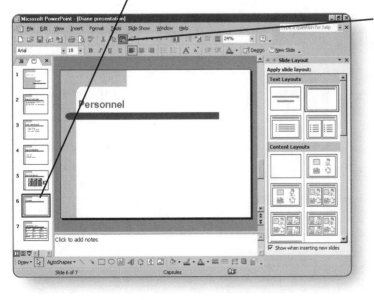

The chart probably will be hard to read because it is too small. You'll need to resize it.

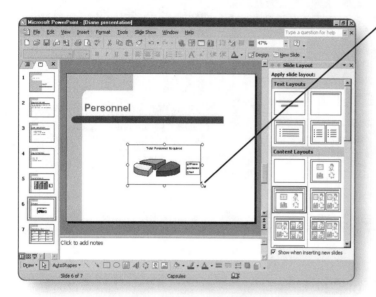

7. Position the **mouse** over one of the handles. The mouse pointer will turn into a double-headed arrow.

TIP

Dragging on a corner handle allows you to resize the chart in both directions (length and width) simultaneously and maintain the chart's proportions. The middle handles resize the chart in a single direction.

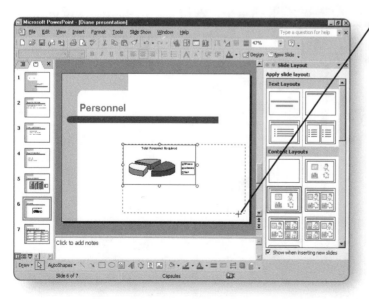

8. Drag a **chart handle** outward. The mouse pointer will change to a cross and a dotted line will indicate the new chart size.

9. Release the **mouse button**. The chart will be resized.

Moving a Chart

You can also move the chart to a different position on the page.

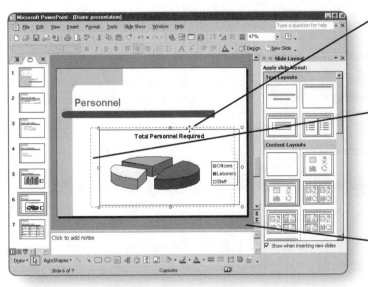

1. **Move** the **mouse pointer** over the chart edge. The mouse pointer will change to a four-headed arrow.

2. **Drag** the **chart** to a different location on the slide. A dotted box indicates the new position.

3. **Release** the **mouse button**. The chart will be moved.

4. **Click anywhere** on the gray area. PowerPoint will cancel the selection.

NOTE

The chart you just inserted will not be updated if you make changes to the version in Excel. To update this slide, you have to make the changes in Excel and then delete the chart on the PowerPoint slide (select it and press the Delete key). Finally, perform the steps in this section to insert the updated chart.

Working with Clip Art

You can add visual interest to your slides by using clip art. When Office was installed, some clip art was copied to your hard drive. Additional clip art is available from the Microsoft Web site (**http://www.microsoft.com**).

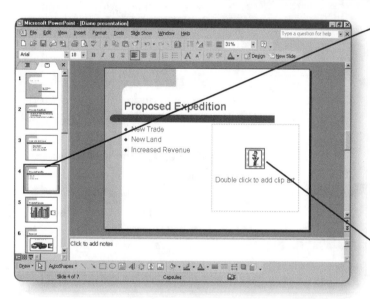

1. **Click on** the **slide** to which you want to add clip art. The slide will be displayed.

TIP

If your slide does not have a clip art button, choose Insert, Picture, and then Clip art.

---

2. **Double-click** on the **button** with the words "Double click to add clip art". The Select Picture dialog box will open.

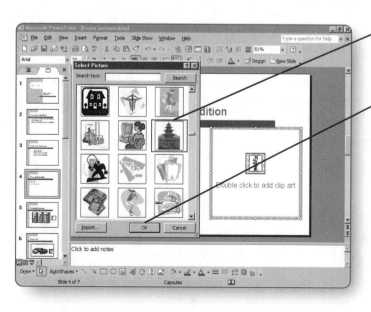

3. **Click** on the **graphic** that you want to use. The graphic image will be selected.

4. **Click** on **OK**. The clip art will be inserted onto your slide.

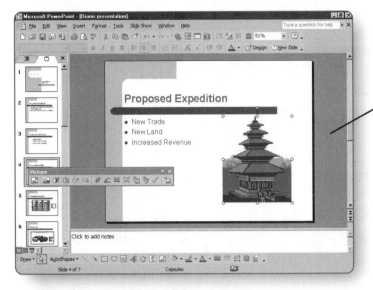

See "Inserting an Excel Chart" earlier in this chapter for examples of resizing and moving an object.

5. Click on the **gray area** outside the slide. PowerPoint will cancel the selection of the image.

Adding Transitions

Transitions are special effects you can use when you're creating a presentation you intend to show as a slide show on a computer. Transitions make the change between slides appear smoother by fading, wiping, or dissolving slides.

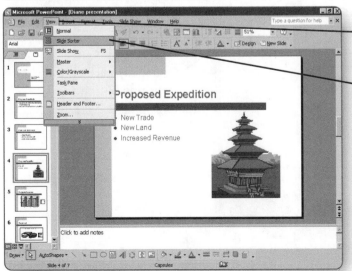

1. Click on **View**. The View menu will appear.

2. Click on **Slide Sorter**. PowerPoint will switch to Slide Sorter view.

3. **Click** on **Edit**. The Edit menu will appear.

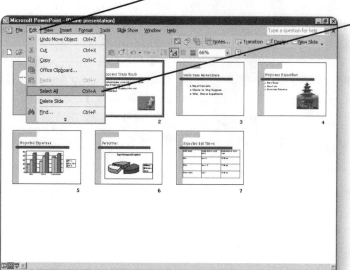

4. **Click** on **Select All**. PowerPoint will select all slides in the presentation.

NOTE

The transition you choose will apply to all slides in the presentation. If you want the transition to apply only to certain slides, select just those slides by holding down the Ctrl key while clicking on each slide.

5. **Click** on **Slide Show**. The Slide Show menu will appear.

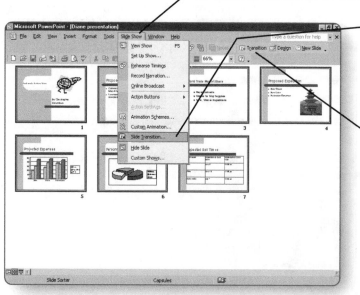

6. **Click** on **Slide Transition**. The Slide Transition Task Pane will open.

TIP

Optionally, click on the Transition button.

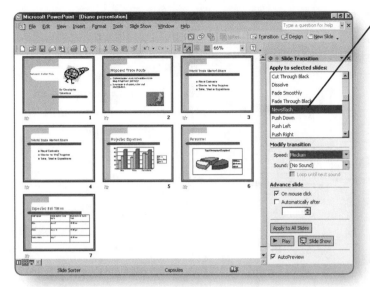

7. Click on an **effect.** The slide sorter view will demonstrate the selected effect.

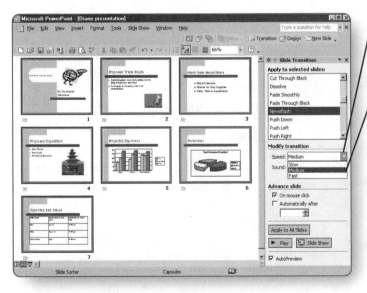

8. Click on the **Speed arrow.** A list of available transition speeds will appear.

9. Click on a **speed** (Slow, Medium, or Fast). The slide sorter view will demonstrate the selected effect speed.

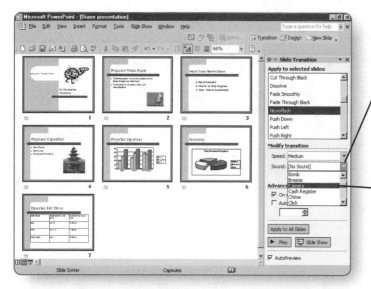

You can also apply sounds to play as each slide moves to the next one.

10. Click on the **drop-down arrow** at the right of Sound. A list of available sounds will display.

11. Click on a **sound**. The sound will be selected.

NOTE

You might be prompted to insert your Microsoft Office CD to install PowerPoint sound effects.

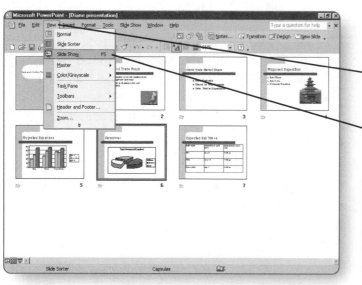

Test all your special effects by displaying a slide show.

12. Click on **View**. The View menu will appear.

13. Click on **Slide Show**. The slide show will display.

TIP

Click the mouse to advance through each slide; press the Esc key to end the show.

Part IV Review Questions

1. What three elements are displayed in Normal view? *See "Using Normal Tri-Pane View" in Chapter 15*

2. Why might you want to create speaker notes? *See "Adding and Viewing Speaker Notes" in Chapter 15*

3. What key can be pressed at any time to end a slide show? *See "Viewing a Slide Show" in Chapter 15*

4. What is each page of a presentation called? *See "Adding Slides" in Chapter 15*

5. How many slides are changed when you change a presentation design? *See "Changing Presentation Designs" in Chapter 16*

6. What happens to remaining slides when a slide is deleted? *See "Deleting Slides" in Chapter 16*

7. What steps must you take to print Speaker Notes? *See "Printing a Presentation " in Chapter 16*

8. Where does a table come from that you add to a slide? *See "Adding Tables" in Chapter 17*

9. If you've created a chart from an Excel worksheet, do you need to recreate it to display it in a PowerPoint presentation? *See "Inserting Charts" in Chapter 17*

10. What are transitions? *See "Adding Transitions" in Chapter 17*

P A R T   V

Using Outlook

18

Getting Started with Outlook

Outlook is the information organizer of Office—you can send and receive e-mail, store names and addresses, maintain a calendar, keep track of things you need to do, review a history of the things you've done, and keep notes. Microsoft has designed Outlook so that you can use it as an information center; you can even use Outlook to open Office documents. It's best to start using Outlook by understanding the Outlook window. In this chapter, you'll learn how to:

- Understand the Outlook window
- Add folders and shortcuts to the Outlook bar
- Reorder shortcuts on the Outlook bar
- Delete Outlook bar shortcuts

Understanding the Outlook Window

In Outlook, you store information in folders. You open a folder in Outlook by clicking on a shortcut for the folder that appears in the Outlook bar. On the Outlook bar, shortcuts are organized into groups.

1. Start Outlook. The Outlook window will open.

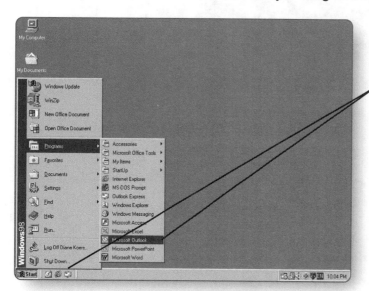

TIP

You might be asked to choose a Profile; select the appropriate profile and accept it by clicking on OK.

Along the left side of the screen, you will see the Outlook bar, which contains shortcuts to folders. The shortcuts you see initially point to folders that are created by default in Outlook. You can add shortcuts to the Outlook bar to organize information in Outlook in a way that suits your work style. When you add new folders, shortcuts for these folders are created automatically by Outlook.

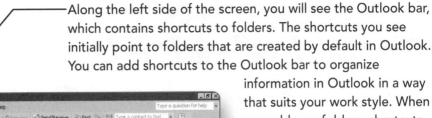

Notice on the Outlook Bar that Outlook organizes shortcuts into groups. The default group that appears is the Outlook Shortcuts group.

Other groups include My Shortcuts and Other Shortcuts.

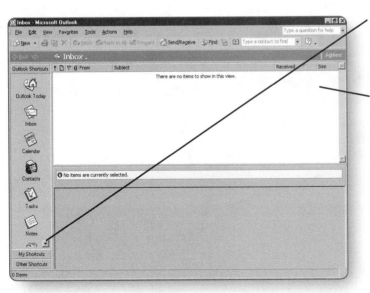

Use the arrows to scroll through the shortcuts on the Outlook bar.

The right side of the window shows the contents of the folder that is currently selected on the left side of the window. When you first start Outlook, you will see the contents of the Inbox, which stores e-mail.

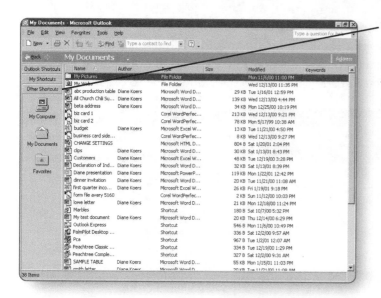

You can also click on the Other Shortcuts group, which contains shortcuts that allow you to open folders on your computer or on any attached network drive.

Viewing Outlook Today

The Outlook Today pane displays a condensed version of your scheduled activities. By default, five days of your calendar appointments appear along with your tasks and a list of mail messages.

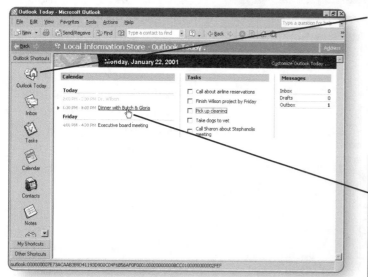

1. Click on **Outlook Today**. Your scheduled activities will appear.

You'll learn in Chapters 20-22 how to enter calendar appointments and tasks as well as check e-mail.

TIP

Click on an item to display a dialog box with additional details about the appointment, task, or e-mail.

Displaying Outlook Folders

The Outlook bar contains shortcuts to folders; it doesn't contain the actual folders. However, you can display the folders as part of the Outlook window. As you'll learn later in this chapter, you can add folders that don't have shortcuts in the Outlook bar or you can create shortcuts in the Outlook bar for folders you add.

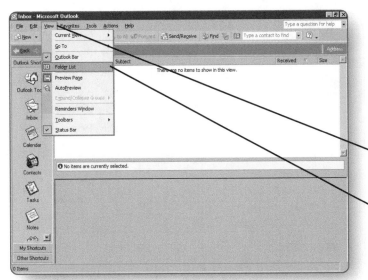

1. Click on **View**. The View menu will appear.

2. Click on **Folder List**. The Folder List panel will appear.

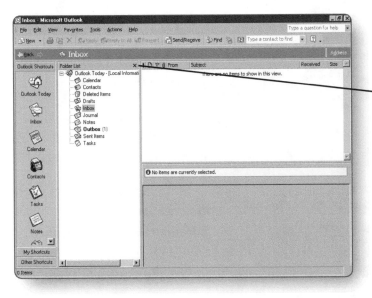

Initially, the folders in the Folder List match the shortcuts that appear in the Outlook bar.

3. Click on the **Folder List Close box**. The Folder list will close.

Adding a Folder in Outlook

To further organize your work in Outlook, you might need additional folders.

1. Click on **File**. The File menu will appear.

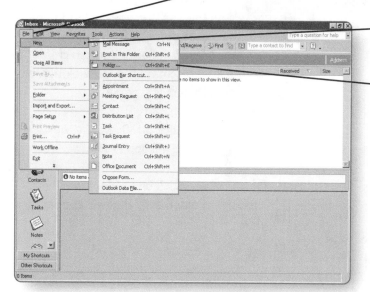

2. Click on **New**. A cascading menu will appear.

3. Click on **Folder**. The Create New Folder dialog box will open.

TIP

You might want to add folders to Outlook to help you organize the e-mail you receive.

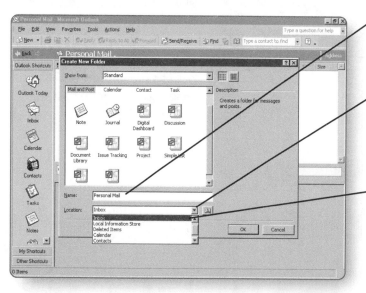

4. Type the **folder name** in the Name text box. The folder name will display in the text box.

5. Click on the **down arrow** of the Location list box. A list of items you can track in Outlook will appear.

6. Click on the **type of information** the new folder will contain.

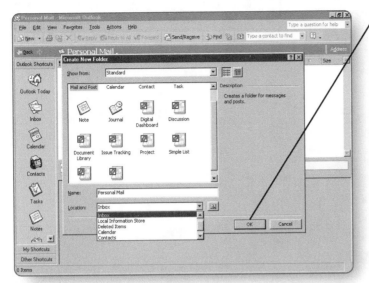

7. Click on **OK**. The Create New Folder dialog box will close and an "Add Shortcut to your Outlook bar?" message box will appear.

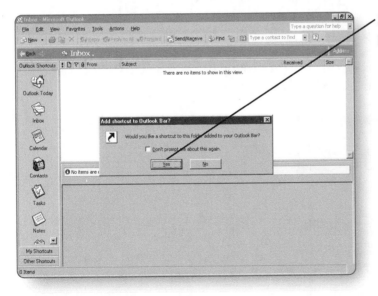

8. Click on **Yes**. The message box will close.

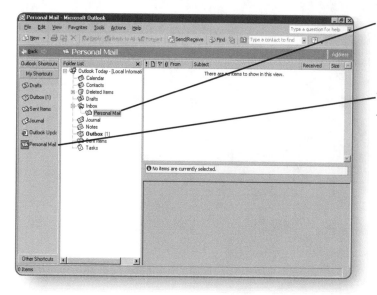

The new folder will appear in the Folder List under the folder you selected.

The shortcut is also added to the My Shortcuts group.

Changing the Order of Outlook Bar Shortcuts

You can move a shortcut up or down on the Outlook bar or move it to a different group.

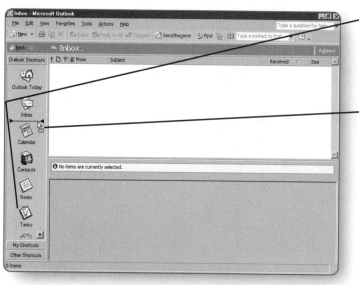

1. Point at the **shortcut** you want to move. A square will appear around the shortcut icon.

2. Click and drag the **shortcut** up or down in the list or to a different group. A black marker will appear between existing shortcuts as the mouse pointer moves over an acceptable spot.

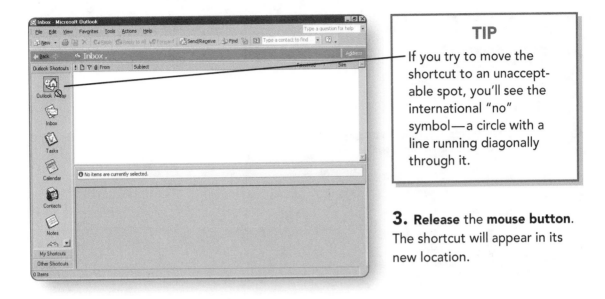

TIP

If you try to move the shortcut to an unacceptable spot, you'll see the international "no" symbol—a circle with a line running diagonally through it.

3. Release the **mouse button**. The shortcut will appear in its new location.

Deleting a Shortcut

If you've created a shortcut on the Outlook bar and decide you no longer need it there, you can easily delete it. Deleting a shortcut icon will only delete the display of the shortcut on the Outlook bar, not the folder itself or its contents.

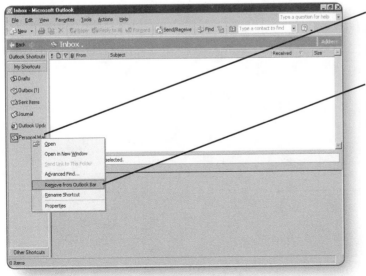

1. Right-click on the Outlook Bar shortcut to be deleted. A shortcut menu will appear.

2. Click on **Remove from Outlook Bar**. A confirmation window will display.

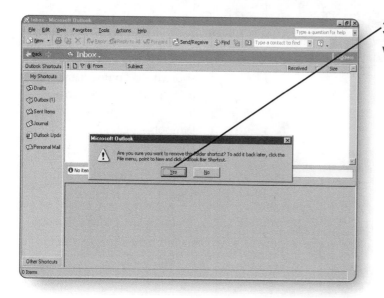

3. Click on **Yes**. The shortcut will be removed.

19

Working with the Address Book

Outlook contains an address book that you can use to maintain information about business and personal contacts. You can use the address book to print a phone or address list, telephone a contact, or send e-mail to a contact. In this chapter, you'll learn how to:

- Add an address book entry
- Print a contact list
- Delete a contact

Adding an Address Book Entry

It is easy to add entries to the address book in Outlook. Initially, the contact list will contain an entry for you and one for Microsoft. Contacts are listed in alphabetical order by last name.

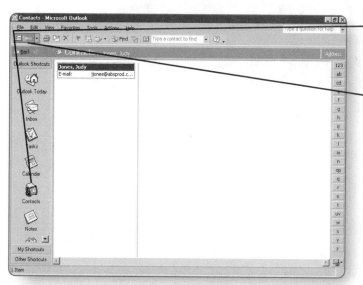

1. **Click** on the **Contacts shortcut**. Your list of entries will appear.

2. **Click** on the **New contact button**. The Contact window will appear.

NOTE

The New button in Outlook is context-sensitive. When you're viewing the Inbox, clicking on New will start a new mail message. When you're viewing Contacts, clicking on New will start a new contact.

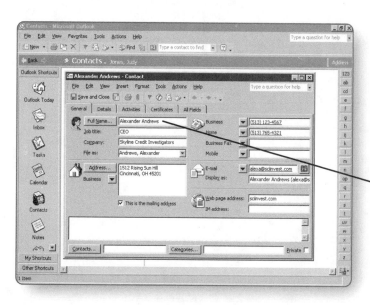

The first tab to be displayed is the General tab. This is where the contact's primary information, such as name and address, is stored.

3. **Type information** in each box on the General tab. Use the Tab key to move from box to box. The data you type will display in the appropriate boxes. All fields are optional except the name.

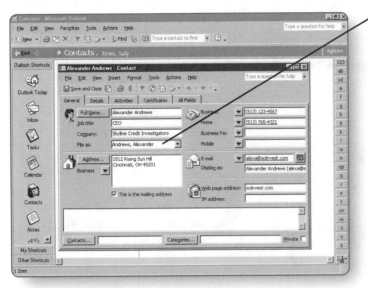

When you enter the full name in the order first name, last name, Outlook will fill in the File As list box in that order too (last name, first name).

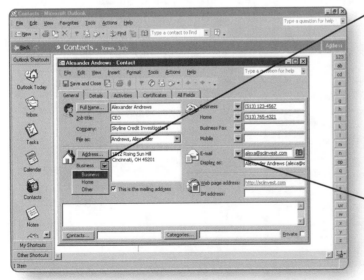

You can enter up to three addresses for each contact by clicking on a selection (Business, Home, or Other) under the Address button. You can enter a different address for each selection but only one address at a time will be displayed on the General tab.

You can enter up to three e-mail addresses by clicking on the down arrow next to the E-mail list box.

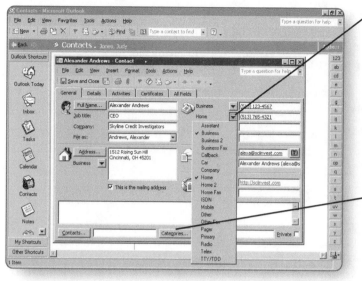

To enter several phone numbers for a category, click on the down arrow next to a phone number list box and click on a selection. Up to four telephone numbers can be displayed at the same time on the General tab—one each for Business, Home, Business Fax, and Mobile.

4. Click on the **Categories button**. The Categories dialog box will open.

Categories can be used to divide your contacts into those with similar characteristics. You can then use that information to produce telephone or mailing lists to specific groups.

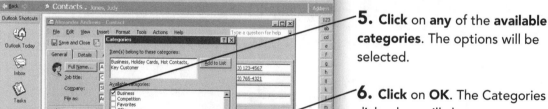

5. Click on **any** of the **available categories**. The options will be selected.

6. Click on **OK**. The Categories dialog box will close.

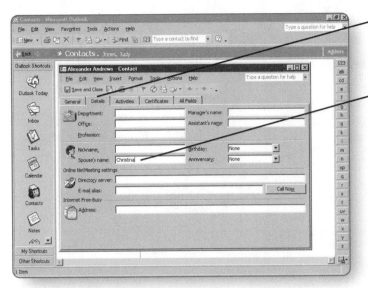

7. Click on the **Details tab**. The Details pane will come to the front.

8. Type any **additional information** about the contact. The data will display in the boxes on the Details tab.

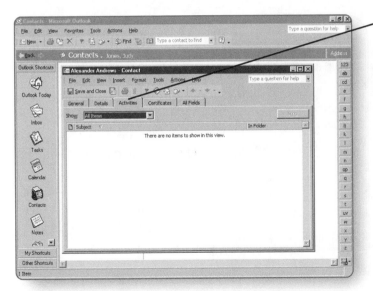

9. Click on the **Activities tab**. The Activities pane will come to the front.

Outlook can use the journal to keep a list of recorded contacts you have made with this person, such as meetings you have scheduled or e-mail you have sent or received. Those journal entries will display in the Activities tab. Because this is a new contact, no journal entries have yet been made.

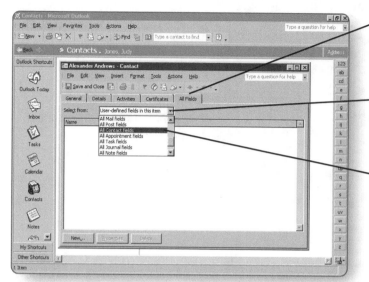

10. **Click** on the **All Fields tab**. The All Fields pane will come to the front.

11. **Click** on the **down arrow** next to the Select From list box. A list of choices will display.

12. **Click** on **All Contact fields**. The option will be selected.

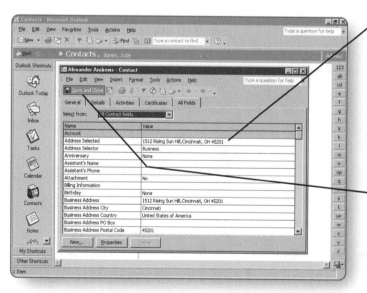

You will now see information about the contact in a tabular format. You can use this table to proofread your entries. To make changes to any entry, just click on the appropriate tab to go back to that pane and then make the changes there.

13. **Click** on the **Save and Close button**. Outlook will save this entry and close the New Contact box.

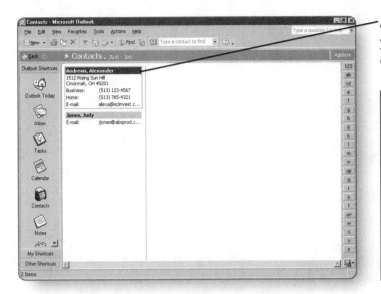

After you enter a new contact, you'll see information about the contact in the Contacts window.

> **TIP**
>
> To open and edit any contact's information, double-click on the contact's name and make any desired changes. Be sure to click on the Save and Close button when you are finished.

Printing a Contact List

You can print the information you store about your contacts in a variety of formats: card style, small booklet style, medium booklet style, memo style, and phone directory style.

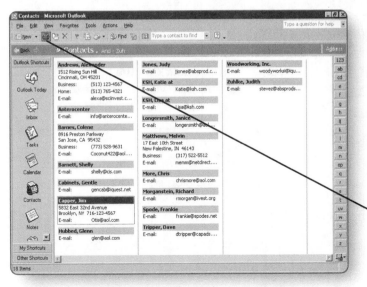

> **TIP**
>
> If you want to print only a portion of your contact list, hold down the Ctrl key and click on the records you want to print. The selected records will be highlighted.

1. Click on the **Print button**. The Print dialog box will open.

TIP

Optionally, click on File, Print.

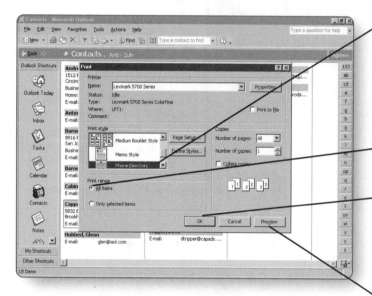

2. Click on a **print style**. The style will be highlighted.

You can elect to print your entire contact list, or only the records you have selected.

3. Click on a **print range**. The option will be selected.

4a. Click on **OK.** The contact list will print with the options you selected.

OR

4b. Click on **Preview**. A preview of your selections will appear.

TIP

Click on the page in preview mode to zoom in and see it clearer.

5. Click on **Print**. The Print dialog box will reappear.

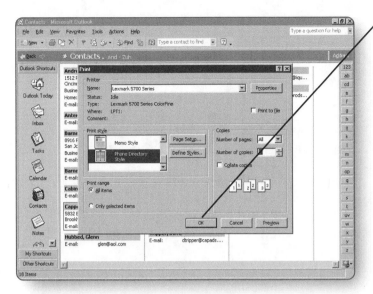

6. Click on **OK**. The contact list will print with the options you selected.

Deleting a Contact

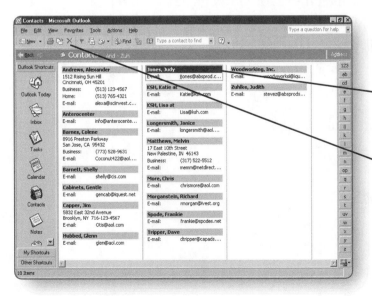

If you no longer want a contact listed in your address book, you can easily delete it.

1. Click on the **contact name** to be deleted. The name will be selected.

2. Click on the **Delete button**. The contact and all its information will be deleted.

TIP

There is no warning prior to deleting an entry, but if you delete the wrong entry, click on Edit and choose Undo to reverse your last action.

20

Using E-mail

Outlook enables you to send and receive e-mail messages. You can also create an e-mail message and check for new mail in Outlook. In this chapter, you'll learn how to:

- Configure Outlook for e-mail
- Create and send an e-mail message
- Respond to an e-mail message
- Manage e-mail messages

Configuring Outlook for Internet E-mail

In order to use Outlook's e-mail process, you must have some type of e-mail, either an internal company e-mail or one through the Internet. Either way, you need to advise Outlook how to connect to your e-mail.

Some of the following steps will require technical information. If you don't have written instructions from your ISP on configuring your e-mail, call them on the phone and have them talk you through the choices you'll need to make for their connection. If you have a network administrator, he or she might also have the required information and be able to assist you.

1. Click on **Tools**. The Tools menu will appear.

2. Click on **Options**. The Options dialog box will open.

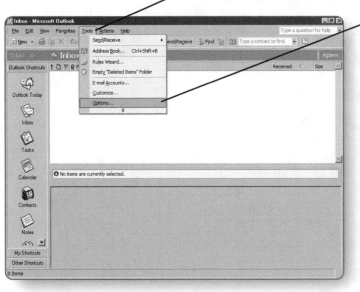

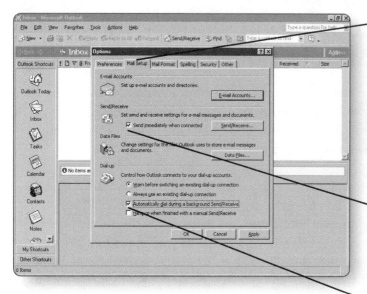

3. Click on the **Mail Setup tab**. The Mail Setup pane will come to the front.

The two options in the following steps speed up the process of sending messages because they require less interaction on your part.

4. Click on the **check box** to send messages immediately when connected. The option will display a check mark.

5. If you are using a dial-up connection (instead of Cable or DSL), **click** on the **check box** to automatically dial during a background send/receive. The option will display a check mark.

Now you'll need to tell Outlook what Internet account to use for your e-mail.

6. Click on the **E-mail Accounts button**. The E-mail accounts wizard will open.

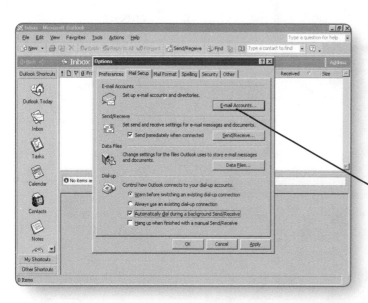

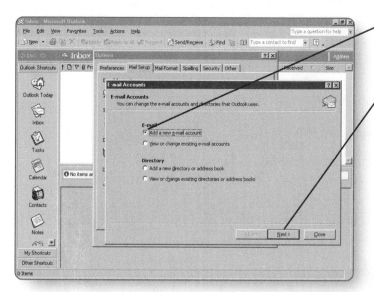

7. Click on **Add a new e-mail account**. The option will be selected.

8. Click on **Next**. The Server Type page will appear.

These next steps are a little trickier. The type of information you enter here will depend on the requirements of your Internet Service Provider (ISP).

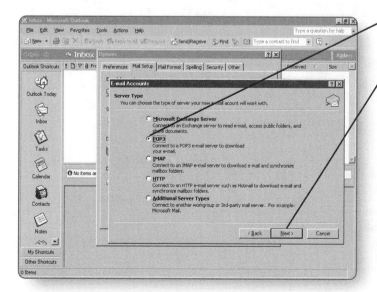

9. Click on a **Server Type**. The option will be selected.

10. Click on **Next**. The Internet E-mail Settings page will appear.

NOTE

Depending on your selections, your screens can vary from the ones displayed in this book.

11. Enter the **information** requested on the e-mail screen. Again, contact your ISP or network administrator if you need assistance.

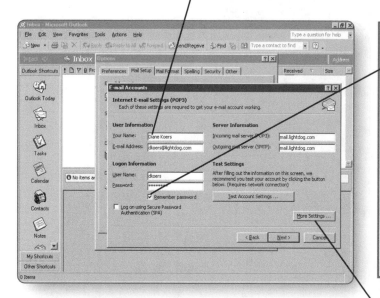

12. Click on **More Settings**. An Internet E-mail settings dialog box will open.

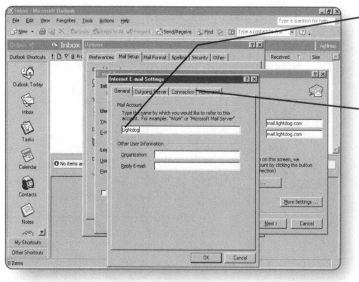

13. Enter the **name** to identify the mail account. For example, AOL or LIGHTDOG or MY INTERNET CONNECTION.

14. Click on the **Connection tab**. The Connection pane will come to the front.

15. Click on a **connection type**. The option will be selected.

Typically, cable modems and DSL use a network connection and modems use telephone line connections.

If you are using a modem/telephone line, you'll need to specify the dial-up connection information.

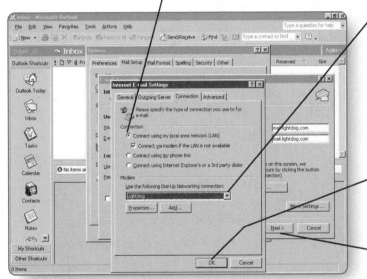

16. Click on the **down arrow** next to use the following dial-up networking connection. A list of your connections will appear.

17. Click on a **connection name**. The name will appear in the selection box.

18. Click on **OK**. The Internet E-mail Settings dialog box will close.

19. Click on **Next**. The final screen of the wizard will appear.

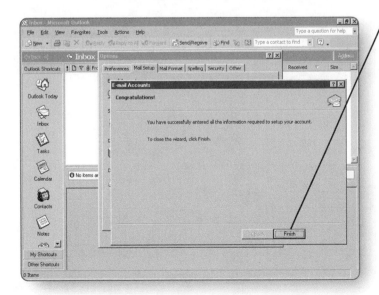

20. Click on **Finish**. The E-mail Accounts dialog box will close.

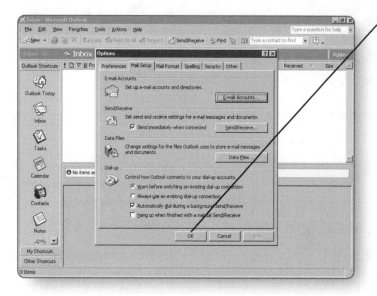

21. **Click** on **OK**. The Options dialog box will close.

Creating an E-mail Message

In Outlook, you can access your e-mail software to send e-mail messages.

1. **Click** on the **Inbox shortcut** in the Outlook bar. The current messages in your Inbox will display.

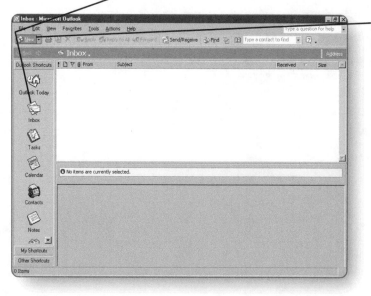

2. **Click** on the **New Mail Message button**. A new mail message window will appear.

3. Click on the **To button**. The e-mail addresses you have stored in the Contact list will appear in the Select Names dialog box.

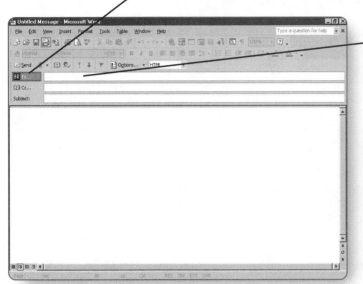

NOTE

If you don't want to use the Address Book, as steps 3 through 6 explain, you can type the recipient's e-mail address in the box next to the To button. For multiple recipients, separate their e-mail addresses with a semicolon. For example: typing **johnj@abs.com**; **susanb@aol.com** would send the message to both johnj and susanb.

Also, if the contact is listed in your Address Book, you can type the name in the To box. Outlook will then look up the e-mail address and display it.

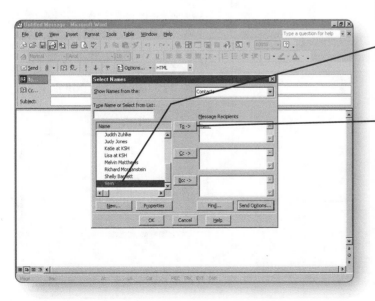

4. Click on the recipient's **name**. The name will be highlighted.

5. Click on the **To button**. The recipient's name will appear in the Message Recipients text box.

6. To send the message to more than one recipient, **repeat steps 4 and 5**.

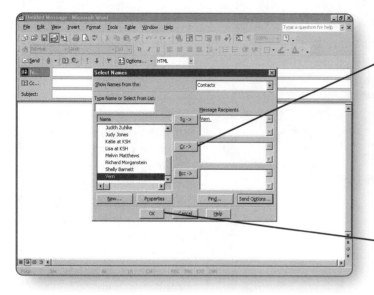

TIP

To send copies of the message to a recipient, repeat the same steps, but click on the Cc button instead of the To button in step 5. Use the Bcc button to send blind copies of the message.

7. **Click** on **OK**. The Select Names dialog box will close. The names you selected will appear in the To and Cc text boxes.

8. **Click** in the **Subject text box**. The insertion point will move to the subject line.

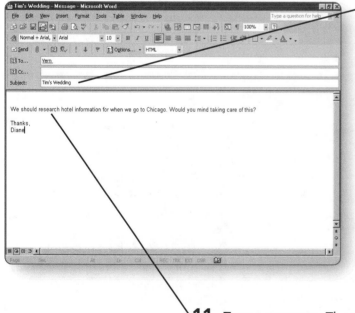

9. **Type** a **subject** for the message. The subject will appear in the Subject text box. It's not required, but messages should have a subject.

10. **Click** in the large **message box**. A blinking insertion point will appear.

TIP

Don't type in ALL CAPS! That's considered SHOUTING.

11. **Type** a **message**. The text will appear in the message box.

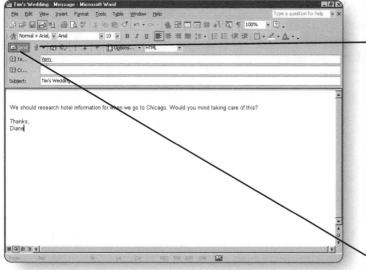

TIP

To attach a file, click on the Insert File button (it looks like a paper clip). The Insert File dialog box will open. Navigate to the folder containing the file and choose the file. When you click on OK, you'll see an icon representing the file in your mail message.

12. **Click** on the **Send button**. The Message window will close and the Inbox window will appear.

NOTE

When sending an e-mail to someone with more than one e-mail address in the Address Book, Outlook will display a dialog box asking you to pick which e-mail address you want to use.

Sending Your Message

Most e-mail messages are sent immediately, however if you're connecting via a modem, Outlook might hold messages in the Outbox until you connect and send your messages.

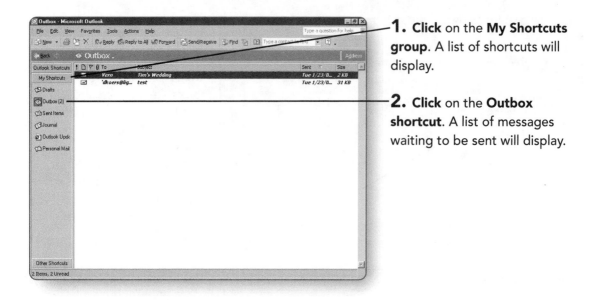

1. Click on the **My Shortcuts group**. A list of shortcuts will display.

2. Click on the **Outbox shortcut**. A list of messages waiting to be sent will display.

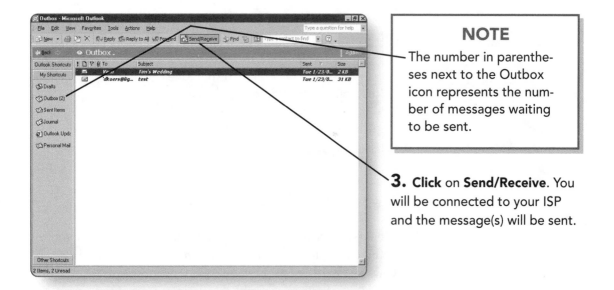

NOTE

The number in parentheses next to the Outbox icon represents the number of messages waiting to be sent.

3. Click on **Send/Receive**. You will be connected to your ISP and the message(s) will be sent.

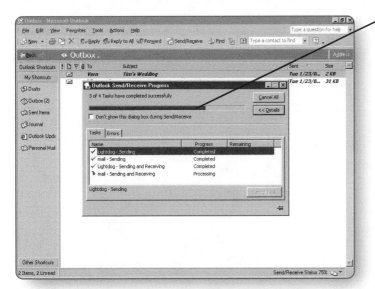

A dialog box that indicates the sending status might appear.

Outlook moves the messages from the Outbox to the Sent Items window.

Checking for Messages

You can check for new mail from Outlook; any e-mail you receive will appear in your Outlook Inbox.

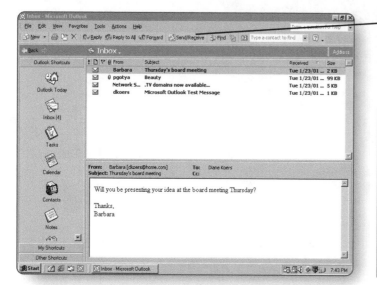

1. **Click** on **Send/Receive.** Outlook will check for new messages and send any messages waiting to be sent.

TIP

If you are always connected to your e-mail system, messages might appear automatically in your Inbox and you won't need to check for messages.

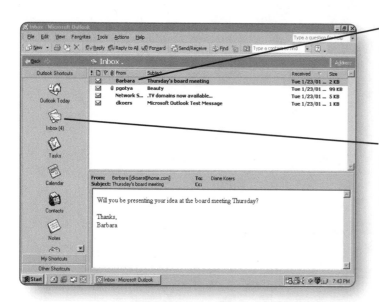

Any new messages you receive will appear in the Outlook Inbox. New messages appear in bold to indicate they have not yet been read.

The number of unread messages in your Inbox appears in parentheses after the Inbox shortcut.

Reading Your Messages

The Inbox window has two panes that you can use to work with messages. The top half of the Inbox lists the messages. The current message is displayed in the bottom half of the window. The first thing you'll want to do is read the message.

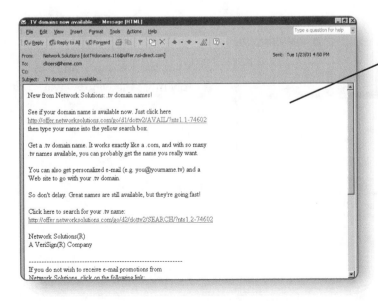

1. Click on the **message** to be read. The message will be displayed in the bottom half of the Inbox window.

2. Click on the **down arrow**. More of the message will be scrolled onto the screen.

TIP

Optionally, if you double-click on a message, the entire message will display in a separate window. This might make some messages easier to read.

Responding to a Message

You can respond to a message in a number of ways: reply to the message, forward the message, or close the message without answering.

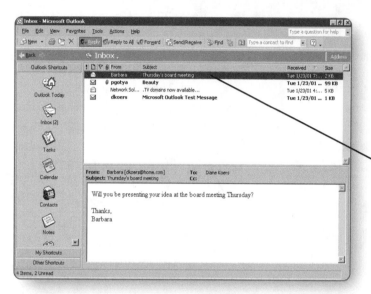

Replying to a Message

Many people consider it a common courtesy to respond to a message they receive.

1. **Click** on a **message**. The message title will be highlighted.

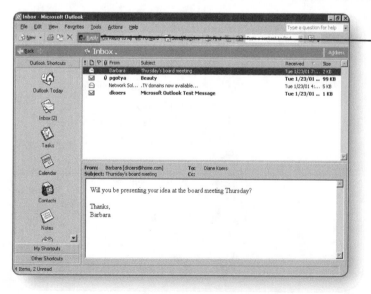

2. **Click** on the **Reply button**. A reply message window will open.

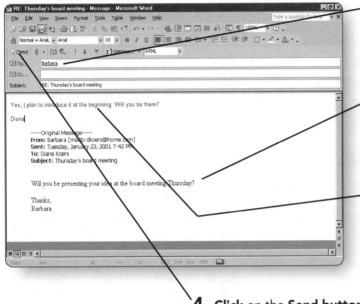

Outlook will fill in the To text box with the address of the original sender as well as the Subject text box.

Outlook will copy the original message and allow you space to add reply information to the top of the message.

3. **Type** the **reply message**. The text will display in the message window above the original text.

4. **Click** on the **Send button**. The reply message will be sent and the reply window will close.

Forwarding a Message

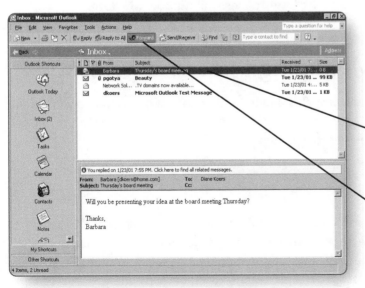

On occasion, information might come to you via e-mail that you want to share with others. In these cases, you can forward the message.

1. **Click** on the **message** to be forwarded. The message title will be highlighted.

2. **Click** on the **Forward button**. A forward message window will open.

Just like in a reply message, Outlook will copy the original message and allow you space to add the forwarding message at the top of the message.

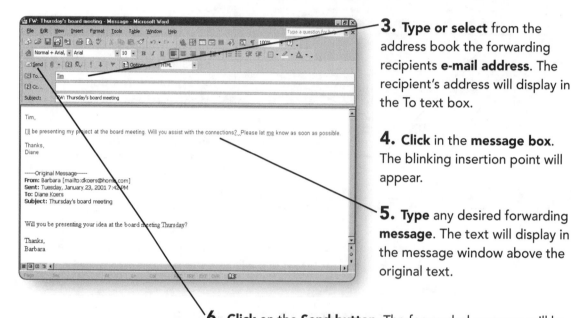

3. Type or select from the address book the forwarding recipients **e-mail address**. The recipient's address will display in the To text box.

4. Click in the **message box**. The blinking insertion point will appear.

5. Type any desired forwarding **message**. The text will display in the message window above the original text.

6. Click on the **Send button**. The forwarded message will be sent and the forward message window will close.

Managing Files and Messages

You'll probably end up getting lots of e-mail. Some you'll want to keep and others you won't. You can elect to store, save, or delete received e-mail.

Managing Messages

In some cases, you might not be ready to respond to a message when you receive it. You might want to answer it later or file the information for future use. You can file messages into different folders; perhaps one you created in Chapter 18, "Getting Started with Outlook."

1. Click on the Outlook bar **group** that contains the folder you want to hold your message (such as My Shortcuts). The folder icon will display in the Outlook bar.

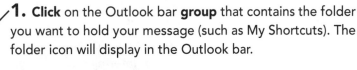

2. Click on the **message** to be stored. The message title will be highlighted.

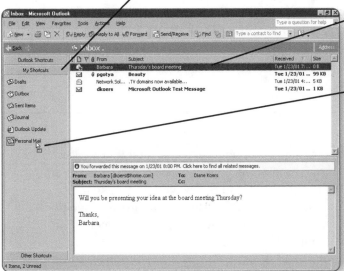

3. Drag the **message** to the storage folder on the left. As you are dragging the mouse, the pointer will become an arrow with a small box under it.

4. Release the **mouse button**. The message will be removed from the Inbox and moved to the folder.

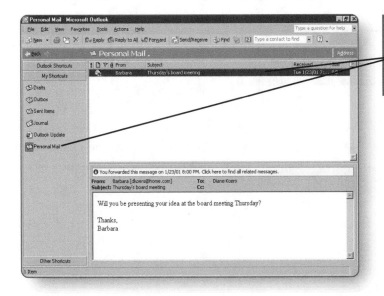

TIP

Click on the folder to see your message.

Managing Attached Files

If someone sends you an e-mail with an attachment, you'll need to determine whether you want to open or save the attachment. If you don't know who sent the attachment, the general rule of thumb is DO NOT OPEN IT! Opening attachments from unauthorized senders is a good way to pick up a computer virus, which can destroy information on your computer.

TIP

Make sure you not only have a reputable anti-virus program running on your computer, but that that anti-virus program is set to review your incoming e-mail. Also, make sure you update your anti-virus definitions every couple of weeks. Refer to the documentation that comes with your anti-virus software.

Messages with an attachment are indicated with a paper clip. They might not include text in the body of the message.

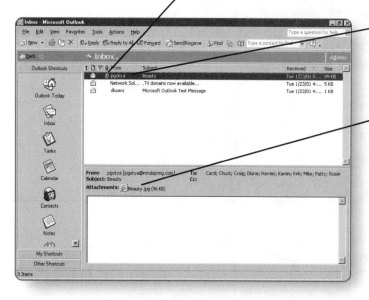

1. Click on the e-mail **message** containing the attachment. The message will be highlighted and will display in the bottom pane.

2. Double-click on the **attachment icon**. The Opening Mail Attachment dialog box will open.

3. Click on an **option**:

- Open it will open the attachment in a separate application window. To open an attachment, you must have an application that supports the same file type. For example, if someone sends you an Excel file, you must have Excel (or an application that can read Excel files) on your machine.

- Saving an attachment stores it on your hard drive in a location you specify for future opening.

4. Click on **OK**. If you elected to save the file, the Save As dialog box will open.

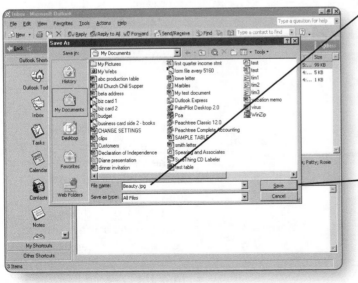

5. Enter a **file name and specify** a **location** to save the file. The file name will display in the File Name text box. Be sure to make note of the directory you are storing the file in (My Documents in this case) so that you can find it later.

6. Click on **Save**. The file will be saved in the location you specify.

Deleting a Message

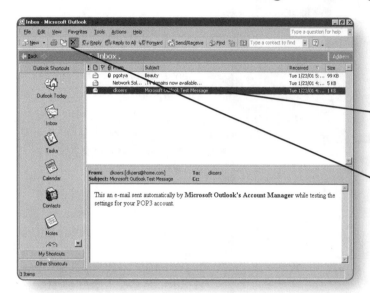

Some messages require no response and you might want to delete them. Others might have outlived their usefulness.

1. **Click** on a **message** to be deleted. The message title will be highlighted.

2. **Click** on the **Delete button**. The message will be deleted from the Inbox.

TIP

Optionally, press the Delete key on your keyboard to delete a selected message.

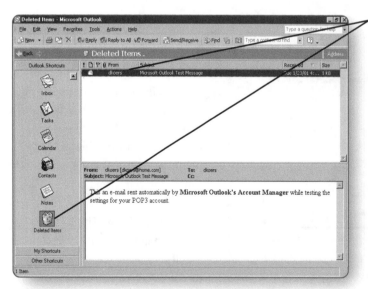

Outlook will move the message from the Inbox to the Deleted Items folder. You can display the contents of that folder and see the deleted message.

TIP

Similar to the Windows Recycle Bin, items remain in the Deleted Items folder until you delete them from that folder. Delete icons from the Deleted Items folder in the same manner you learned in steps 1 and 2, however deleting them from the Deleted Items folder is permanent.

Finding Messages

Outlook tracks replies and forwarding messages sent from an e-mail you received. You can ask Outlook to find all messages related to a single message.

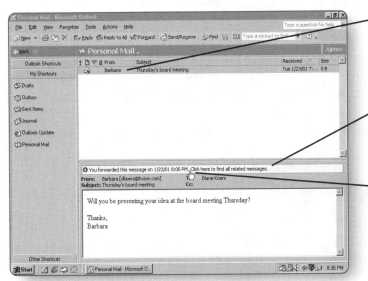

1. Click on the **message** from which you want to find other messages. The message will be highlighted.

The yellow bar above the message indicates sent or replied messages are available.

2. Click on the **yellow bar**. The Advanced Find dialog box will open.

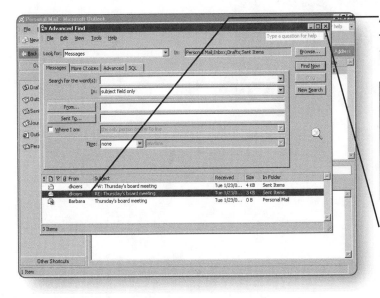

A list of all messages attached to the original message appears in the bottom of the dialog box.

TIP
Double-click on any message you want to review; the message will open in a separate window.

3. Click on the **Close box**. The Advanced Find dialog box will close.

E-mailing Files from Windows

Although this feature actually originates with your Windows operating system, it uses Outlook to manage your e-mailing. You have the ability to send any file to an e-mail recipient without having to actually launch Outlook.

1. In Windows, **open** a **folder** that contains the file you want to send. You can open the folder with Explorer or My Computer, or even just open the My Documents folder on your Windows desktop if it contains the necessary file.

2. Right-click on the **file** you want to send. A shortcut menu will appear.

3. Click on **Send To**. A submenu will appear.

4. Click on **Mail Recipient**. An e-mail message will appear on-screen.

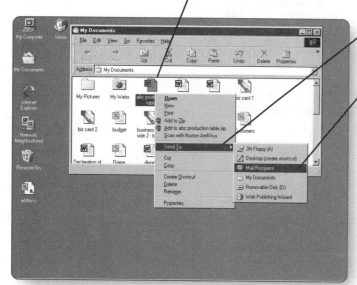

5. **Enter** the **recipient and any message** you want to send along with the file.

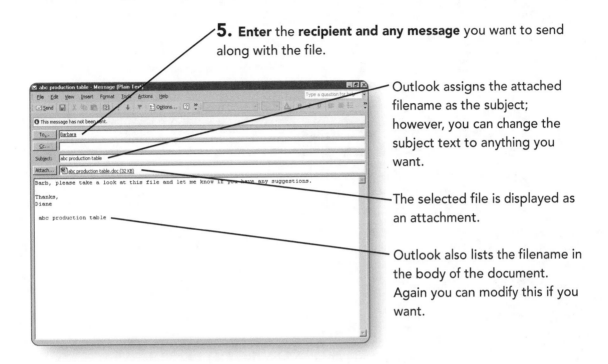

Outlook assigns the attached filename as the subject; however, you can change the subject text to anything you want.

The selected file is displayed as an attachment.

Outlook also lists the filename in the body of the document. Again you can modify this if you want.

6. **Click** on **Send**. The message will be sent along with the file attachment.

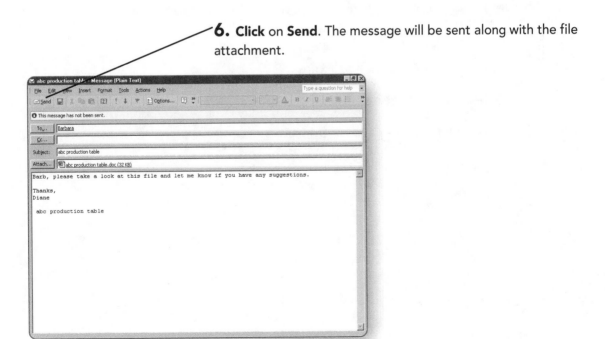

21

Using the Calendar

You can use the Outlook Calendar to schedule appointments, meetings, and events. You can also use the Outlook Calendar for individual or group scheduling. In this chapter, you'll learn how to:

- Change the Calendar's display
- Schedule an appointment or meeting
- Create a recurring appointment
- Reschedule and delete appointments
- Print the Calendar

Viewing the Calendar

You can view your Calendar from several perspectives: one day at a time, one week at a time, one month at a time, and in a tabular format. You can switch to these views in different ways.

Changing the Calendar's View

1. Click on the **Calendar shortcut** in the Outlook bar. The Calendar will appear in the day view.

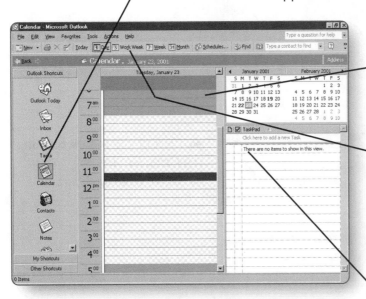

> ### TIP
> Times that appear darker are not standard "business hours."

2. Click on the **Work Week button**. The Calendar view will change to display one work week at a time without Saturday and Sunday.

> ### NOTE
> The Task Pad also appears. You'll learn about the Task Pad in Chapter 22 "Using Outlook to Keep Organized."

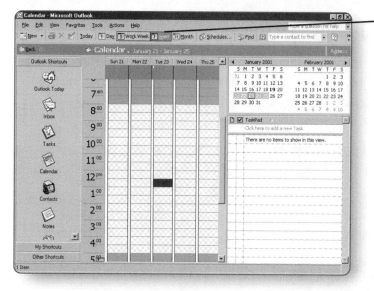

3. **Click** on the **Week button**. The Calendar view will change to display one week at a time—this time, including the weekend.

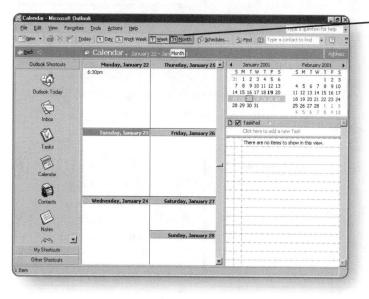

4. **Click** on the **Month button**. The Calendar view will change to display one month at a time.

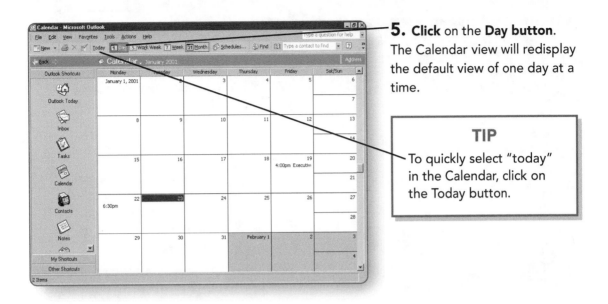

5. Click on the **Day button**. The Calendar view will redisplay the default view of one day at a time.

Using the Date Navigator

The Date Navigator helps you quickly switch between Calendar views and select days, weeks, or months to view.

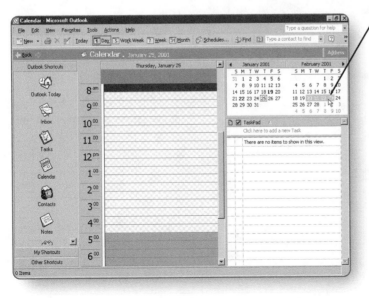

1. Click and drag the mouse **across the days** you want to view. The Calendar view will display that time frame.

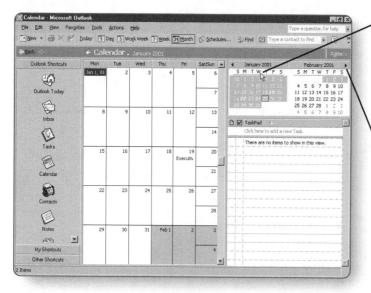

2. Click anywhere on the day of the week headings for the month you want to view. The Calendar view will display that month.

NOTE

If you need to see a different month, click on the left or right arrows that appear next to the month names.

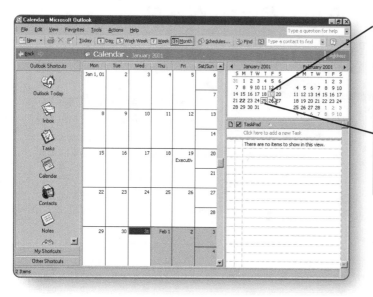

3. Click on the **day** you want to view. The Calendar view will show that day.

TIP

The current day is surrounded by a square so you can easily identify it.

Looking at the Calendar in Table View

Sometimes, seeing a list of appointments on the Calendar works better than any of the views.

1. Click on **View**. The View menu will appear.

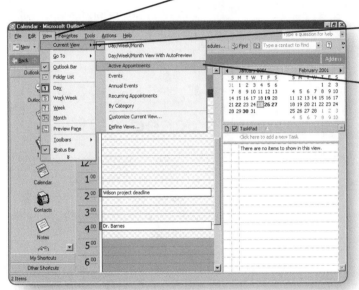

2. Click on **Current View**. A submenu will appear.

3. Click on **Active Appointments**. The table view of your Calendar will appear in the Calendar window.

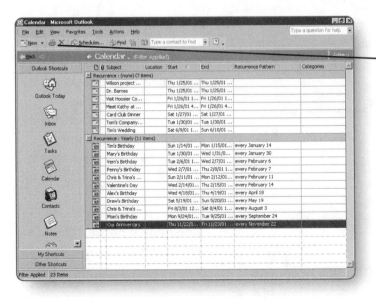

TIP

Click on the Print button to print the table view of your Calendar.

You'll find it just as easy to return to the appointment view.

4. Click on **View**. The View menu will appear.

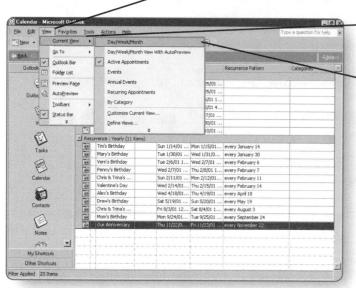

5. Click on **Current View**. A submenu will appear.

6. Click on **Day/Week/Month**. The standard calendar view will redisplay.

Setting Your Schedule

With Outlook you can schedule a one-time appointment, an all day event, a recurring occasion, or even schedule a meeting with coworkers.

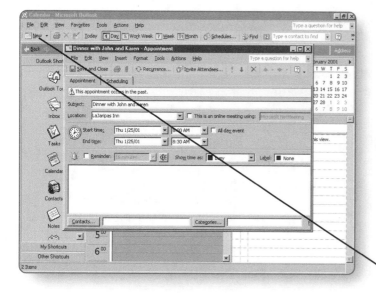

Making an Appointment

An *appointment* is an entry in the Calendar that reserves time for an activity; appointments do not include other people (for that, you need to set up a meeting; see the next section). To make a new appointment, make sure you are viewing the Calendar.

1. Click on the **New Appointment button**. The Appointment window will appear.

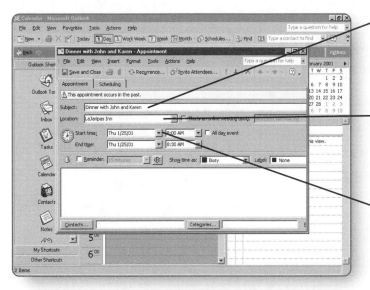

2. Type a **description** for the appointment in the Subject text box. The text will display in the text box.

3. Optionally, **type** a **location** for the appointment in the Location text box. The text will display in the text box.

4. Click on the **down arrow** next to the Start Time list box. A small calendar will appear from which you can select a date for the appointment.

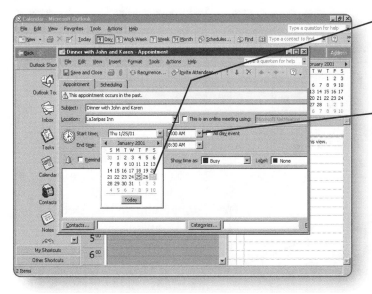

5. Click on the **date** for the appointment. Outlook will insert the date into the Start Time list box.

6. Click on the **down arrow** next to the Start Time list box. A list of available times will appear.

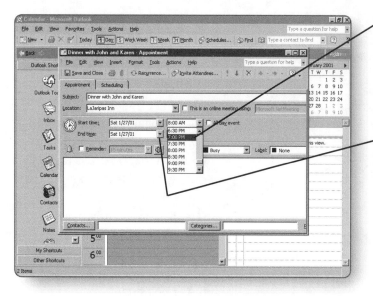

7. Click on a **start time** for the appointment. The selected time will display.

TIP

To set an end time, repeat steps 6 and 7 using the down arrows next to the End Time list boxes.

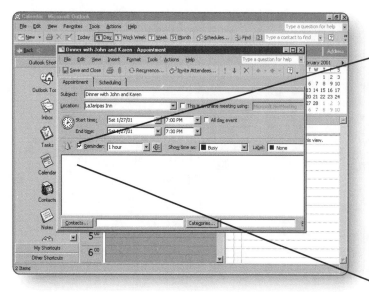

NOTE

Click to place a check mark in the Reminder check box to tell Outlook to remind you of the appointment by playing a sound. If you do this, you can use the Reminder list box to specify the amount of time prior to the appointment that Outlook will remind you.

8. Click in the **text box** at the bottom of the window. The blinking insertion point will appear.

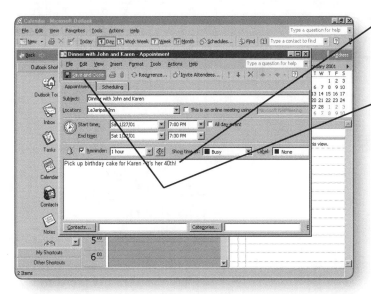

9. Optionally, **type** any **notes** about the appointment. The text will display in the text box.

10. **Click** on the **Save and Close button**. Outlook will save the appointment on the day and at the time you scheduled it.

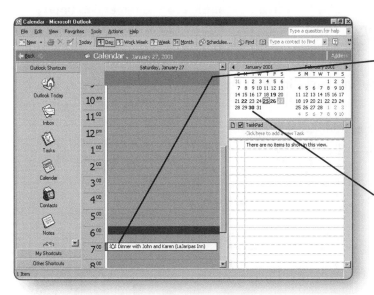

TIP

To view the appointment, switch to the scheduled day, week, or month view containing the appointment. To edit the appointment, double-click on it.

In the Date Navigator, future dates containing appointments appear in bold.

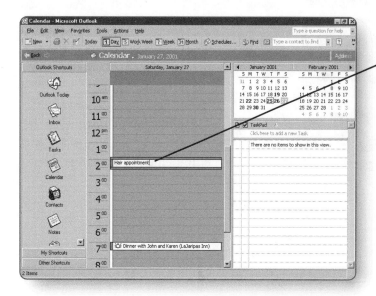

TIP

Another quick and easy way to schedule an appointment is to simply click on the desired time slot and type the appointment.

Scheduling a Meeting

Meetings are entries for which you schedule time and invite others to attend. When you invite others who are using Outlook, Outlook lets you look at their schedules and determine whether they have free time at the proposed meeting time. When you schedule the meeting, you send an e-mail to each person and place a tentative activity on each person's Calendar.

If you want to invite someone who is not using Outlook, you won't be able to check for free time; however, if you have stored that person's e-mail address in your Outlook address book, you can send an e-mail requesting attendance.

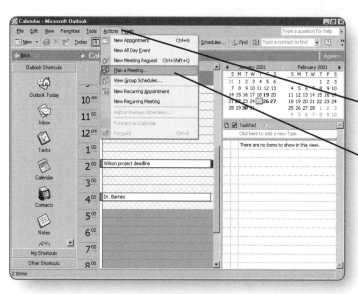

1. Click on **Actions**. The Actions menu will appear.

2. Click on **Plan a Meeting**. The Plan a Meeting dialog box will open.

First, you can invite anyone in your Outlook contacts list.

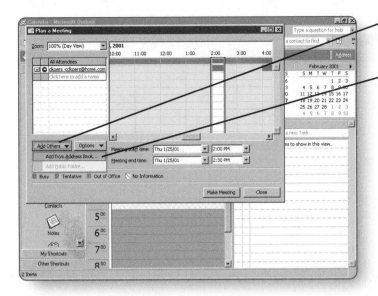

3. Click on **Add Others**. A drop-down list will appear.

4. Click on **Add from Address Book**. The Select Attendees and Resources dialog box will open.

A list of contacts from your Outlook contact list will display.

5. Click on the **name** of the first person to attend the meeting. The person's name will be highlighted.

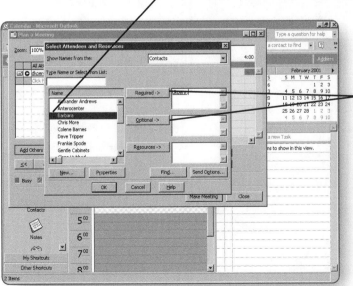

Either a person will be required to attend the meeting, or his/her presence is optional.

6. Click on **Required or Optional**. The attendee's name will appear in the selected box.

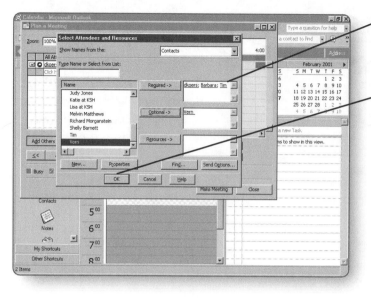

7. Repeat these steps for each attendee. Selected names will display in the boxes.

8. Click on **OK**. The dialog box will close.

The people you selected will appear on the Plan a Meeting attendee list.

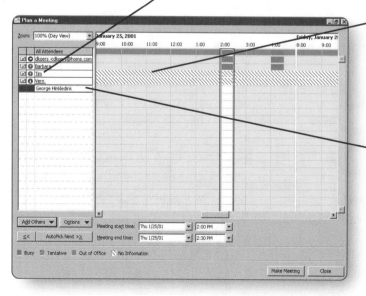

If their schedules are not available (either because they are not using Outlook or because they are not on the network), you'll see diagonal lines through their schedule.

9. Click the **mouse** in the next available line in the All Attendees list. The blinking insertion point will display.

10. Type any additional attendees' **names**. The names will appear in the All Attendees list.

You can invite people to attend a meeting even if you don't have an e-mail address for them; you simply tell Outlook not to send an e-mail message.

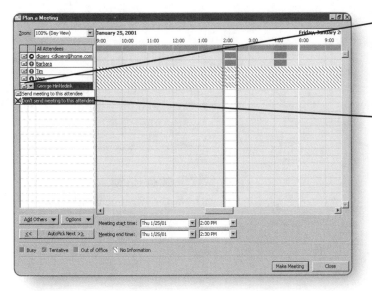

11. **Click** on the **envelope** next to the name of the person to whom you *do not* want to send e-mail. A list box will open.

12. **Click** on the **option**: Don't send meeting to this attendee. Outlook will place an X over the envelope next to the attendee's name.

Now you need to set a meeting date and time.

13. **Click** on the **Meeting Start Time**. A calendar will appear.

14. **Click** on a **Meeting date**. The selected date will appear in the Meeting Start Time box.

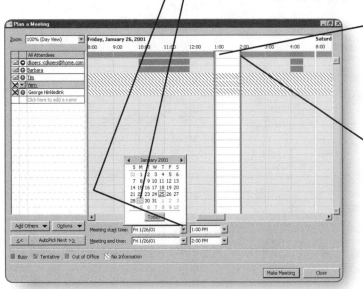

15. **Click** on the desired meeting **time**. A one-half hour increment of time will be blocked off.

TIP
Click and drag the time bars to increase or decrease the meeting length.

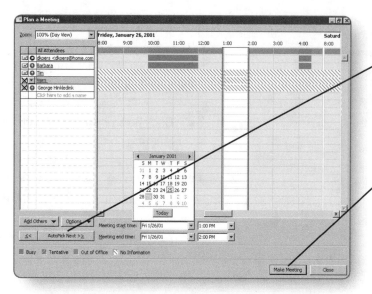

TIP

Optionally, click on AutoPick Next to let Outlook find a mutually available time for all attendees.

16. **Click** on **Make Meeting**. The appointment window will display.

Notice that Outlook has placed the recipients who are to be notified in the To list.

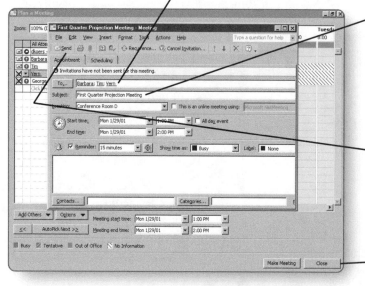

17. Complete any other notations, such as the subject and location, to specify the meeting information. The information will display in the appointment window.

18. **Click** on **Send**. Outlook will send e-mail messages to the proposed attendees and the meeting will be placed on your schedule.

19. **Click** on **Close**. The Plan a Meeting window will close.

Responding to a Meeting Call

When someone schedules a meeting, the recipients called to the meeting will receive an e-mail notifying them of the upcoming meeting. Each person can respond to the meeting call.

Meeting call e-mail received by recipient.

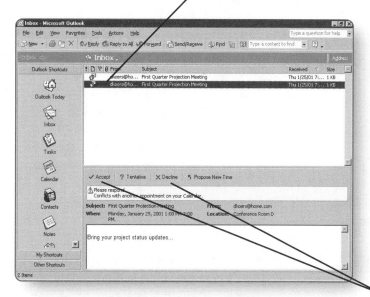

If the recipients have Outlook, they can then accept or decline the invitation or they can respond with a tentative acceptance or even suggest a new meeting time.

TIP

If the recipients do not use Outlook, they can reply to the message in a normal e-mail method.

1. Click on **Accept or Decline**. A message box will appear.

2a. Click on **OK**. The message accepting the meeting will be sent to the meeting originator and the meeting will be added to your Outlook schedule.

OR

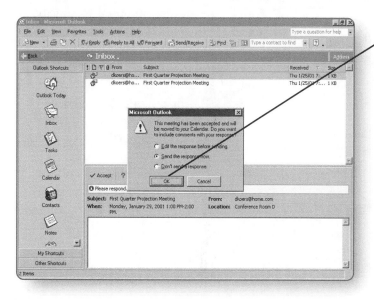

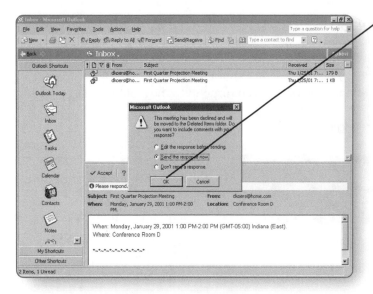

2b. **Click** on **OK**. The message declining the meeting will be sent to the meeting originator and the incoming mail message will be deleted.

Creating Recurring Entries

Recurring entries are useful for recording appointments, meetings, or events that occur on a regular basis. Weekly meetings or birthdays are good examples of recurring entries.

1. Click on the **New Appointment button**. The Appointment window will appear.

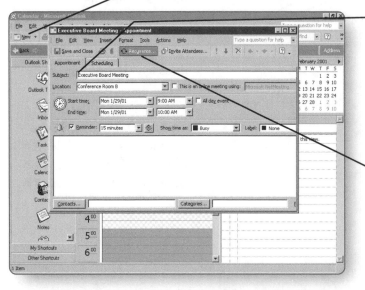

2. Type to complete **text boxes** for a subject, location, starting and ending times, and any other notations to specify the event information. The information will display in the appointment window.

3. Click on the **Recurrence button**. The Appointment Recurrence dialog box will open.

The Recurrence pattern changes, depending on the frequency you choose on the left side of the dialog box. After you choose a frequency, you must specify how often the entry will occur.

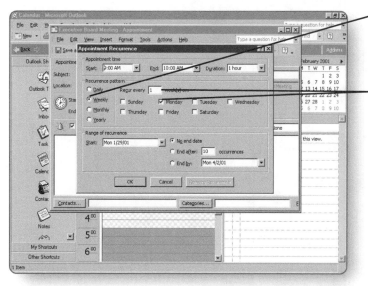

4. **Click** on a **Recurrence pattern**. The options for that pattern will display.

5. **Click** on the desired recurrence **options**. The options will be selected.

At the bottom of the dialog box, set the period over which the recurring entry will appear on your Calendar.

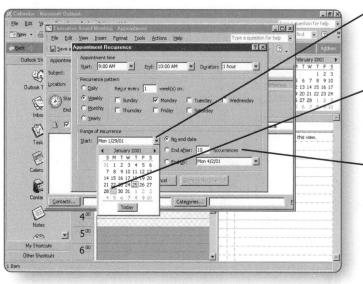

6. **Click** on the **down arrow** next to the Start list box. A calendar will display.

7. **Click** on a **start date**. The date will display in the Start list box.

8. Optionally, **specify** an **end date or** a total **number of occurrences**. The options will display in the Range of recurrence section.

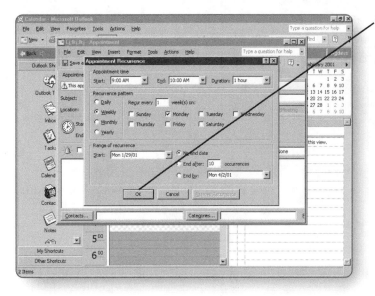

9. **Click** on **OK**. The Appointment Recurrence window will close.

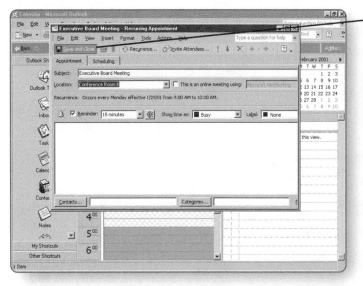

10. **Click** on **Save and Close**. The Appointment window will close and Outlook will display the recurring entry on your Calendar.

Editing an Appointment

If you need to reschedule an appointment, you can drag the appointment to the new date or time. If the appointment to be edited or deleted is recurring, Outlook will ask you if you want the change to affect all occurrences of the appointment or only the current one.

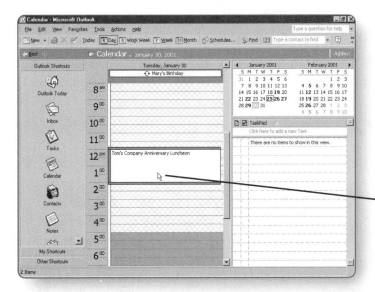

Moving Appointments to a Different Time

If you're moving your appointment to a different time in the same day, move it in the day view.

1. Position the **mouse pointer** over an appointment to be moved. The mouse will be a white arrow.

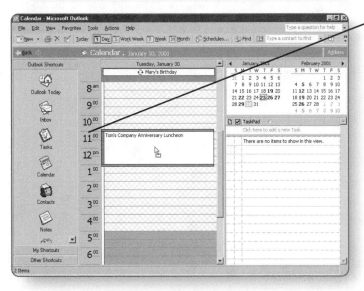

2. Click and drag the **event** to the desired time slot. The event will appear at the new time.

3. Release the **mouse button**. The event will be moved.

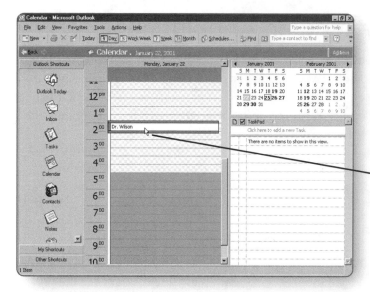

Moving to a Different Date

If your company picnic has been postponed to the next weekend, move it by using the Date Navigator.

1. Position the **mouse pointer** over the event to be moved. The mouse will be a white arrow.

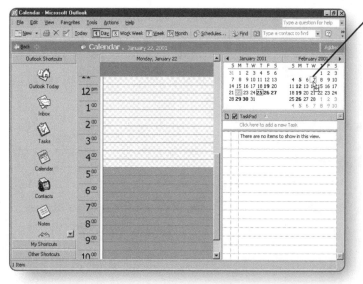

2. Drag the **event** to the desired day on the monthly calendar. The selected day will have a small box around it.

3. Release the **mouse button**. The event will be moved.

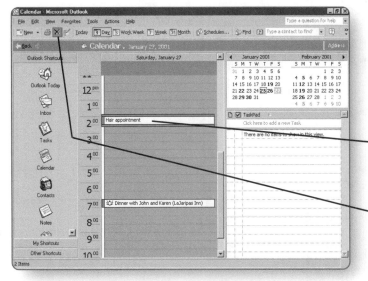

Deleting an Appointment

If you need to cancel an appointment, use the Outlook Calendar toolbar.

1. Click on the **appointment** to be deleted. The appointment will be selected.

2. Click on the **Delete button**. The event will be deleted. Recipients will be notified via e-mail.

Printing the Calendar

You can print a daily, weekly, monthly, or tri-fold Calendar.

1. Click on the **Print button**. The Print dialog box will open.

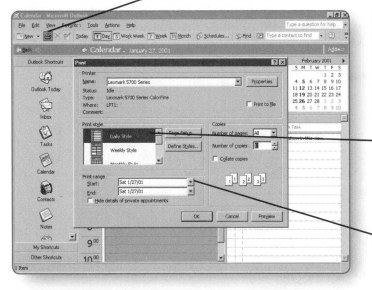

TIP

Optionally, click on File, Print to open the Print dialog box.

2. Click on a **Print style** (Daily, Weekly, Monthly, Tri-fold, or Calendar Details Style). The option will be highlighted.

3. Click on **down arrow** to the right of the Start list box. A calendar will display.

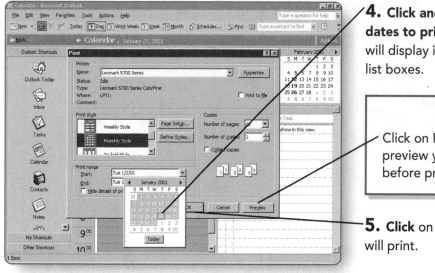

4. Click and drag across the dates to print. The date range will display in the Start and End list boxes.

TIP

Click on Preview to preview your selection before printing.

5. Click on **OK**. Your Calendar will print.

22

Using Outlook to Keep Organized

Using the Tasks folder, you can create a To Do list to make sure things don't "fall through the cracks." The Notes folder provides a place where you can store miscellaneous information—perhaps the kind of information you usually place on a sticky note. In this chapter, you'll learn how to:

- Create and delete tasks
- Print your task list
- Use the Notes folder to store miscellaneous information

Working with Tasks

A *task* is something you need to get done. It doesn't necessarily have a due date, but it is something you want to get done and don't want to forget. The task list is frequently referred to as a To Do list. Outlook helps keep your task list organized.

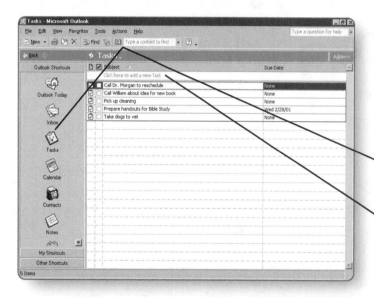

Creating a One-Time Task

Some tasks only need to be listed once whereas other tasks recur at regular intervals.

1. Click on the **Tasks shortcut**. The Tasks window will display.

2. Click on the **first line** of the Subject text box to add a new task. A blinking insertion point will display.

3. Type a **subject** for the task. The text will display in the Subject text box.

4. Click on the **Due Date text box**. A blinking insertion point will display with a down arrow next to it.

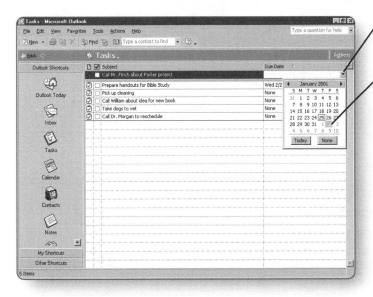

5. Click on the **down arrow**. A calendar will display.

6. Click on a **date**. The date will display in the Due Date text box.

7. Press the **Enter key** or **click** in the **task list**. The task will be listed with any others you've created.

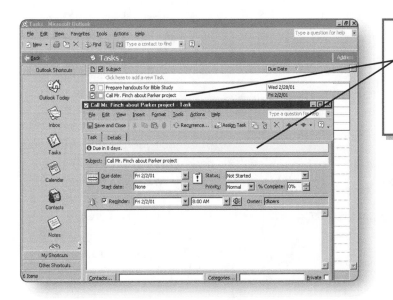

TIP

Optionally, double-click on a task to assign more information to it such as a priority or reminder.

Creating Recurring Tasks

Sometimes, you need to do the same task at regular intervals, so you should set it up as a recurring task.

1. **Click** on the **New Task button**. The Task window will appear.

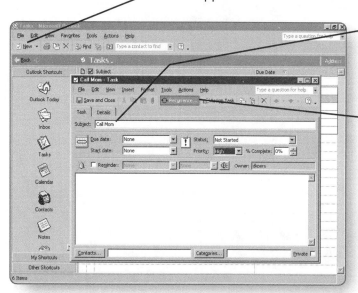

2. **Type** a **subject** and other information needed to set up the task. The information will display in the Task windows.

3. **Click** on the **Recurrence button**. The Task Recurrence dialog box will open.

Setting options in the Task Recurrence dialog box is similar to the options you selected in the Outlook Calendar in Chapter 21, "Using the Calendar."

The Recurrence choices will change depending on the frequency you choose. After you choose a frequency, you must specify how often it will occur.

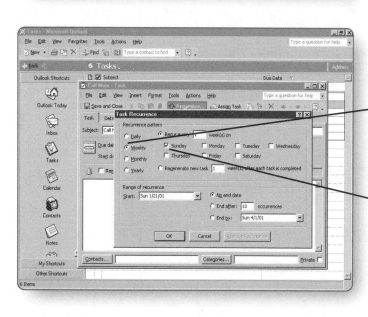

4. **Click** on a **recurrence pattern** (Daily, Weekly, and so on). The options for that pattern will be selected.

5. **Click** on the desired recurrence **options**. The options will be selected.

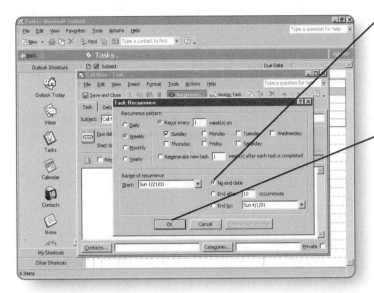

6. Optionally, **specify** an **end date** or a total **number of occurrences**. The options will be selected in the Range of recurrence section.

7. Click on **OK**. The Task Recurrence dialog box will close and the Task window will redisplay.

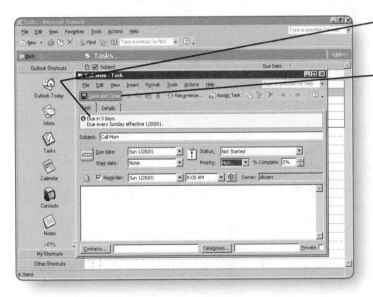

The recurrence details display at the top of the task.

8. Click on **Save and Close**. The recurring task will be added to your list.

Printing a Task List

You might want to create a paper copy of your task list to carry with you.

1. Click on the **Print button**. The Print dialog box will open.

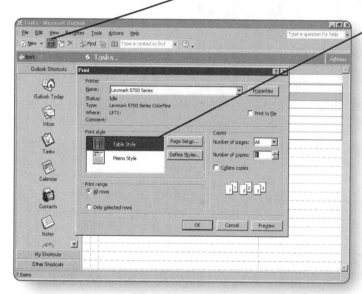

2. Click on a **Print style** for your list. The option will be highlighted.

- **Table Style:** Prints a list of all tasks showing their subject and due date.

- **Memo Style:** Prints all available information on a single task.

Next, specify whether you want to print the entire task list, or only a portion of it.

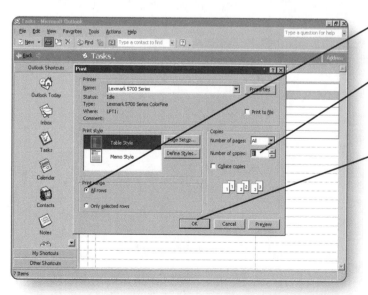

3. Click on a **Print range**. The option will be selected.

4. Click on a **number of copies**. The number will display in the copies box.

5. Click on **OK**. The task list will print.

Changing the Task List View

By default, the task list will display both active and completed items. You might only want to see active items. With Outlook, you can filter the display of your tasks.

1. Click on **View**. The View menu will appear.

2. Click on **Current View**. A submenu will appear.

3. Click on **Active Tasks**. All completed tasks will disappear from the list.

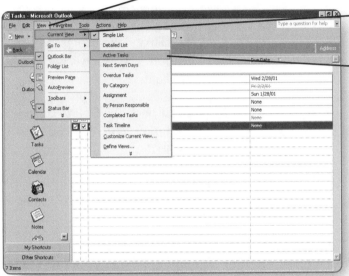

TIP

You can return to the Current View list and display only the completed tasks, or choose Simple List to see both completed and active tasks.

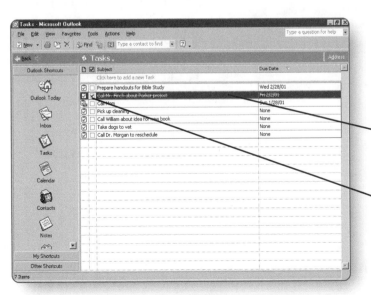

Completing a Task

When a task is complete, you'll want to check it off your To Do list.

1. Click on the **completed task**. The task will be highlighted in the task list.

2. Click in the **check box** just to the left of the subject. A check mark will display in the check box.

Completed items are crossed off the list.

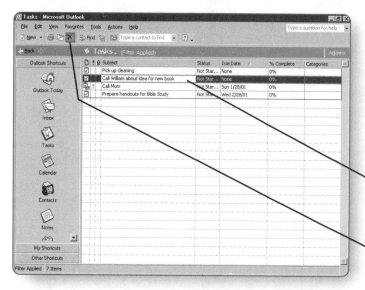

Deleting a Task

If you change your mind or no longer need to accomplish a certain task, you can delete it from the list. You might also want to delete completed tasks to remove them from your task list.

1. Click on the **task** to be deleted. The task will be highlighted.

2. Click on the **Delete button**. The task will be removed from the list.

Making Notes

Think of the Notes window in Outlook as your electronic sticky notepad. Here you can record ideas you have, conversations you want to remember, and any other miscellaneous information that just doesn't fit into any other category.

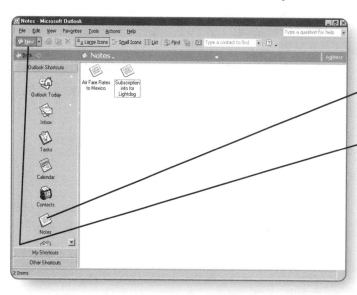

1. Click on the **Notes shortcut**. The Notes window will appear.

2. Click on the **New Note button**. A small "sticky note" window will appear.

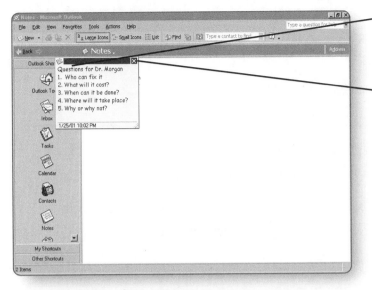

3. Type the note **information**. The text will display in the note window.

4. Click on the **Close box**. The note window will close.

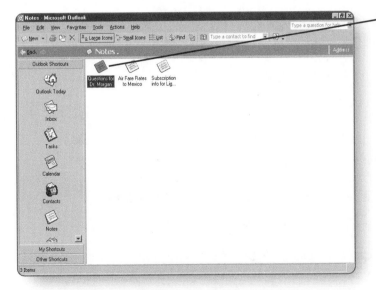

The note will appear in the Notes window.

Notes can be further modified in the following ways:

- **Edit a note**. To edit or read a note, double-click on it.

- **Delete a note**. To delete a note, click on it once and then press the Delete key.

- **Move a note**. To move a note, click on it once and drag it to a different location on the window.

Part V Review Questions

1. What is Outlook? *See "Getting Started with Outlook" in Chapter 18*

2. When you add a folder to the Outlook bar, which group is it added to? *See "Adding a Folder in Outlook" in Chapter 18*

3. How many different telephone numbers can be stored in a single Address Book Entry? *See "Adding an Address Book Entry" in Chapter 19*

4. How do you print a phone directory of your address book entries? *See "Printing a Contact List" in Chapter 19*

5. Can e-mail be sent to only those you have listed in your Outlook Address Book? *See "Creating an E-mail Message" in Chapter 20*

6. Do you have to start Outlook before you can e-mail a file? *See "E-mailing Files from Windows" in Chapter 20*

7. What happens when you schedule a meeting using Outlook? *See "Scheduling a Meeting" in Chapter 21*

8. How do you schedule recurring events using Outlook? *See "Creating Recurring Entries" in Chapter 21*

9. What does Outlook call a To Do list? *See "Working with Tasks" in Chapter 22*

10. What is Outlook's version of the sticky note? *See "Making Notes" in Chapter 22*

PART VI

Using Access

23

Creating an
Access Database

The Access application of Office includes a powerful but easy-to-use database. There is one major difference between Access and Word, Excel, and PowerPoint. Access only allows you to have one database open at a time. In this chapter, you'll learn how to:

- Understand database terms
- Create a database using a wizard
- Add, edit, and delete records
- Find records
- Print standard reports

Understanding Database Terms

Before you can work with a database, you should become familiar with some terms that are used in Access.

- **Database.** A *database* is a collection of information that is similar in nature. A telephone book, a list of your videos, and an inventory list are all examples of a database.

- **Records.** A *record* is all the information about one item. For example, in an address book, the entire sheet of information about Diane Koers is the record.

- **Fields.** *Fields* are categories of information. In the address book example, the last name and fax number are examples of fields.

- **Tables.** A *table* is a matrix, similar in appearance to a spreadsheet, that's used to store database information. All databases require at lease one table whereas many databases require several tables, linked together; such as one to store a client's address and telephone numbers and another one to track all the phone calls made to the client.

- **Forms.** A *form* is used for easy data entry. Forms usually display one record at a time.

- **Queries.** A *query* is a subset of data that meets certain criteria. An example might be a query of all clients named Smith who live in the city of Chicago. Queries are also known as *filters*.

- **Reports.** A *report* summarizes data in a format suitable for printing. A mailing label is an example of a report.

Using the Database Wizard

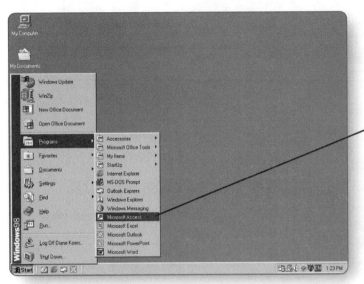

The fastest, easiest method to create a database is to start with one of the databases available from the Access Wizard.

1. Open the **Access** application. Use one of the methods you learned in Chapter 1, "Welcome to Office XP." The Microsoft Access dialog box will open with a Task Pane on the right.

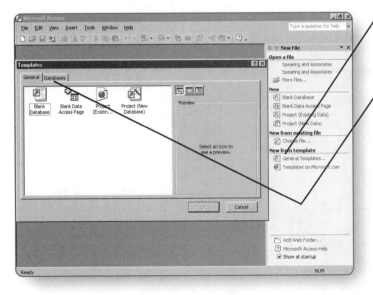

2. Click on **General Templates**. The Templates dialog box will open.

3. Click on the **Databases tab**. A selection of database templates will appear.

Access provides many sample databases.

4. Click on the **database sample** you want to start with. The database will be highlighted.

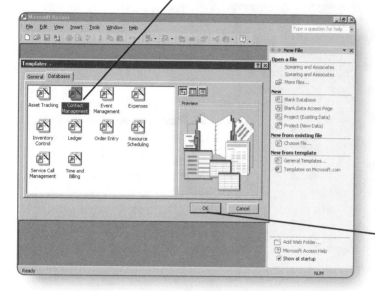

NOTE

For this chapter and the next one, you'll be working with the Contact Management database. Please be aware that if you select a different database, your screens will look a little different.

5. Click on **OK**. The File New Database dialog box will open.

An Access database must be named and saved before it is even created.

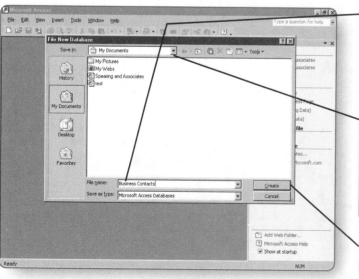

6. Type a **file name**. The file name will display in the File Name text box.

TIP

Optionally, click on the down arrow of the Save In list box and select a different location for the database.

7. Click on **Create**. The Database Wizard will begin.

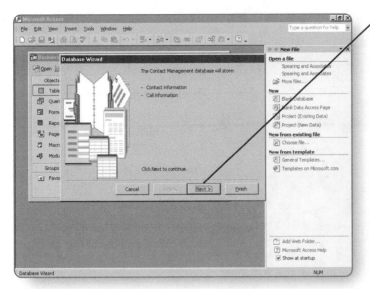

8. Click on **Next**. The next page of the wizard will display.

A list of predefined tables in the database will display.

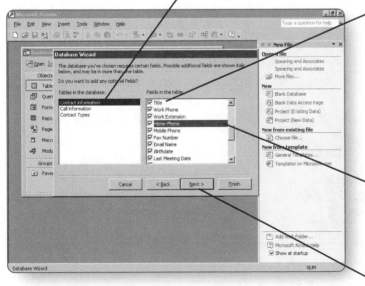

A list of the fields that can be included in each table will display.

You can select any additional fields you'd like to include in the database. Optional fields are displayed in italics.

9. Click on any **field names** that you want to use. A check mark beside the field names will appear.

10. Click on **Next**. The next page of the Wizard will display.

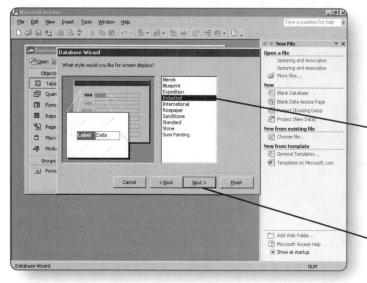

You now need to select a background appearance for your database. These backgrounds do not print; they are for decorative purposes only.

11. Click on a **style**. The style name will be highlighted and a sample will display in the preview box on the left of the screen.

12. Click on **Next**. The next page of the wizard will display.

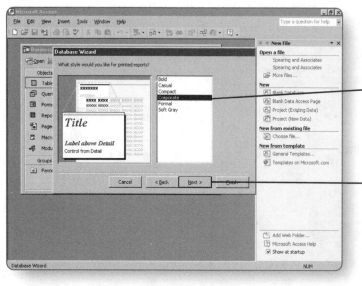

Next, you need to determine the overall appearance for your reports.

13. Click on a **report style**. The style name will be highlighted and a sample will display in the preview box.

14. Click on **Next**. The next page of the wizard will display.

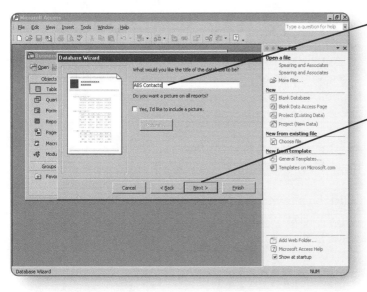

15. Optionally, **enter** a custom **name** for the database. The name will appear in the text box.

16. Click on **Next**. The final page of the wizard will display.

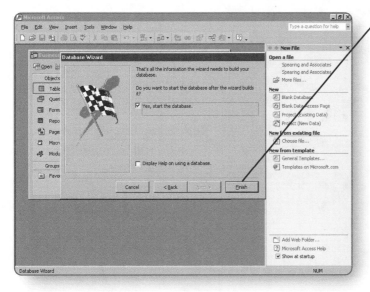

17. Click on **Finish**. The Database Wizard will close. After a few moments, the database will be created and the opening screen of the database will display.

Looking at the Switchboard

When you use the Database Wizard to create your database, Access creates an opening screen called the *switchboard*. The switchboard is a form that acts as a menu for you to easily move from place to place in your database.

The switchboard has buttons that you can click on to open forms, tables, and reports.

1. Click on a **Switchboard button**. Depending on which button you click on and the particular switchboard that is displayed, one of the following actions will take place.

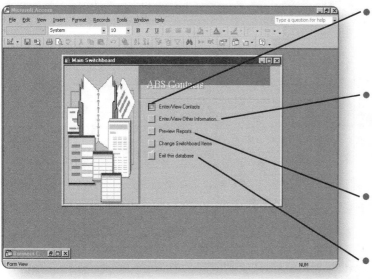

- A database screen will display. Click on the Close box to return to the main switchboard.

- A different switchboard might appear with further options. Click on Return to Main Switchboard to return to the main switchboard.

- A dialog box will open. Click on Cancel to return to the main switchboard.

- The current database will close. You'll need to reopen the database to display the main switchboard.

Working with Records

To successfully use your database, you'll need to be able to add, edit, and delete records. You'll also want to be able to quickly locate information in the database.

Adding Records

The data entry form is the easiest way to enter records.
Because you used the Database Wizard to create your
database, a data entry form is automatically created for you.
The data entry form is accessed
from the Main Switchboard.

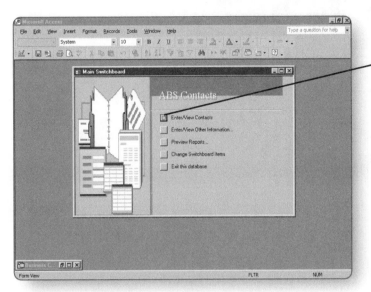

1. Click on **Enter/View
Contacts**. The Contacts form
will display with a blank entry.

NOTE

Remember that this book
demonstrates working
with the Contact Manage-
ment database. If you've
selected a different one,
your options will vary
slightly.

TIP

If the current record is not
blank, click on one of the
two New Record buttons
or choose New Record
from the Insert menu.

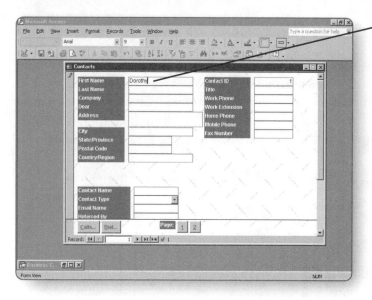

2. Type the **first field** of information. In this example, it's the First Name of the contact. The text will display in the first field box.

3. Press the **Tab key**. The insertion point will move to the next field.

4. Type the **next field** of information. The text will display in the second field box.

5. Repeat steps 3 and 4 until all fields that you want to fill out are completed.

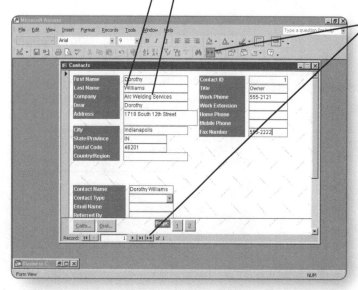

6. Click on one of the two **New Record buttons**. A new blank record will appear for you to fill out.

NOTE

A database is different from many other types of files in that you don't have to keep clicking on the Save button. The database is automatically saved each time you add or edit a record.

Viewing Records

Once you have your records entered, you'll want to be able to look at them. Access gives you two distinct views to use when viewing records: Form View and Datasheet View.

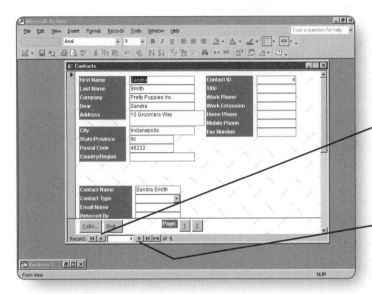

Navigating Around in a Form

Form View allows you to see one record at a time.

1a. Click on the **Previous Record button**. The previous record will display.

OR

1b. Click on the **Next Record button**. The next record will display.

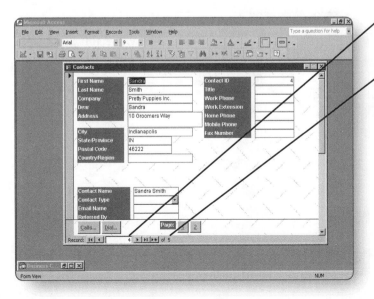

This counter is showing which record is currently displayed.

This counter is showing the total number of records.

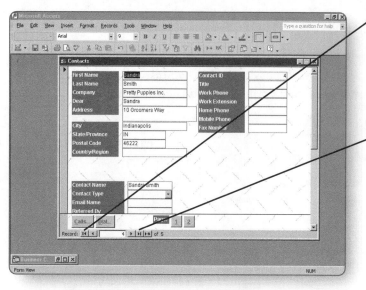

2a. Click on the **First Record button**. The first record you entered in your database will display.

OR

2b. Click on the **Last Record button**. The last record of your database will display.

Viewing from the Datasheet

In Datasheet view, you'll see many records on a single sheet, similar to an Excel spreadsheet.

1. Click on **View**. The View menu will appear.

2. Click on **Datasheet View**. The records will display in Datasheet View.

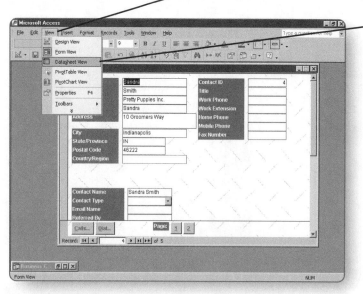

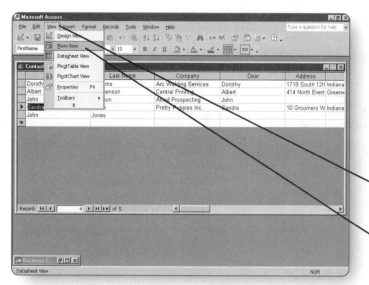

3. Click on **View**. The View menu will appear.

4. Click on **Form View**. The Form View will return to the form.

Editing Records

Editing a record is as easy as locating a record and typing a correction.

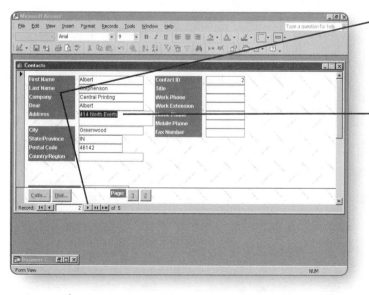

1. Click on the **navigation buttons** until the record to be edited is displayed. The record will display on the screen.

2. Click and drag across the **data** you want to modify. The existing data will be highlighted.

3. Type a **correction**. The corrected data will be saved with the record.

Deleting Records

If you need to delete a record from your database, the entire record will be deleted.

1. Display the **record** to be deleted. The record will display on the screen.

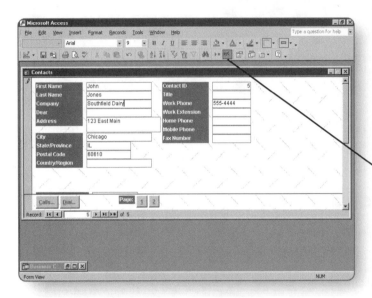

TIP

If you are working in Datasheet view, click anywhere in the record you want to delete before proceeding to step 2.

2. Click on the **Delete Record button**. A confirmation message will appear. The message you see can vary, but if any of the information in this record is tied to other tables in the database, the message will warn you that deleting this record will also affect those tables.

TIP

Optionally, choose Delete Record from the Edit menu.

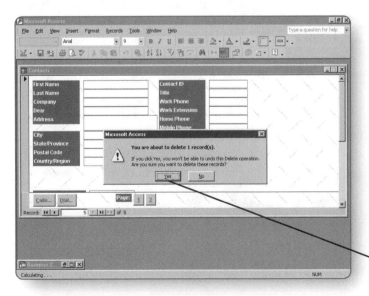

NOTE

Once you delete a record, you cannot undo it.

3. Click on **Yes**. The record will be deleted.

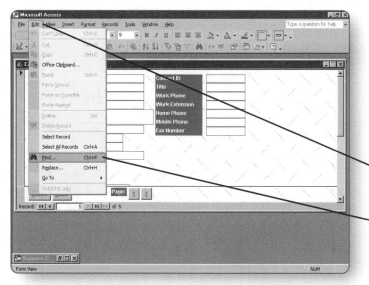

Finding Records

When many records have been entered, you might want to quickly locate one of them. Use the Find function to track down your record.

1. Click on **Edit**. The Edit menu will appear.

2. Click on **Find**. The Find and Replace dialog box will open.

TIP

Optionally, press Ctrl+F to display the Find and Replace dialog box.

---

3. Type a piece of **information** contained in the record you're searching for. The text will appear in the Find What text box.

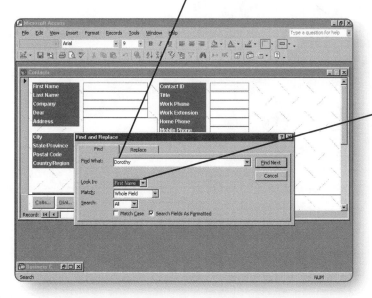

You'll need to tell Access where to look for the text—either search the current field or the entire database.

4. Click on the **drop-down arrow** next to the Look In list box. Two options will appear: the current field or the name of your database.

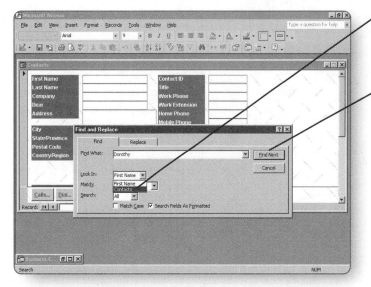

5. Click on an **option**. The selection will display in the Look In text box.

6. Click on **Find Next**. The record with the first occurrence of the matched text will display.

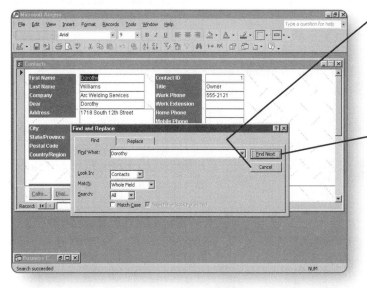

7a. Click on **Cancel** if this is the record you're searching for. The Find and Replace dialog box will close.

OR

7b. If you need to search further, **click** on **Find Next**. The next occurrence will display.

Printing Database Reports

Most people will need all or some of the database information in printed form. If you created your database with the wizard, you'll have some pre-designed reports that can provide useful summary information.

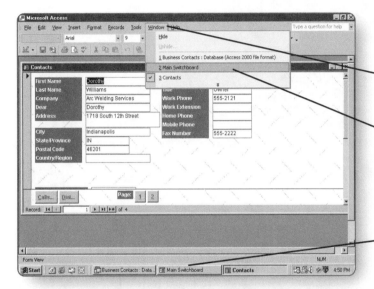

Reports are accessed from the main switchboard.

1. Click on **Window**. The Window menu will appear.

2. Click on **Main Switchboard**. The main switchboard will redisplay.

TIP

A quick way to access the switchboard is to click on it from the Windows taskbar.

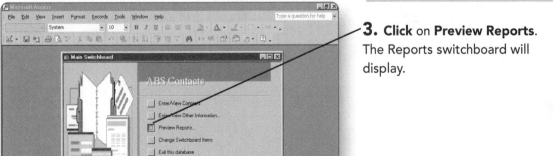

3. Click on **Preview Reports**. The Reports switchboard will display.

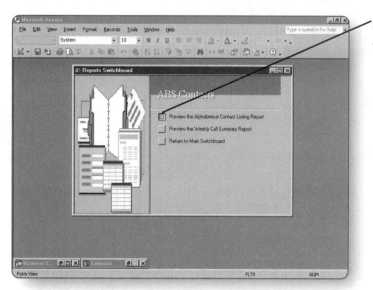

4. Click on a **report**. The report will appear on your screen.

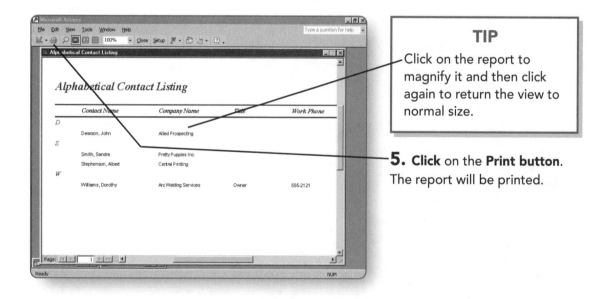

TIP
Click on the report to magnify it and then click again to return the view to normal size.

5. Click on the **Print button**. The report will be printed.

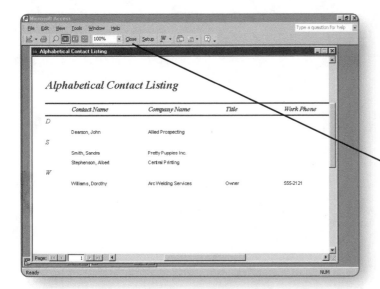

TIP

Optionally, choose File, Print to display the Print dialog box and make specific print specifications.

6. Click on **Close**. The view will return to the Reports switchboard.

24

Modifying an Access Database

Sometimes a database created with the wizard will provide everything you need, but other times, you find yourself wishing for more reports, additional fields, or other tables and forms. Each database can be modified to meet your needs. In this chapter, you'll learn how to:

- Add and delete fields from a table
- Modify a form
- Create mailing labels

Modifying Table Structure

Whether you're going to add a new table or modify an existing one, you'll need to work with a window called the Database window. The Database window has been hiding behind your main switchboard window. When a table is first created, you might not know exactly which fields you want and where you want them placed. You can choose to modify the structure of an existing table.

Adding Fields to a Table

Add as many additional fields as you need. In the Contacts Management database, for example, you'll add a field for the contact's birthday.

1. Click on **Window**. The Window menu will appear.

2. Click on a **Database**. The name of the database will precede the word "Database." The Database window will display.

TIP

You can also access the Switchboard anytime by choosing Windows, Main Switchboard.

3. **Click** on **Tables**. The database tables will be listed.

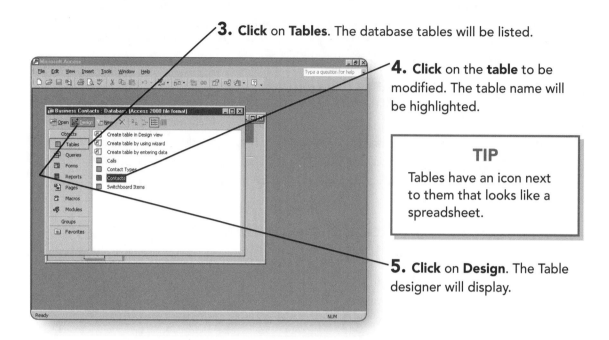

4. **Click** on the **table** to be modified. The table name will be highlighted.

> ### TIP
> Tables have an icon next to them that looks like a spreadsheet.

5. **Click** on **Design**. The Table designer will display.

6. **Click** on the **grid** for the row where you want the new field to be located. The new field will be inserted above the one you select. A blinking insertion point will display.

An arrow indicates the selected field.

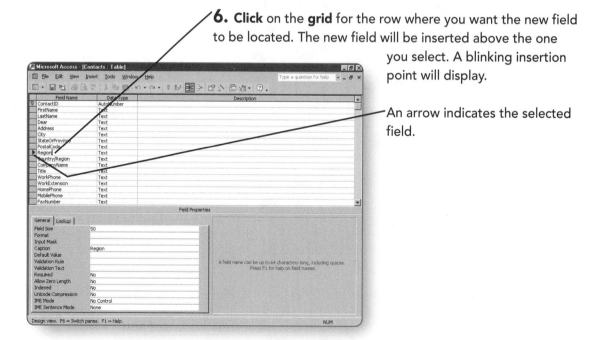

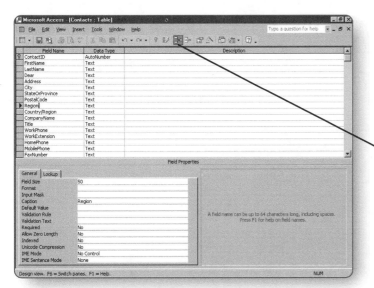

TIP

Optionally, click on the Insert menu and click on Rows.

7. Click on the **Insert Rows button**. A blank row will be inserted above the insertion point.

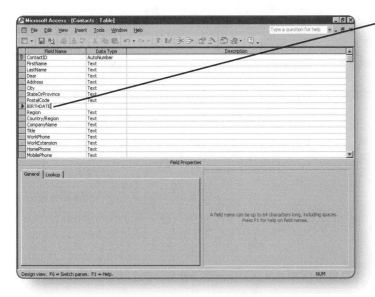

8. Type a **name** for the new field. Field names cannot have any spaces in them. The text will display in the Field Name column.

9. Press the **Tab key**. The insertion point will jump to the Data Type column.

You need to tell Access what type of data is going to be placed in this field. Examples include text, date, or numbers.

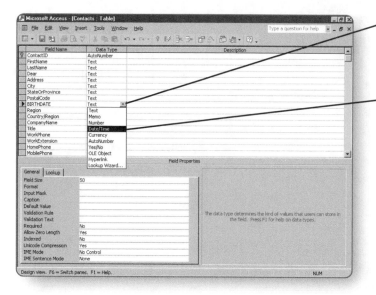

10. **Click** on **drop-down arrow** under the Data Type. A list of choices will display.

11. **Click** on a **Data Type**. The drop-down list will close.

The options in the Field Properties area will change according to the Data Type you select.

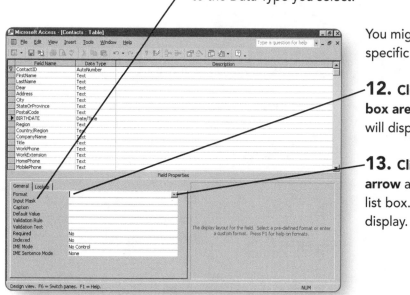

You might want to set some specific formats for the field.

12. **Click** in the **Format list box area**. A drop-down arrow will display.

13. **Click** on the **drop-down arrow** at the right of the Format list box. A list of choices will display.

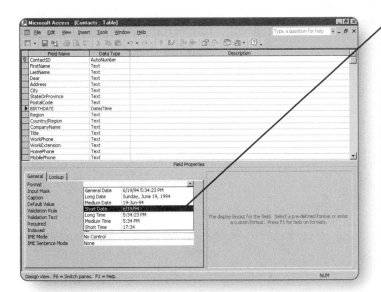

14. **Click** on a **Format**. The format will display in the Format list box area.

NOTE

The format choices displayed vary with the data type you selected in step 11.

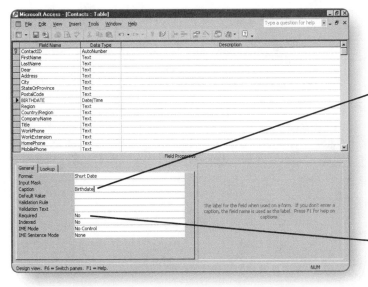

15. **Click** in the **Caption text box**. A blinking insertion point will display.

16. **Type** the **caption** you'd like to see displayed on your forms. It can be the same as the actual field name or you can call it something else.

TIP

If you want to require that information be entered in the new field, click on the Required box and choose Yes from the drop-down list. This means that the field cannot be left blank.

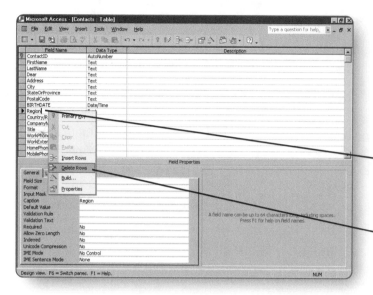

Deleting Table Fields

When you delete a field, you'll also delete any record data stored in the field.

1. Right-click on the **field** you want to delete. A shortcut menu will appear.

2. Click on **Delete Rows**. A confirmation box will open.

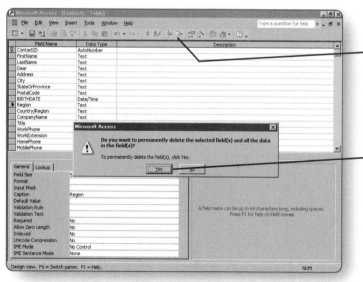

TIP

Optionally, click on the field you want to delete and click on the Delete Rows button.

3. Click on **Yes**. The field and its data will be deleted.

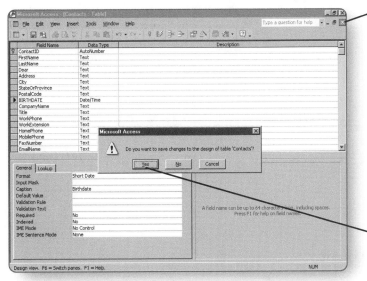

4. Click on the **Table Close box**. A warning message will display.

In the previous chapter, you learned that Access automatically saves data as you enter it. When modifying database design however, you must tell Access whether to save your changes.

5. Click on **Yes**. The design changes will be saved and the Database window will redisplay.

Modifying a Form

You might want to modify a form to match additions or changes to your database. Changes you make to tables do not necessarily reflect on your forms.

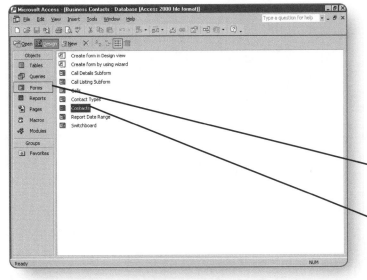

Adding a Field to a Form

Even though you added a field to a table, you'll still need to modify any forms that you want to include the new field.

1. Click on **Forms**. A list of available forms will display.

2. Click on the **form name** to be modified. The form name will be highlighted.

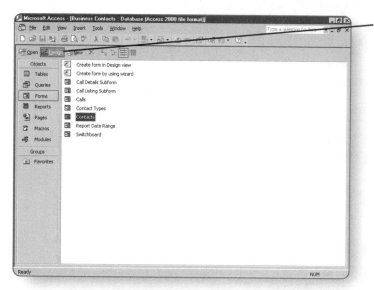

3. **Click** on the **Design button**. The form will display in the Form Design window.

4. **Click** on **View**. The View menu will appear.

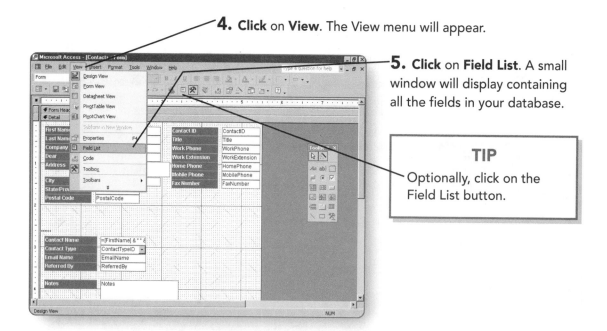

5. **Click** on **Field List**. A small window will display containing all the fields in your database.

TIP

Optionally, click on the Field List button.

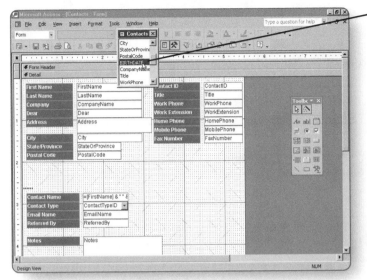

6. Click on the **field name** that you want to add to the form. The field name will be highlighted.

You'll use the mouse to transfer the field to a new location.

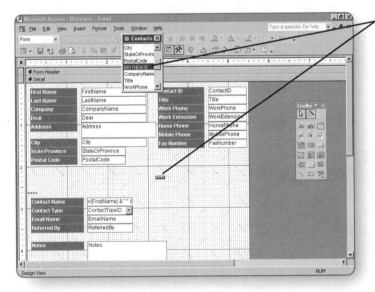

7. Click and **drag** the **field name** onto the form. The mouse pointer will look like a small rectangular box.

8. Release the **mouse button**. The field will be placed on the form along with the caption you created earlier.

Moving a Form Field

Form fields can easily be moved. Again, you'll use the mouse to direct the field to a new location.

1. Click on the field to be moved. The field and the caption will be selected with small handles around each object.

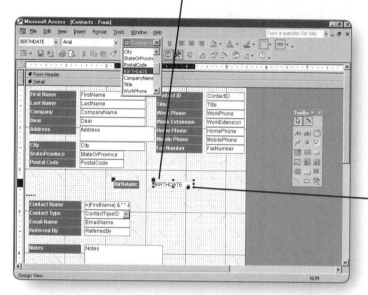

TIP

Be sure to click on the field, not just the field caption. Clicking on the caption will select only the caption, not both field and caption.

2. Position the **mouse pointer** on the bottom edge of the field. The mouse pointer will turn into a small black hand.

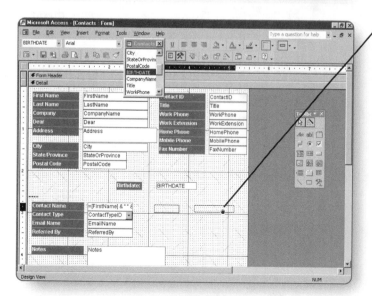

3. Click and **drag** the **field** and its caption to the new position. A dotted box will indicate the new position.

4. Release the **mouse button**. The field will be moved.

Deleting a Field from a Form

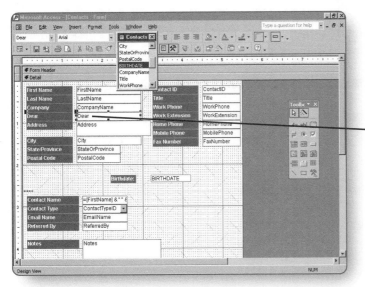

When deleting a field from the form, no data will be lost. This just means that the particular data cannot be accessed from the form anymore.

1. Click on the field to be deleted. The field and the caption will be selected with small handles around each object.

2. Press the **Delete key**. The field and its caption will be removed from the form.

When you've finished making changes to the form design, you'll need to close the form window.

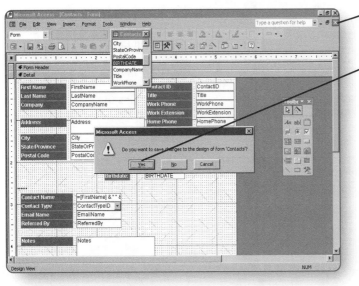

3. Click on the **Close box**. A warning message will display.

4. Click on **Yes**. The form designer will close and the Database window will redisplay.

Creating Mailing Labels

One popular use of a database is to create mailing labels for each record in your database. Access includes a Label Wizard to assist you in setting up your labels.

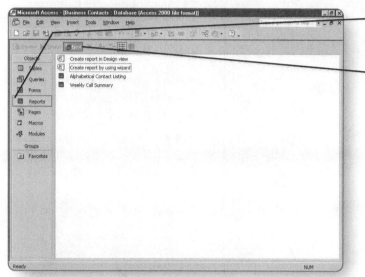

1. **Click** on **Reports**. A list of current reports is displayed.

2. **Click** on **New**. The New Report dialog box will display.

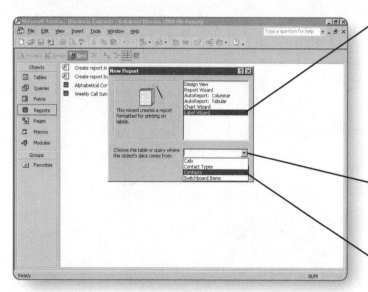

3. **Click** on **Label Wizard**. Label Wizard will be highlighted.

Because most databases have several tables in them, you'll need to indicate which table has the fields that you will use to create labels.

4. **Click** on the **drop-down arrow** to choose the table. A list of existing tables will display.

5. **Click** on the **table** you want to use. The table name will display in the text box.

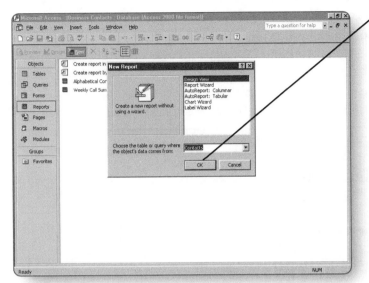

6. Click on **OK**. The first screen of the Label Wizard will display.

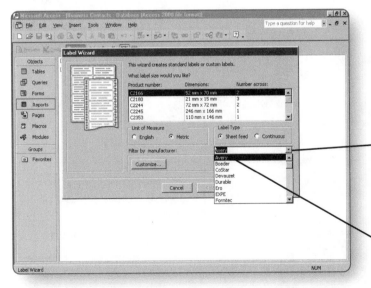

Because there are many label manufactures in the market today, you'll need to tell Access which label you plan to use. First, you'll need to choose the label manufacturer.

7. Click on the **drop-down arrow** at the right of Filter by Manufacturer. A list of label brands will display.

8. Click on the **label brand** you're going to use. The brand name will display.

Next, you'll need to choose which label size you intend to use. Most manufacturers include their label product number on the outside of the box.

9. Click on the label **product number** you're going to use. A description of the labels will be displayed including dimensions and the number of labels across the width of a page.

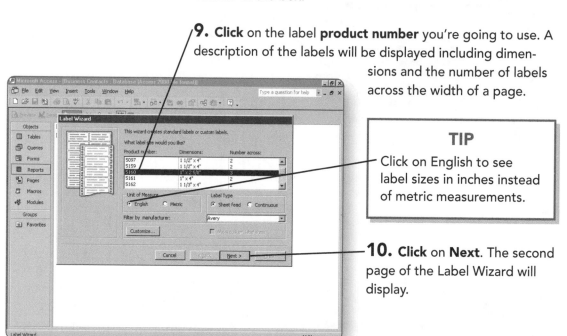

> **TIP**
>
> Click on English to see label sizes in inches instead of metric measurements.

10. Click on **Next**. The second page of the Label Wizard will display.

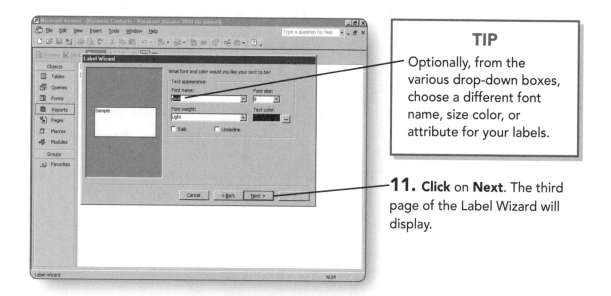

> **TIP**
>
> Optionally, from the various drop-down boxes, choose a different font name, size color, or attribute for your labels.

11. Click on **Next**. The third page of the Label Wizard will display.

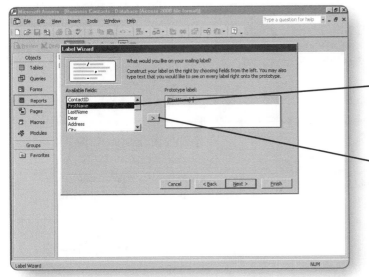

On this screen, you'll need to tell Access what fields you want to place on the label.

12. Click on the **first field** that you want to include. The field name will be highlighted.

13. Click on the **right arrow**. The field name will be added to the label layout.

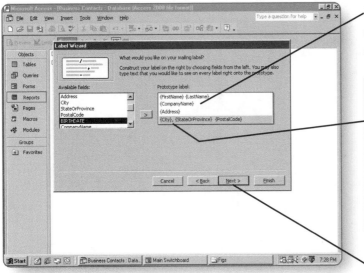

14. Continue adding any desired **fields**. The fields will be added to the label layout.

NOTE

Press any spaces, type any punctuation or text, or press the Enter key as needed to make sure the fields are placed where you want them.

15. Click on **Next**. The next screen of the Label Wizard will display.

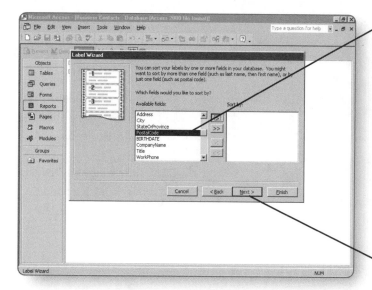

16. Double-click on a **field** to sort your labels in the Available Fields list box. The field name will display in the Sort By area.

TIP

When doing a bulk mailing, the USPS requires the documents sorted by postal code.

17. Click on **Next**. The final screen of the Label Wizard will display.

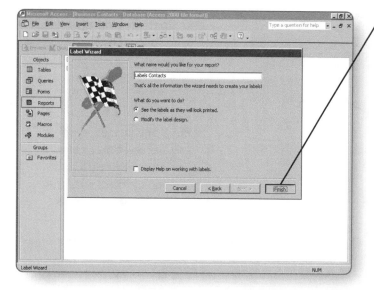

18. Click on **Finish**. The labels will be previewed on your screen.

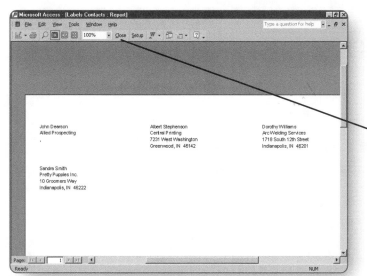

TIP

Click on the page to zoom in.

19. Click on the **Close box**. The Preview window will close and the Database window will redisplay.

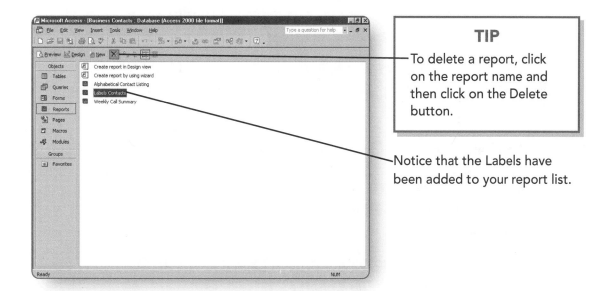

TIP

To delete a report, click on the report name and then click on the Delete button.

Notice that the Labels have been added to your report list.

Part VI Review Questions

1. What is a database? *See "Understanding Database Terms" in Chapter 23*

2. How many tables are required in an Access database? *See "Understanding Database Terms" in Chapter 23*

3. What happens to the database each time you add or edit a record? *See "Adding Records" in Chapter 23*

4. Which Access database view allows you to see many records together on the same page? *See "Viewing from the Datasheet" in Chapter 23*

5. How do you access the predefined database reports? *See "Printing Database Reports" in Chapter 23*

6. What is the name of the Window you need to work with when modifying tables or forms? *See "Modifying Table Structure" in Chapter 24*

7. Can field names include spaces? *See "Adding Fields to a Table" in Chapter 24*

8. Name an example of data type. *See "Adding Fields to a Table" in Chapter 24*

9. What happens to record data when a field is deleted? *See "Deleting Table Fields" in Chapter 24*

10. Which feature of Access helps you create mailing labels? *See "Creating Mailing Labels" in Chapter 24*

PART VII

Discovering Office Productivity Tools

25

Saving Office Documents as Web Documents

In Word, Excel, and PowerPoint, you can create documents that can be published as Web documents. Web documents are those that will appear on the Internet. They follow a different standard than the documents you typically create—to be able to read a document on the Internet, you must insert HTML tags. Because inserting HTML tags is cumbersome, you don't want to insert them while creating a document. So, Office programs let you create a document as you normally do and then, when you save the document as a Web document, the Office application will insert the HTML tags for you. In this chapter, you'll learn how to:

- Save a Word, Excel, or PowerPoint document as a Web document
- View the document in Internet Explorer
- Edit a Word Web document

Saving an Existing Document as a Web Document

When a document is saved as a Web document, Office will insert the HTML tags for you—you won't even see them.

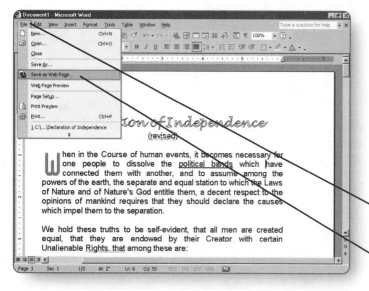

You don't need to create HTML documents from scratch if you want to use a document you've already created.

1. Open or create the Word, Excel, or PowerPoint **document** you want to save as a Web page. The document will display on the screen.

2. Click on **File**. The File menu will open.

3. Click on **Save As Web Page**. The Save As dialog box will open.

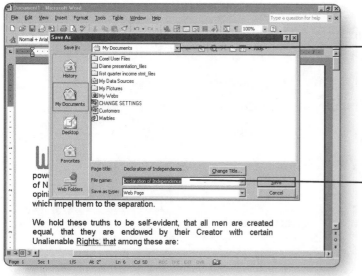

TIP

Optionally, click on the drop-down arrow next to the Save In list box to specify the folder in which you want to save the Web document.

4. Type a **name** for the file. The name will display in the File Name text box.

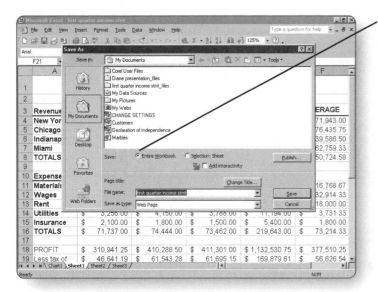

When using Excel, you can save the entire workbook or just the current page. Click on an option to the right of the Save area. The option will be selected.

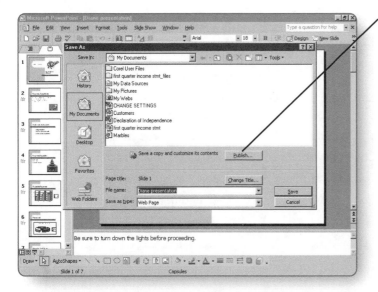

PowerPoint assumes you want to save all the slides in the presentation unless you click on the Publish button and select which slides to include.

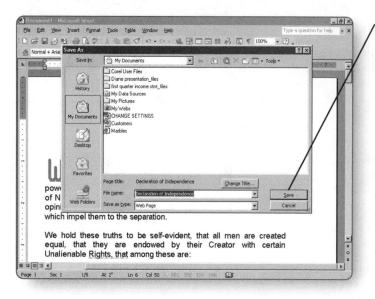

5. Click on **Save**. The document will be converted to HTML format.

Most Word formatting choices are acceptable in a Web document; however, there are a few formats that most Web browsers cannot support. The following table lists a few of the specialized character formats that do not convert properly when converting a Word document to HTML.

Format	Reaction in a Web Browser
Animated text	No animation and will appear as italicized text
Emboss or engrave	Will turn into a light gray shaded text
Shadowed text	Text will become bold
Character borders	No border around text
Special underlining	Appears as a single underline
Color underline	Black underline
Small caps	All caps

If you have any of the non-supported formats in your Word document, a dialog box will advise you what will happen to the non-supported formats.

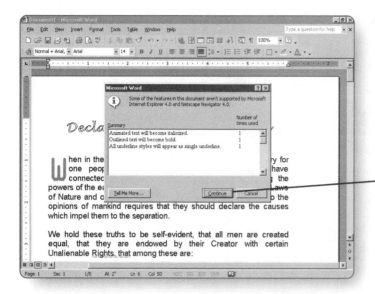

NOTE

Excel and PowerPoint documents don't advise you if you are going to lose any formatting features.

6. Click on **Continue**. The conversion will continue and the document will be displayed in Web Layout view.

Viewing the Document in Internet Explorer

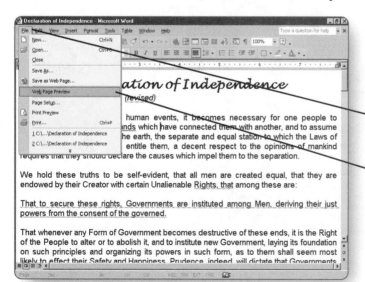

Now that the document has been saved as HTML, it's time to see what it looks like in Internet Explorer.

1. Click on **File**. The File menu will appear.

2. Click on **Web Page Preview**. The Internet Explorer window will display and you'll see the document as viewed through Internet Explorer.

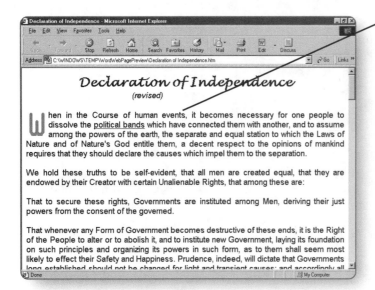

This is a Word document as viewed in Internet Explorer.

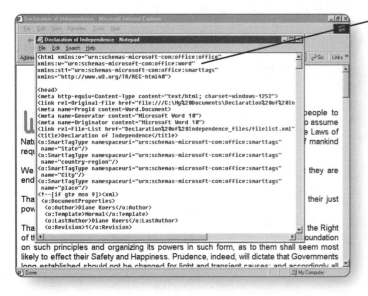

To view the HTML source code, from the Internet Explorer window, click on View, Source. A window will open with all the HTML tags. Aren't you glad you have Office to do all this work for you!

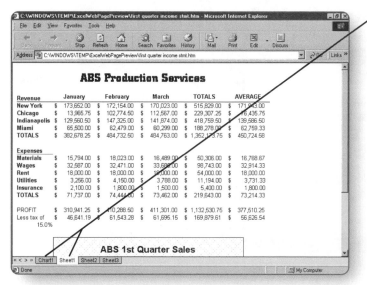

If you elected to save your entire Excel workbook when you saved to HTML, Internet Explorer (and most Web browsers) will display the worksheet very similarly to the way it is displayed in the Excel program. Tabs will be placed along the bottom of the screen to view the different worksheet or chart pages.

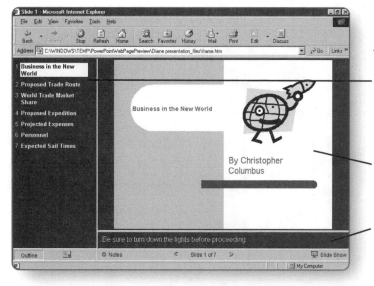

From PowerPoint, the HTML document includes three frames:

- **An Outline frame.** By default, the Outline frame only includes the slide titles, not the text.

- **A Slide frame.** The currently selected slide on the outline appears in the Slide frame.

- **A Notes frame.** Any speaker notes created for the current slide will appear.

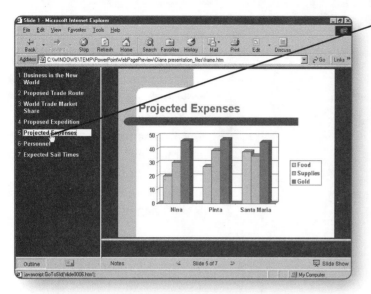

3. Position the **mouse pointer** over an outline title. The mouse pointer will change to a hand because each title is a hyperlink to that slide.

4. Click on an **Outline title**. The slide associated with that title will display.

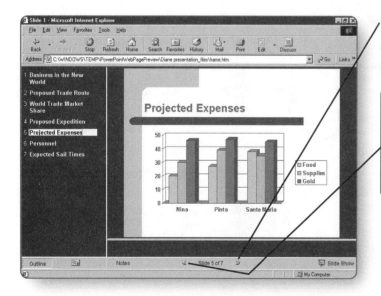

5. Click on the **Next Slide arrow**. The next slide in the presentation will display.

TIP

Similarly, click on the Previous Slide arrow. The previous slide will display.

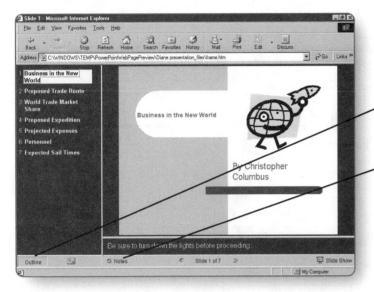

If you don't want the outline or the speaker notes frame to display, you can hide either or both of them.

6. Click on the **Outline button**. The Outline frame will hide.

7. Click on the **Notes button**. The Speaker Notes frame will hide.

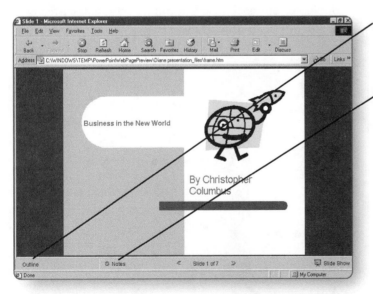

8. Click on the **Outline button** again. The Outline frame will redisplay.

9. Click on the **Notes button** again. The Speaker Notes frame will redisplay.

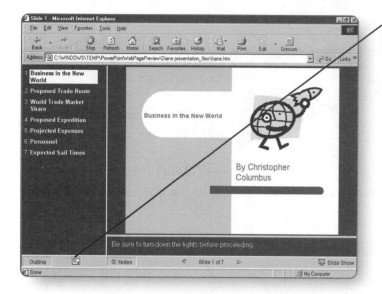

10. **Click** on the **Expand/Collapse Outline button**. The Outline text will display in full.

If your outline is longer than will fit on the screen, a vertical scroll bar will display for the Outline frame.

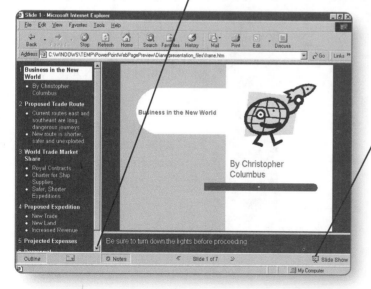

TIP

Click on Expand/Collapse Outline again to display only slide titles.

Web surfers can also enjoy a PowerPoint presentation as a slide show by clicking on the Slide Show button. PowerPoint does not have to be installed on a viewer's computer to view the slide show.

Editing a Word Web Document

After you've previewed your Microsoft Word document as a Web document, you might find you want to make changes to it. Editing the text in the document is the same as any other Word document, but Word includes some special effects that are quite nice for Web pages.

Adding Scrolling Text

Scrolling text on a Web page provides quite a dramatic effect. Unfortunately, not all Web browsers support scrolling text. Any surfer who happens to be using a browser that doesn't support scrolling text will see regular text.

To create scrolling text, you'll need to use the Web Tools toolbar.

1. Open the **Word document** to include scrolling text. The document will display on the screen.

2. Click on **View.** The View menu will appear.

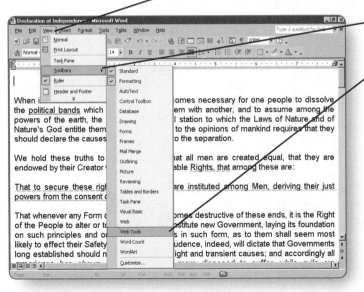

3. Click on **Toolbars**. The Toolbars submenu will appear.

4. Click on **Web Tools**. The Web Tools toolbar will display.

5. Click the location where you want the scrolling text. The blinking insertion point will appear.

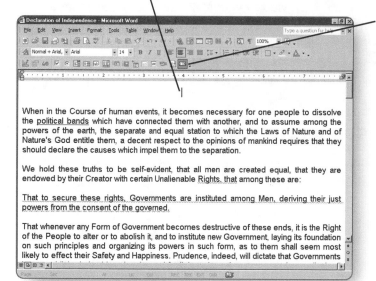

6. Click on the **Scrolling Text tool** from the Web Tools toolbar. The Scrolling Text dialog box will open.

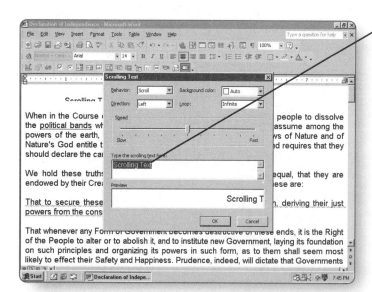

7. Select the words **Scrolling Text** in the "Type the scrolling text here" text box. The text will be highlighted.

8. Type the **text** you want to appear. The new text will replace the original text.

9. **Click** on the **drop-down arrow** to the right of the Behavior list box. A list of choices will appear.

10. **Click** on a **method** of scrolling. The selection will appear in the Behavior list box.

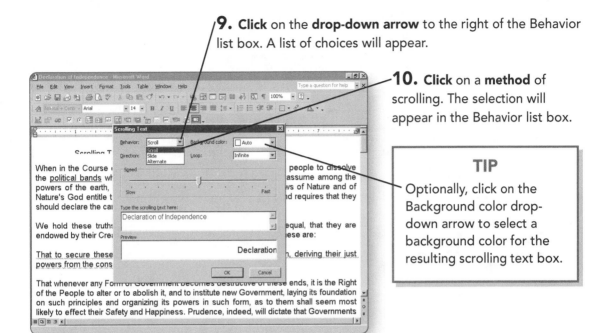

11. **Click** on the **drop-down arrow** to the right of the Direction list box. A list of choices will appear.

12. **Click** on a **direction** for the text to scroll. The selection will appear in the Direction list box.

13. **Drag** the **speed knob** to the left or right. Dragging to the left will slow down the speed of the scrolling text, whereas dragging to the right will increase the speed.

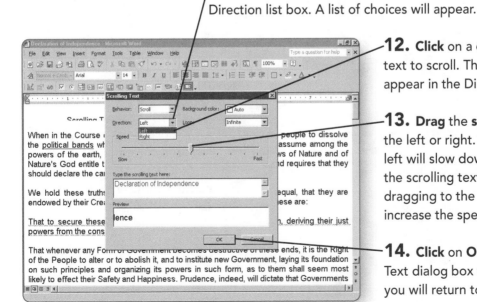

14. **Click** on **OK**. The Scrolling Text dialog box will close and you will return to your Web page.

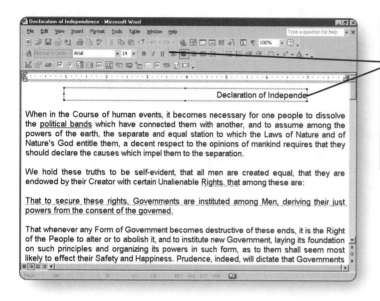

TIP

You can now further edit the scrolling text object. Click on the appropriate choices from the Standard toolbar to edit the size, font, or color.

Using a Web Theme

Themes are a collection of background colors/patterns, bullet styles, line styles, heading styles, and font styles. When you select a theme, you make available, in your document, all the styles associated with the theme. Most people use themes when designing Web pages in Word.

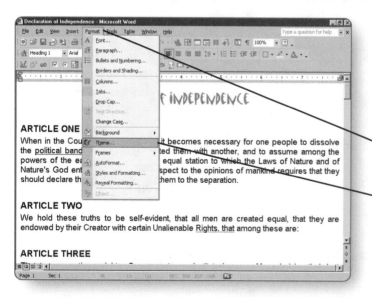

1. Click on **Format**. The Format menu will appear.

2. Click on **Theme**. The Theme dialog box will open.

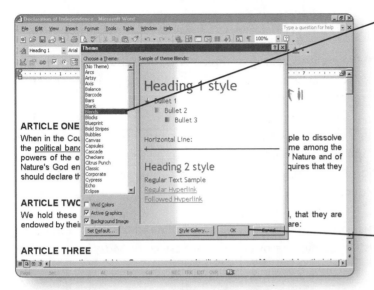

3. Click on a **theme**. The theme name will be highlighted and a sample will display in the preview window.

NOTE

You might need your Office CD to install some of the themes.

4. Click on **OK**. Word will apply the background and other formatting choices to the document.

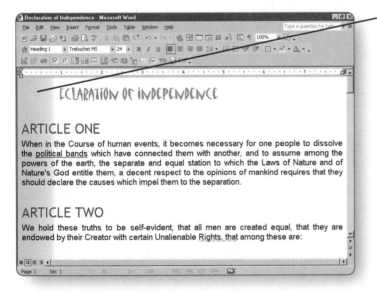

Notice the changes to the headings and background.

Publishing Web Documents

You've created your Web documents; now the issue becomes how to make your Web pages accessible to your company's Intranet or on the Web.

You'll need to save your Web pages and their related files (the graphics, lines, bullets, and so on) to a *Web folder*, which is a shortcut to a Web server. The Web server must support Web folders.

This varies between servers so you'll need to check with your system administrator or Internet Service Provider.

26

Streamlining Office Activities

The Microsoft Office Shortcut Bar contains a series of toolbars that help speed up your work. For example, using these toolbars, you can quickly open Office documents or create new Office documents or access, from any Office program, a shortcut on your Desktop. In this chapter, you'll learn how to:

- Use the Office Shortcut Bar
- Move the Office Shortcut Bar
- Customize the Office Shortcut Bar

Working with the Office Shortcut Bar

The Office Shortcut Bar provides you with quick access to the resources you use most often on your computer. When you first see the Office Shortcut Bar, it will appear at the side of your screen, but you can move it. By default, the Office Shortcut Bar remains visible at all times, regardless of the program(s) in which you are working. However, you can hide it, making it available but not always visible. You can also close it.

Understanding and Using the Office Shortcut Bar

The first time you use the Office Shortcut Bar, you'll need to select it from the menu.

1. **Click** on **Start**. The Start menu will appear.

2. **Click** on **Programs**. The Programs submenu will appear.

3. **Click** on **Microsoft Office Tools**. The Microsoft Office Tools submenu will appear.

4. **Click** on **Microsoft Office Shortcut Bar**. A dialog box will open.

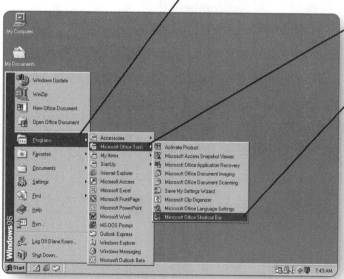

TIP

If you do not have Microsoft Office Shortcut Bar listed in the Microsoft Office Tools menu, add it via the Control Panel, Add/Remove programs feature. See Appendix B.

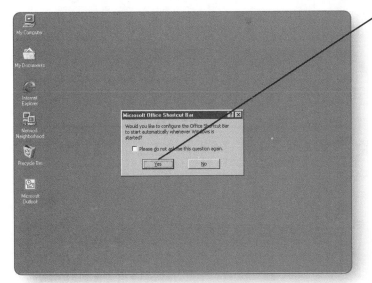

5. Click on **Yes**. The Office Shortcut Bar will launch.

The Office Shortcut Bar will appear on the right side of your screen and consists of two main sections:

- **The Control Menu Button.** You can click here to do any customizing to the Shortcut Bar.

- **Shortcut Bar Buttons.** You'll click on these to make various applications launch: those provided by Microsoft and some of your own you'll add later in this chapter.

Moving the Office Shortcut Bar

The Office Shortcut Bar will appear, by default, at the side of your screen. Many people find this cumbersome because it can block the vertical scroll bar of your applications. You can place the Office Shortcut Bar anywhere on-screen.

1. Position the **pointer** onto a gray or black area on the Shortcut Bar. Make sure you're not pointing at any buttons.

2. Drag the **Shortcut Bar** to a new location. A red box indicates the new position.

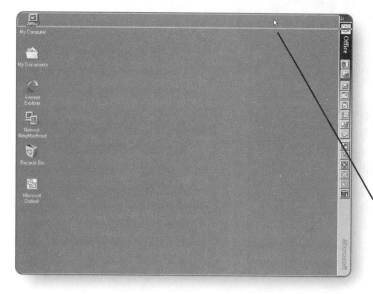

TIP

For best results, move the Shortcut Bar to an edge of your screen. The box will change shape from an almost square box to a long thin rectangular box.

3. Release the **mouse button**. The Shortcut Bar will appear wherever you drop it.

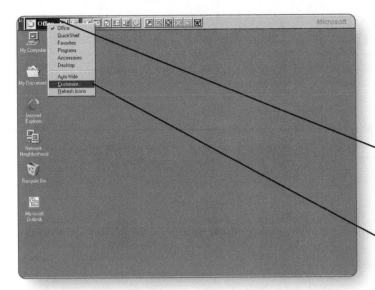

Resizing the Office Shortcut Bar

To make the Office Shortcut Bar easier to use, you might want to enlarge the buttons.

1. Right-click on any gray or black area of the **Shortcut Bar**. The Shortcut Bar menu will appear.

2. Click on **Customize**. The Customize dialog box will open.

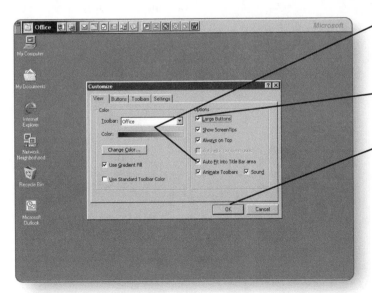

3. Click on the **check box** next to the Auto Fit into Title Bar area. The option will be selected.

4. Click on **Large Buttons**. The option will be selected.

5. Click on **OK**. The Shortcut Bar will enlarge to fill the top of your screen.

The Office Shortcut Bar contains buttons to help you quickly get whatever you need. Pause the mouse pointer over any icon to get a description of the icon function.

● Click on these buttons to create new Office documents and to open existing Office documents.

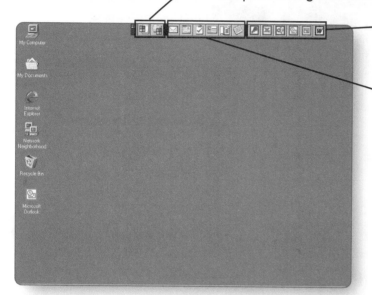

● Click on these buttons to open Microsoft Office applications.

● Click on these buttons to create new Outlook events.

Hiding the Office Shortcut Bar

By default, the Office Shortcut Bar will appear on-screen all the time. If you aren't using Auto Fit and you don't want to see the Shortcut Bar all the time, you can temporarily hide it.

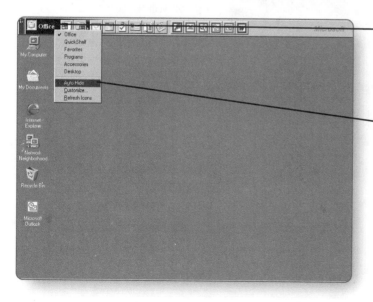

1. Right-click on any gray or black area of the **Shortcut Bar**. The Shortcut Bar menu will appear.

2. Click on **Auto Hide**. The shortcut menu will disappear.

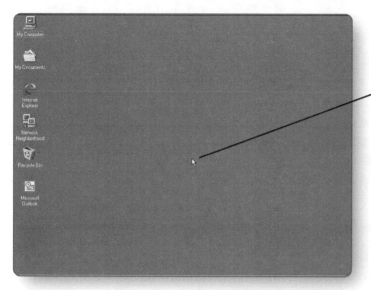

Your Desktop will adjust itself as though the Office Shortcut Bar were not there.

3. Point the **mouse anywhere** on the Desktop except on the Shortcut Bar. The Office Shortcut Bar will roll up into an edge of the screen and disappear.

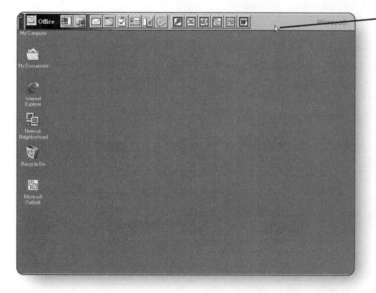

4. Move the **mouse pointer** to the location where the Office Shortcut Bar used to appear. The Office Shortcut Bar will reappear and remain visible as long as the mouse pointer stays somewhere over it.

If you hide the Office Shortcut Bar, it might cover some portion of your application screen when it reappears.

TIP
Repeat steps 1 and 2 to turn off the Auto Hide feature.

Closing the Office Shortcut Bar

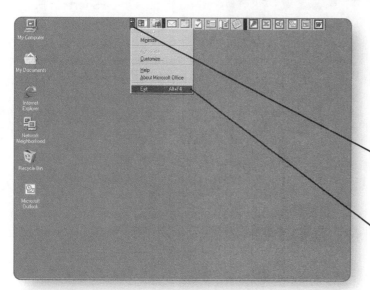

If you're working on a project that won't require the Shortcut Bar, you can close it so it's not visible. You can make the closing of the Office Shortcut Bar temporary or permanent.

1. Right-click on the **Control Menu button**. The Office Shortcut Bar menu will appear.

2. Click on **Exit**. A message box will display.

3a. Click on **Yes**. The Shortcut Bar will close but will reappear the next time you restart Windows.

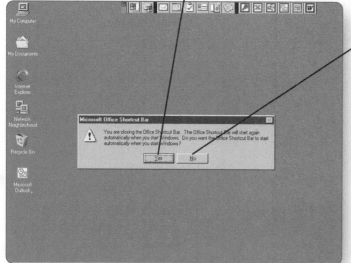

OR

3b. Click on **No**. The Shortcut Bar will close and will not reappear the next time you restart your computer.

TIP

If you choose no, and then decide you want to restart the Office Shortcut Bar, click on Start, Programs, Microsoft Office Tools, and then choose Microsoft Office Shortcut Bar.

Customizing the Office Shortcut Bar

Do you have a program, folder, or document that you use all the time and you want to place it on one of the toolbars on the Office Shortcut Bar? You can add a button to a toolbar. To add a button to a toolbar, that toolbar must be visible.

TIP

If your Office Shortcut Bar is not visible, click on Start, Programs, Microsoft Office Tools, and then choose Microsoft Office Shortcut Bar.

---

1. Right-click on the **gray or black area** of the Office Shortcut Bar. A shortcut menu will appear.

2. Click on **Customize**. The Customize dialog box will open.

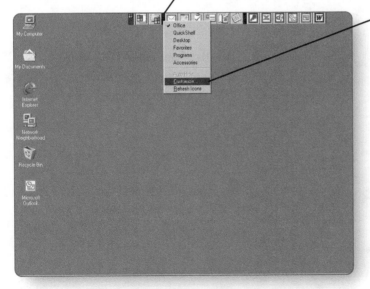

3. Click on the **Buttons tab**. The Buttons tab will come to the front.

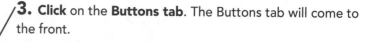

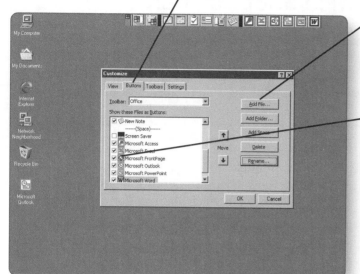

4. Click on **Add File**. The Add File dialog box will open.

TIP

Buttons that appear on the selected toolbar have a check mark next to them. Remove the check mark to remove the item from the toolbar. You will not delete the program, only the icon showing on the Office Shortcut Bar.

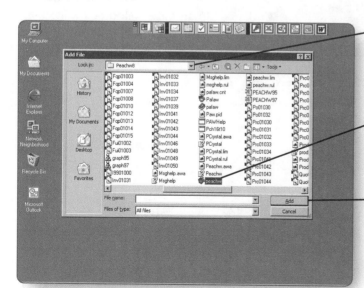

5. Navigate to the **folder** containing the file or program for which you want to add a button.

6. Click on the **file** for which you want to add a button. The file will be selected.

7. Click on **Add**. The Add File dialog box will close.

The Customize dialog box will reappear with the file you chose appearing as a button at the top of the list.

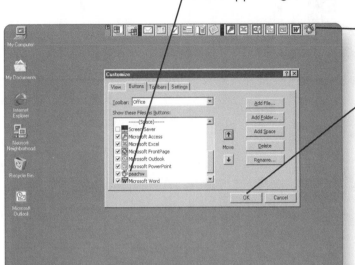

A button for the file will also appear at the end of the toolbar.

8. Click on **OK**. The Customize dialog box will close, and you'll have a new button on the toolbar.

Renaming a Toolbar Button

The name you saw in the Customize dialog box in the previous task was the file name as it is stored on your computer. This is the name that will appear in the ScreenTip when you move the mouse pointer over the button. You can rename the button.

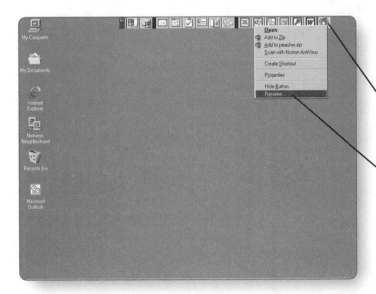

1. Right-click on the **item** you want to rename. A shortcut menu will appear.

2. Click on **Rename**. The Rename dialog box will open.

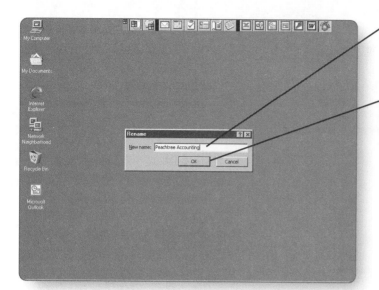

3. **Type** a new **name**. The new name will replace the existing name.

4. **Click** on **OK**. The Rename dialog box will close.

5. **Move** the **mouse pointer** over the button to see its ScreenTip. The ScreenTip will match the new name you supplied.

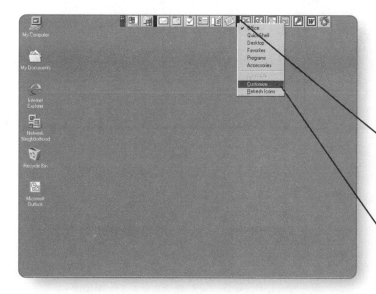

Moving a Toolbar Button

You can place toolbar buttons anywhere on the toolbar.

1. Right-click on the **gray or black area** of the Office Shortcut Bar. A shortcut menu will appear.

2. Click on **Customize**. The Customize dialog box will open.

3. Click on the **Buttons tab**. The Button tab will come to the front.

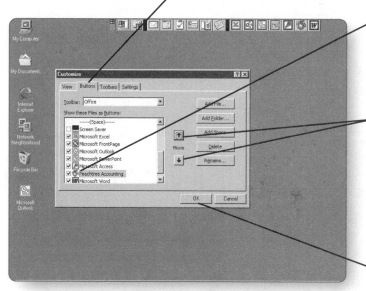

4. Click on the **file name** for the button you want to move. The file name will be highlighted.

5. Click on the **Move arrows** in the direction you want to move. Each time you click, the button will move up or down (depending on which direction you choose) in the Customize dialog box and on the toolbar.

6. Click on **OK**. The Customize dialog box will close and the button will appear in its new location on the toolbar.

Using the Office Shortcut Bar

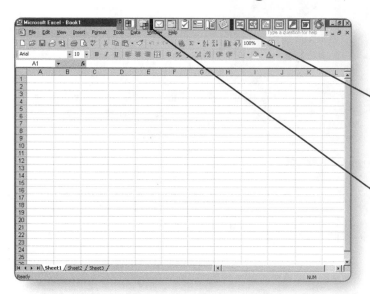

Now that you have the Office Shortcut Bar setup, how can you put it to use?

1. Click on any Office Shortcut Bar **button**. The application associated with that button will launch.

Unless you have the Auto Hide feature active, the Office Shortcut Bar will remain on top of the open application.

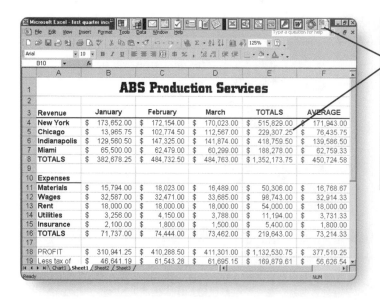

TIP

If you add a button for a specific file instead of a program, the Office Shortcut Bar not only launches the application that created the document, but opens the file as well.

27

Speaking with Office

Microsoft Office XP now supports speech recognition technology. With speech recognition, you can dictate directly into a microphone and Office applications will either type the information you've dictated into a document or follow your menu commands.

Because speech recognition is still a relatively new technology, you probably won't find it 100 percent accurate in understanding your words; however, the one included with Microsoft Office XP beats the competition hands down! With proper training, you can expect about a 95% accuracy rate, meaning it should correctly identify 95 out of every 100 words you dictate.

The only drawback is that you won't like speech recognition on an older, slower computer. Your computer needs at least 128MB of RAM memory (more memory increases speech recognition performance) and to be at least a Pentium II, 400Mhz to effectively handle speech recognition. You'll also need a microphone, preferably a headset unit. In this chapter, you'll learn how to:

- Install the speech recognition components
- Train speech recognition to your voice
- Record and correct dictation
- Instruct Excel to read data back to you

Installing Speech

By default, the speech function is not installed with Microsoft Office. The first time you access speech, you'll be prompted to install it.

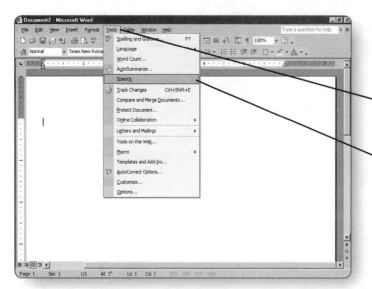

1. Open an **Office Application**. The application and its menu will appear on-screen.

2. Click on **Tools**. The Tools menu will appear.

3. Click on **Speech**. A message will display.

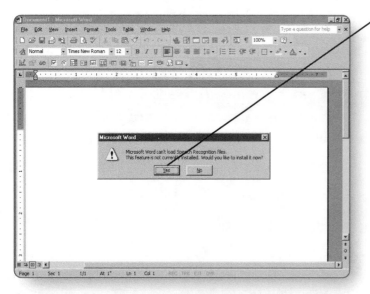

4. Click on **Yes**. The Welcome to Speech Recognition dialog box will open. Your first step is to adjust your microphone.

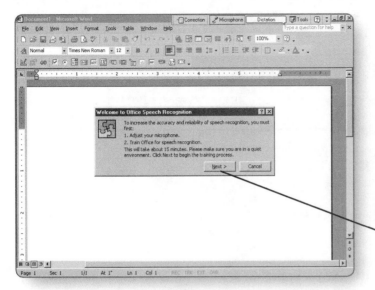

Setting Up Your Microphone

To increase accuracy, you'll need to set up your microphone and teach speech recognition about your speech patterns. You'll also get better performance if you use a good quality headset microphone.

1. Click on **Next**. The Microphone Wizard will launch.

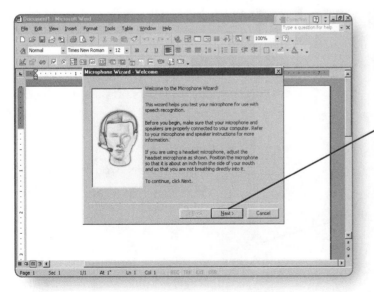

Position your microphone headset on your head. If you're using a hand-held microphone, hold it in a position for you to speak into it.

2. Click on **Next**. You'll be asked to adjust your microphone volume.

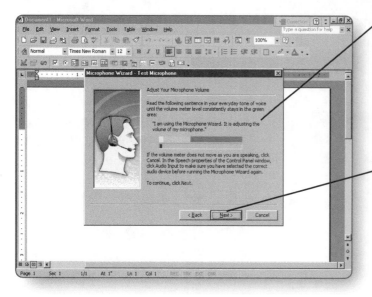

3. Repeat the **sentence** displayed on your screen. The volume meter will monitor your volume. Repeat the sentence as necessary to keep your volume in the green area of the volume meter.

4. Click on **Next**. The Test Positioning box will appear.

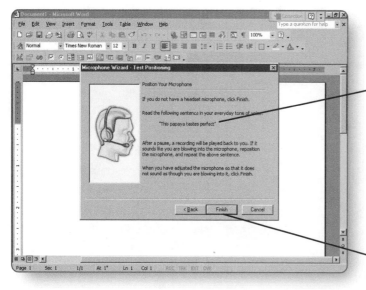

If you are using a headset microphone, you'll need to test the microphone position.

5. Say the **sentence** displayed on the screen. The recording will be played back to you.

If it sounds like you're blowing back into the microphone, move the headset microphone slightly and try the sentence again.

6. Click on **Finish**. The Default Speech Profile box will appear.

Training Speech Recognition

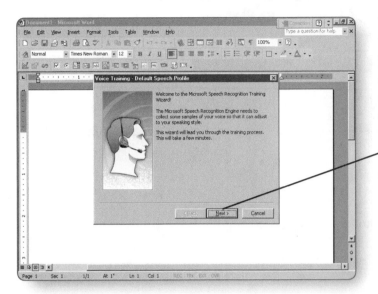

The speech recognition wizard next needs to collect samples of your voice. The training steps are the most important steps to making speech recognition work effectively.

1. **Click** on **Next**. The next screen of the Default Speech Profile box will appear.

In order to accurately recognize your voice, speech recognition must determine your age and gender.

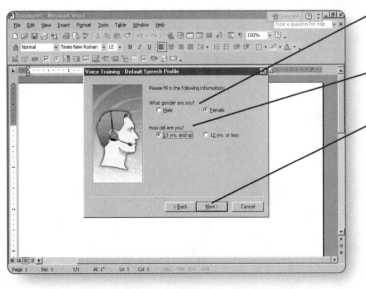

2. **Click** on a **gender**. The option will be selected.

3. **Click** on an **age bracket**. The option will be selected.

4. **Click** on **Next**. The next screen of the Default Speech Profile box will appear.

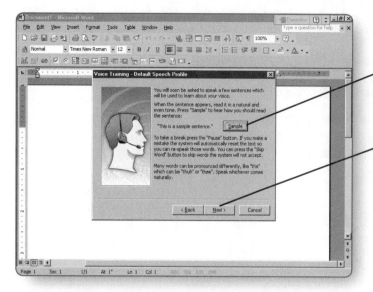

The sample speech illustrates how you should speak.

5. Click on the **Sample button**. You will hear sample text from your computer speakers.

6. Click on **Next**. The next screen of the Default Speech Profile box will appear.

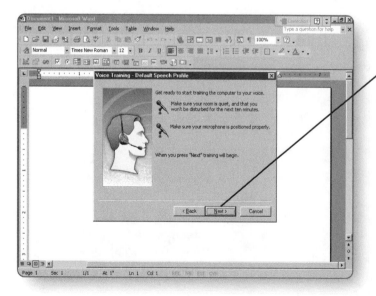

You're ready to begin speech recognition training.

7. Click on **Next**. The first paragraph of text will appear, ready for you to read.

8. Speak the highlighted **word or phrase**. Speech recognition will highlight the next word or phrase.

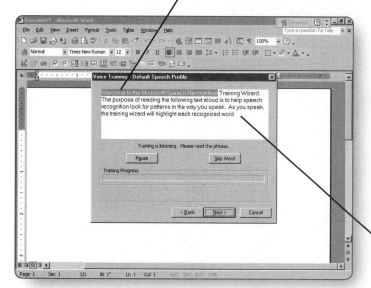

TIP

If speech recognition doesn't move to the next word or phrase, you'll need to repeat the word or phrase until Word recognizes it or you can click on the Skip Word button.

9. Continue reading aloud the paragraph. When you've read the entire paragraph, the next paragraph will automatically display on the screen.

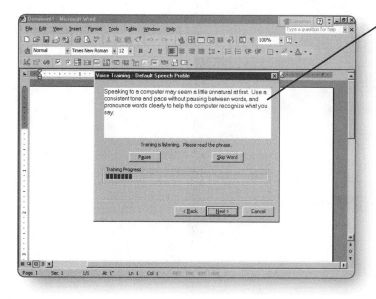

10. Read the **next paragraph**. Speech recognition will display several different paragraphs for you to read.

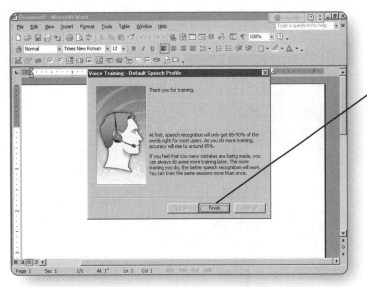

When you've completed all the reading, speech recognition will collect and save the data.

11. **Click** on **Finish**. A Welcome to Speech recognition video will appear.

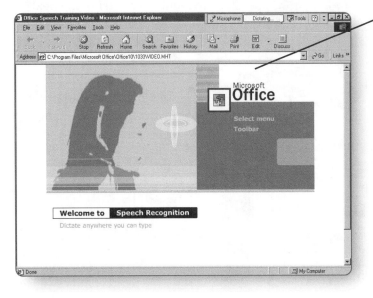

The video will run automatically and explain the basics of working with speech recognition.

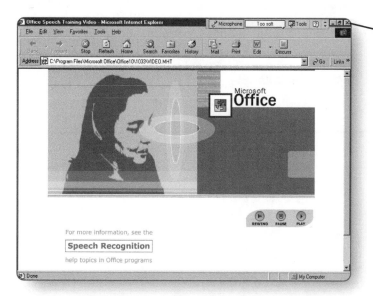

12. Click on the **Close box**. The video window will close and the Office XP application will reappear.

Understanding the Language Bar

Speech recognition includes its own toolbar called the Language Bar. The Language Bar lays on top of the Office application title bar, making it easily visible.

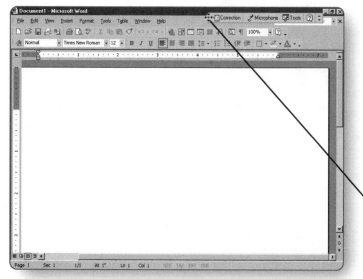

Moving the Language Bar

If the Language Bar is in an inconvenient location, you can easily move it to a better one.

1. Position the **mouse** along the left edge of the Language Bar. The mouse pointer will turn into a four-headed arrow.

2. Click and drag the **Language Bar** to a new location. The Language Bar will move as you drag the mouse.

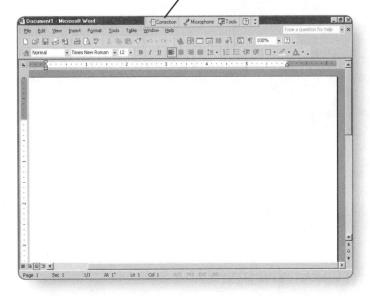

3. Release the **mouse button**. The Language Bar will remain in the new position.

Hiding the Language Bar

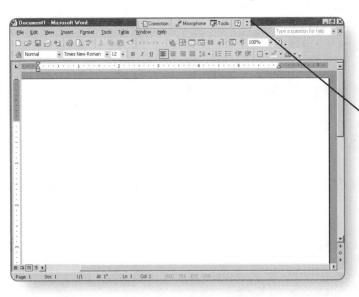

If you don't need to use the speech recognition at the moment, you can minimize the Language Bar to hide it.

1. Click on the **Minimize button**. It's the top arrow on the right side of the Language Bar. The Language Bar will disappear from your screen.

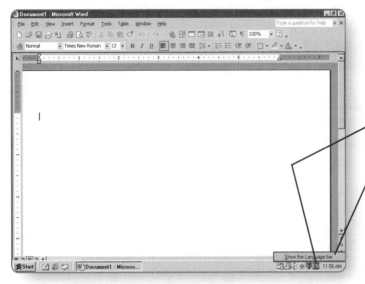

The Language Bar doesn't minimize like other applications. Instead, it locates itself in the System Tray and is represented by a small blue icon.

2. Click on the **Language Bar icon**. A menu will appear.

3. Click on **Show the Language Bar**. The Language Bar will reappear at its previous location.

Speaking Into Office

Speech recognition is available for all the Office XP applications, but you'll probably use it most in Word or Outlook. The steps to use the speech recognition are the same no matter which application you use. For demonstration purposes, I use Microsoft Word.

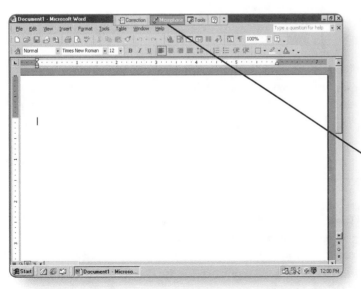

Before you can dictate, you need to make sure the microphone is activated.

1. Click on the **Microphone button**. The Language Bar will expand to show a Dictation button and a Voice Command button.

TIP

Try to keep the microphone in the same position. Moving it around can cause speech recognition to misunderstand your voice.

---

2. Click on the **Dictation button**. Speech recognition will activate Dictation mode.

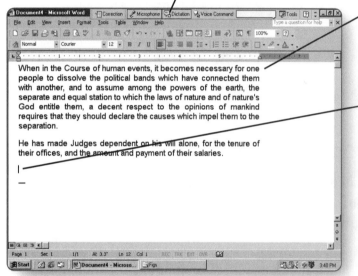

For the purpose of illustration, the text in this figure shows the text I will read into the microphone.

3. Click in the **document** where you want the dictation to begin. The blinking insertion point will appear.

4. Speak into the **microphone**. The results will print on the screen.

Dictate into the microphone speaking in a fairly normal consistent tone, pronouncing your words clearly, but not separating each syllable in a word. Because a phrase is easier for the computer to interpret than a single word, speak without pausing between words.

NOTE

The computer might not display your words on the screen immediately. Continue speaking and pause at the end of each sentence. The computer will display the recognized text on the screen after it finishes processing your voice.

The following table lists commands you can use during dictation.

Say This	To Do This
New line	Start text on the next line.
New paragraph	Start a new paragraph.
Tab	Press the Tab key once
Enter	Press the Enter key once
Spelling mode	Spell out the next word. For example, say this before you spell out a company name or a person's name. Pause after spelling out the word to revert to normal dictation mode.
Forcenum	Enter a number or symbol instead of spelling it out. For example, say this to enter "7" instead of "seven." Pause after saying the number or symbol to revert to normal dictation mode.

In addition to the previous commands, you can also say most punctuation marks. Examples include:

Say This	To Get This	Say This	To Get This
Comma	,	Open bracket	[
Question mark	?	Close bracket	]
Exclamation point	!	Slash	/
Colon	:	Backslash	\
Semicolon	;	Dollar sign	$
Ellipsis	...	Number sign	#
Open paren	(	Ampersand	&
Close paren	)		

TIP

If you want the document to include words or keys such as period, Tab, semicolon and so forth, you have to type them manually because speech recognition interprets them as punctuation marks or commands.

The blue highlight indicates the dictation text is being processed. After processing, the words will appear as text on your screen.

5. Click on the **Microphone button** again. The microphone will turn off and the Dictation button will disappear from the Language Bar.

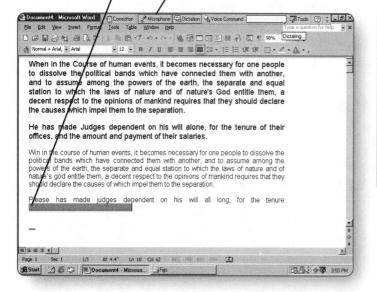

NOTE

If your headset has a Mute button that enables you to turn your microphone on or off, the headset's Mute button overrides the button on the Language Bar.

Making Corrections

Speech recognition is not designed for completely hands-free operation. There are going to be items you'll need to correct by using your keyboard and mouse.

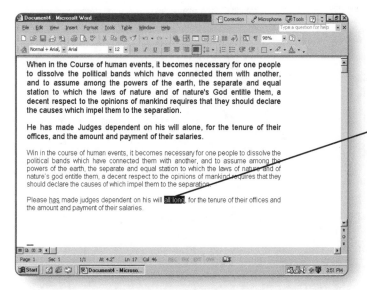

Correcting Manually

Make corrections to dictated text in the same manner as if you typed it yourself.

1. Select any **incorrect text**. The text will be highlighted.

2. Type a **correction**. The incorrect text will be replaced with the corrected text.

Selecting Correction Words

If speech recognition misunderstood you, you might be able to select the correct words from a supplied list.

1. Select the **incorrect word or phrase**. The text will be highlighted.

2. Click on the **Correction button**. Speech recognition will repeat the word through your computer speakers.

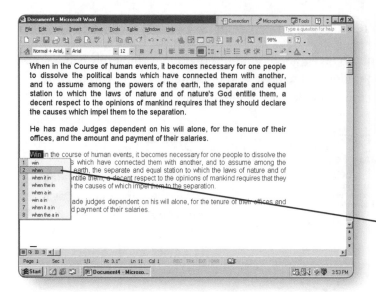

A list of alternative words will appear.

3. Click on a **correction**. The correction will replace the incorrect word.

Creating Special Words

Perhaps you have an unusual name, or a technical term that speech recognition doesn't recognize. You can train it for specific words.

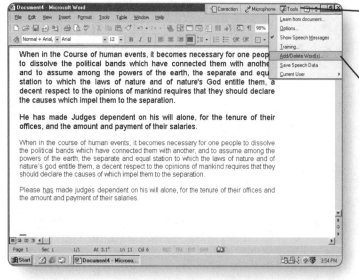

1. Click on the **Tools button** on the Language Bar. A menu will appear.

2. Click on **Add/Delete Words**. The Add/Delete Words dialog box will open.

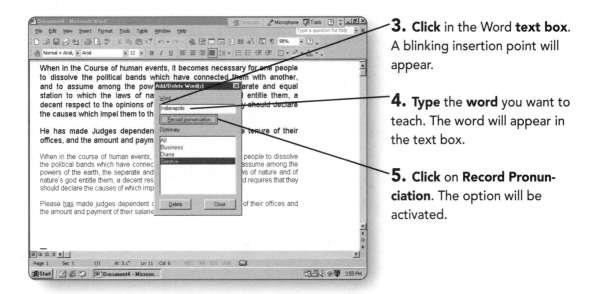

3. Click in the Word **text box**. A blinking insertion point will appear.

4. Type the **word** you want to teach. The word will appear in the text box.

5. Click on **Record Pronunciation**. The option will be activated.

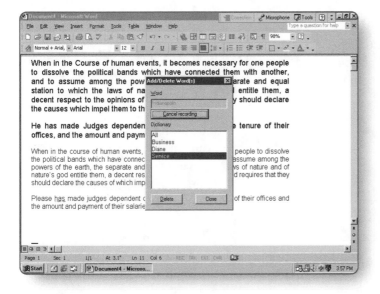

6. Say the **word you typed**. Speech recognition learns the word and adds it to the word list.

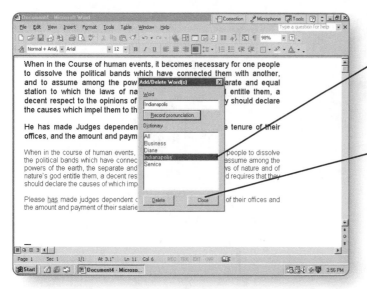

7. Click on **Close**. The Add/ Delete Words dialog box will close.

Dictating Menu Commands

Speech recognition can also understand voice commands such as File, Save or Edit, Undo. It can even make selections from a dialog box.

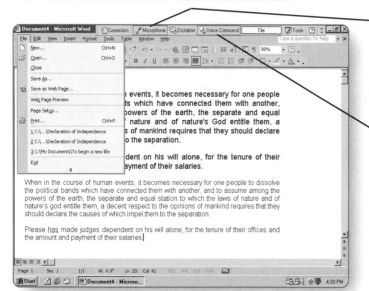

1. Click on the **Microphone button**. The Language Bar will expand to show a Dictation button and a Voice Command button.

2. Click on the **Voice Command button**. The Voice Command mode will become activated.

3. Say a **menu command**. For this example, the command File was spoken so the File menu opened.

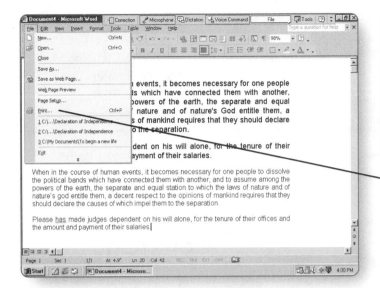

4. Say the **next menu command**. For this example, the command Print was spoken, so the Print dialog box opened.

5. Issue a **command** into the dialog box by dictating them as you see them on the screen. For example, from the Print dialog box, to print only the current page, say Current Page.

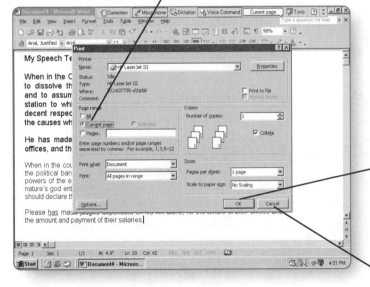

6a. Say OK. Office will accept the choices and execute the command.

OR

6b. Say Cancel. Office will close the dialog box without any action being taken.

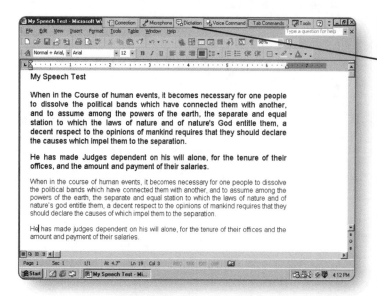

Working with the Keyboard Commands

Speech recognition includes several keyboard commands to assist you with your dictation. These keystrokes include using the Windows button on your keyboard (located on the bottom row of your keyboard and features a flying Windows logo as shown in the margin) along with a standard Windows key , which results in a speech recognition action.

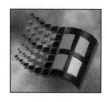

- **Windows key + V**—Turns the microphone on and off.

- **Windows key + T**—Toggles between Dictation mode and Voice Command mode.

- **Windows key + C**—Activates Correction mode.

Discovering Text to Speech

So far in this chapter, you've learned how to speak into the microphone and have your computer translate your speech into data on your screen. What about the reverse? What if your computer can read back to you what is on the screen? It can! This is a huge help when you need to check the data you entered against a hard copy of the data. This feature presently however, is only available in Excel.

1. Open an **Excel worksheet**. The worksheet will be displayed on your screen.

2. Click on **Tools**. The Tools menu will appear.

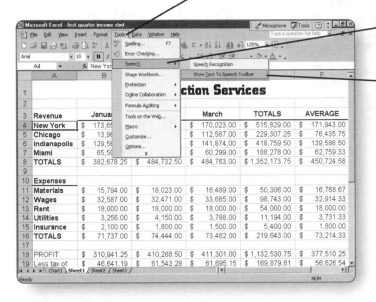

3. Click on **Speech**. The Speech submenu will appear.

4. Click on **Show Text to Speech Toolbar**. The Text to Speech toolbar will appear.

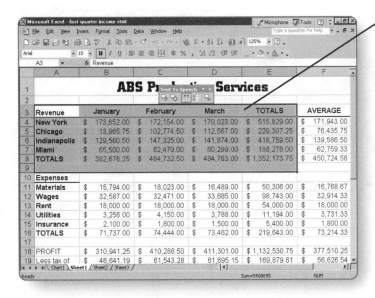

5. Select the **cells** you want Speech to read. The cells will be highlighted. (If you don't select cells, speech will read the current cell.)

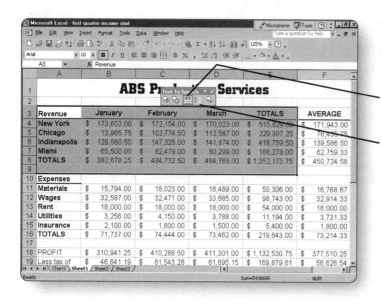

6. Click on a **pattern button**. One of these patterns will be selected:

- Read across the selected rows first.

- Read down the selected columns first.

7. Click on **Speak Cells**. Speech will begin reading your selected cells.

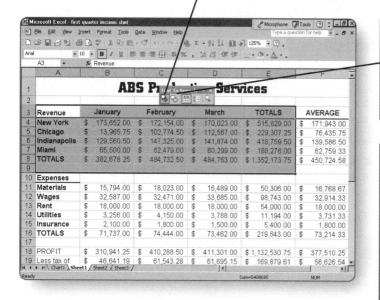

TIP

Click on the Stop Speaking button to interrupt the reading.

NOTE

One final note to mention here is that Office XP also includes the capability to read your handwriting when using a special tablet attached to your computer. Handwriting recognition and tablets are beyond the scope of this book.

Part VII Review Questions

1. When saving a document as an HTML document, which Office application will advise you what will happen to non-supported formats? *See "Saving an Existing Document as a Web Document" in Chapter 25*

2. By default, how many frames appear when viewing a PowerPoint presentation in Internet Explorer? *See "Viewing the Document in Internet Explorer" in Chapter 25*

3. Do all Web browsers support scrolling text? *See "Adding Scrolling Text" in Chapter 25*

4. Which Office feature can provide you with quick access to items you use most often? *See "Working with the Office Shortcut Bar" in Chapter 26*

5. When closing the Office Shortcut Bar, is it permanent or temporary? *See "Closing the Office Shortcut Bar" in Chapter 26*

6. What is the minimum amount of RAM (memory) required to work with the Speech feature? *See "Speaking with Office" in Chapter 27*

7. What is the preferred type of microphone to work with Speech? *See "Speaking with Office" in Chapter 27*

8. When running the speech recognition wizard, what personal information must you include? *See "Training Speech Recognition" in Chapter 27*

9. What is the name of the toolbar provided with Speech? *See "Understanding the Language Bar" in Chapter 27*

10. What keyboard command turns the microphone on and off? *See "Working with the Keyboard Commands" in Chapter 27*

PART VIII

Appendixes

A

Using Keyboard Shortcuts

You might have noticed the keyboard shortcuts listed on the right side of several of the menus. You can use these shortcuts to execute commands without using the mouse to activate menus. You might want to memorize these keyboard shortcuts. Not only will they speed your productivity, but they will also help decrease wrist strain caused by excessive mouse usage. In this appendix, you'll learn how to:

- Get up to speed with frequently used keyboard shortcuts
- Use keyboard combinations to edit text

Learning the Basic Shortcuts

Trying to memorize all these keyboard shortcuts isn't as hard as you might think. Windows applications all share the same keyboard combinations to execute common commands. Once you get accustomed to using some of these keyboard shortcuts, try them out on some of the other programs.

Common Office Shortcuts

The following table shows you a few of the more common keyboard shortcuts that you might want to use when working with documents, spreadsheets, or other Office applications.

To Execute This Command	Do This
Use Help	Press the F1 key
Use the What's This? Button	Press Shift+F1
Create a new document	Press Ctrl+N
Open a different document	Press Ctrl+O
Switch between open documents	Press Ctrl+F6
Save a document	Press Ctrl+S
Print a document	Press Ctrl+P
Close a document	Press Ctrl+W
Cut selected text or objects	Press Ctrl+X
Make a copy of selected items	Press Ctrl+C
Paste the copied or cut items	Press Ctrl+V
Undo an action	Press Ctrl+Z
Redo an action	Press Ctrl+Y
Make the menu bar active	Press F10 or Alt

Using Word Shortcut Keys

Word has many shortcuts available to speed up data entry and formatting.

To Execute This Command	Do This
Highlight an entire word	Press Ctrl+Shift+Right Arrow
Highlight an entire line	Press Shift+End
Highlight a paragraph	Press Ctrl+Shift+Down Arrow
Select an entire document	Press Ctrl+A
Go to a specific page	Press Ctrl+G
Spell check a document	Press the F7 key
Find text in a document	Press Ctrl+F
Replace text in a document	Press Ctrl+H
Change the font	Press Ctrl+Shift+F
Change the size of the font	Press Ctrl+Shift+P
Make selected text bold	Press Ctrl+B
Make selected text italic	Press Ctrl+I
Make selected text underlined	Press Ctrl+U
Remove character formatting	Press Ctrl+Spacebar
Single space a paragraph	Press Ctrl+1
Double space a paragraph	Press Ctrl+2
Set 1.5 line spacing	Press Ctrl+5
Center a paragraph	Press Ctrl+E
Left align a paragraph	Press Ctrl+L
Right align a paragraph	Press Ctrl+R
Left indent a paragraph	Press Ctrl+M
Remove paragraph formatting	Press Ctrl+Q

Using Excel Shortcuts

Whether you need to move around in the large Excel spreadsheet or make your data look great, Excel has shortcuts to make the process faster.

To Execute This Command	Do This
Move to the row beginning (typically column A)	Press Home
Move to the worksheet beginning (typically cell A1)	Press Ctrl+Home
Move down one screen	Press Page Down
Move up one screen	Press Page Up
Move left one screen	Press Alt+Page Up
Move right one screen	Press Alt+Page Down
Move to next sheet in workbook	Press Ctrl+Page Down
Move to previous sheet	Press Ctrl+Page Up
Complete a cell entry	Press Enter
Start a new line in the same cell	Press Alt+Enter
Fill data down	Press Ctrl+D
Fill data to the right	Press Ctrl+R
Edit a cell entry	Press F2
Start a formula	Press = (equals sign)
Insert the AutoSum formula	Press Alt+= (equals sign)
Enter the date	Press Ctrl+; (semicolon)
Enter the time	Press Ctrl+Shift+: (colon)
Display the Format Cells dialog box	Press Ctrl+1
Apply currency format	Press Ctrl+Shift+$
Apply percentage format	Press Ctrl+Shift+%
Apply general number format	Press Ctrl+Shift+~
Apply date format	Press Ctrl+Shift+#
Apply time format	Press Ctrl+Shift+@
Apply number format	Press Ctrl+Shift+!
Apply outline border	Press Ctrl+Shift+&

To Execute This Command	Do This
Hide rows	Press Ctrl+9
Hide columns	Press Ctrl+0 (zero)
Unhide rows	Press Ctrl+Shift+((opening parenthesis)
Unhide columns	Press Ctrl+Shift+) (closing parenthesis)
Select an entire column	Press Ctrl+Spacebar
Select an entire row	Press Shift+Spacebar
Select an entire worksheet	Press Ctrl+A
Extend selection one cell	Press Shift+arrow key
Extend the selection to the last used cell on the worksheet (lower-right corner)	Press Ctrl+Shift+End

Using PowerPoint Shortcuts

Powerful PowerPoint presentations can be created using many of the available shortcut keys.

To Execute This Command	Do This
To move to the next title or body text placeholder	Press Ctrl+Enter
To move to the beginning of a text box	Press Ctrl+Home
To center a paragraph of text	Press Ctrl+E
To left align a paragraph	Press Ctrl+L
To right align a paragraph	Press Ctrl+R
To change font	Press Ctrl+Shift+F
To change font size	Press Ctrl+Shift+P
To apply bold formatting	Press Ctrl+B
To apply italics formatting	Press Ctrl+I
To apply underline formatting	Press Ctrl+U
To promote a paragraph	Press Alt+Shift+Left Arrow
To demote a paragraph	Press Alt+Shift+Right Arrow

To Execute This Command	Do This
To select all objects in the slide view	Press Ctrl+A
To select all slides in the slide panel	Press Ctrl+A
To select all slides in the slide sorter view	Press Ctrl+A
To select all text in the outline pane	Press Ctrl+A
To advance a slide in a slide show	Press N
To return to the previous slide in a slide show	Press P
To display a black screen during a slide show	Press B
To return from a black screen during a slide show	Press B
To display a white screen during a slide show	Press W
To return from a white screen during a slide show	Press W
To see a list of slide show controls during a slide show	Press F1

Using Outlook Shortcuts

Like the other Office applications, Outlook includes shortcuts to speed up your tasks, whether it's working with e-mail, editing a To Do list, or scheduling a meeting.

To Execute This Command	Do This
Display the address book	Press Ctrl+Shift+B
Switch to the Inbox	Press Ctrl+Shift+I
Switch to the Outbox	Press Ctrl+Shift+O
Create or open an appointment	Press Ctrl+Shift+A
Create or open a contact	Press Ctrl+Shift+C
Create or open a message	Press Ctrl+Shift+M
Create or open a task	Press Ctrl+Shift+K
Create or open a note	Press Ctrl+Shift+N
Dial a contact	Press Ctrl+Shift+D
Reply to a mail message	Press Ctrl+R
Mark a message as read	Press Ctrl+Q

To Execute This Command	Do This
Add bullets to a message	Press Ctrl+Shift+L
Increase indent of text	Press Ctrl+T
Decrease indent of text	Press Ctrl+Shift+T
Apply bold to text	Press Ctrl+B
Apply italics to text	Press Ctrl+I
Apply underline to text	Press Ctrl+U
Left align text	Press Ctrl+L
Center align text	Press Ctrl+E
View one day on the calendar	Press Alt+1
Switch to week view	Press Alt+- (hyphen)
Switch to month view	Press Alt+= (equals sign)
Go to the next day	Press the right arrow key
Go to the previous day	Press the left arrow key
Go to the same day in the next week	Press Alt+down arrow

Using Access Shortcuts

Whether you need to move from one view to another or enter data, Access includes shortcuts to assist you.

To Execute This Command	Do This
To switch to Form View from Design View	Press F5
To switch from Edit mode and Navigation Mode	Press F2
To select the next field	Press Tab
To select a column in Datasheet View	Press Ctrl+Spacebar
To select all records	Press Ctrl+A
To enter the current date	Press Ctrl+; (semicolon)
To enter the current time	Press Ctrl+: (colon)

To Execute This Command	Do This
To insert the value from the same field in the previous record	Press Ctrl+' (apostrophe)
To add a new record	Press Ctrl++ (plus sign)
To delete the current record	Press Ctrl+– (minus sign)

Using Speech Shortcuts

In Chapter 27 "Speaking with Office," you learned how to dictate text and commands into Office components. Here's a few commands to help when working with speech. These keyboard shortcuts work with the Windows key, located on the bottom row of your keyboard and features a flying Windows logo.

To Execute This Command	Do This
Turn the microphone on and off	Windows key + V
Toggle between Dictation mode and Voice Command mode	Windows key + T
Activates Correction mode	Windows key + C

B

Installing Microsoft Office XP

When installing Microsoft Office, you can elect to install the entire Office suite, or you can install only desired components such as Microsoft Word. Installing Office XP is practically automatic. In this appendix, you'll learn how to:

- Install Office XP on your computer
- Choose which Office components you want to install
- Detect and repair problems
- Reinstall Office XP
- Add and remove Office XP components
- Uninstall Office XP

Understanding System Requirements

The following is a list of minimum requirements to install and run Microsoft Office XP:

- Microsoft Windows 98, Windows 98 Second Edition, Windows Me, Windows NT 4.0 with Service Pack 6 or greater, or Windows 2000. On systems running Windows NT 4.0 with Service Pack 6, the version of Internet Explorer must be upgraded to at least 4.01 with Service Pack 1.

- RAM requirements depend upon the operating system used. 64MB to 128MB is suggested.

- Hard-disk space requirements will vary depending on configuration. If you have Windows 2000, Office will require 115MB of available hard-disk space for the default configuration of Office Professional with FrontPage. If you don't have Windows 2000, Windows Me, or Office 2000 SR1, Office will require an extra 50MB of hard-disk space for the Office System Pack. Custom installation choices might require more or less hard-disk space.

- A CD-ROM drive is required for installation.

- You must have a super VGA monitor (800x600) or higher-resolution with 256 colors or more.

- You must have a Microsoft Mouse, Microsoft IntelliMouse, or compatible pointing device.

- You must have a Pentium 133MHz or higher processor.

- A multimedia computer is required for sound and other multimedia effects. A hardware accelerated video card or MMX processor will provide improved graphical rendering performance. Pentium II 400MHz or higher processor, 128MB or more of RAM, close-talk microphone, and audio output device required for speech recognition.

Installing Office XP

Before installing Microsoft Office, be sure to close any open applications and temporarily disable any anti-virus programs running on your computer.

Installing Office XP is quick and easy and will require very little decision-making on your part. In most cases, you can simply follow the instructions on-screen.

1. **Insert** the Office **Setup CD** into your computer's CD-ROM drive. The Office Setup Wizard will begin and the User Information box will open.

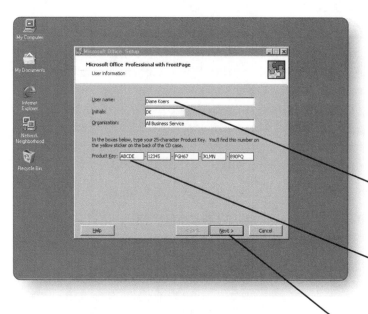

TIP

If the Office Setup Wizard does not automatically begin, double-click on the CD icon in the My Computer window.

---

2. **Enter** your **customer information.** Press Tab to move from field to field.

3. **Enter** your **Office CD Key**. You'll find the CD key number on a sticker on the back of the Office CD case.

4. **Click** on **Next.** The License Agreement will display.

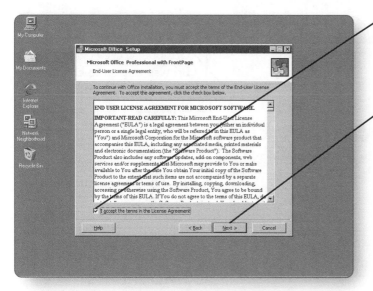

5. After reading the agreement, **click** on **I accept the terms in the License Agreement**. The option will be selected.

6. Click on **Next**. The next installation screen will display.

Installing with Default Settings

The fastest method to install is using the Install Now utility, which will install the most commonly used features of Office including Word, Excel, PowerPoint, Access, Front Page, and Outlook Express.

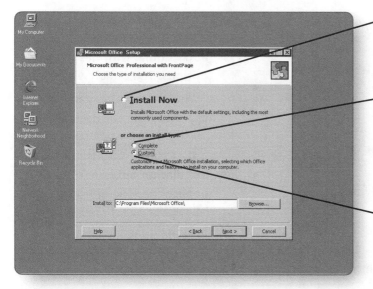

1a. Click on **Install Now**. The option will be selected.

OR

1b. Click on **Complete** if you want to install Office and all components on your system. The option will be selected.

OR

1c. Click on **Custom**, if you want to choose which components to install or where to install them. The option will be selected.

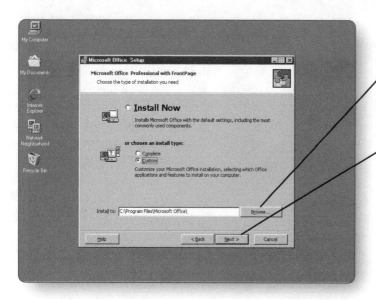

2. Click on **Next**. The screen you see next will depend on which installation option you selected in step 1.

Installing Office Components

If you are not going to be using all the components of Office XP, you can customize the installation process and elect to only install the portions you want to use.

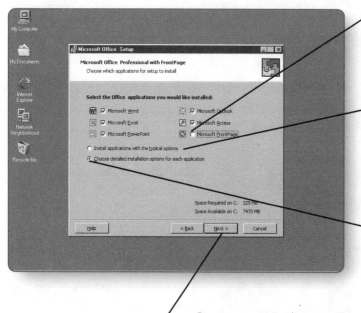

1. Click on any **application** you do **not** want to install. The check mark will be removed from the option.

2a. Click on **Install applications with the typical options.** The option will be selected.

OR

2b. Click on **Choose detailed installation options for each application**. The option will be selected.

3. Click on **Next**. The screen you see next will depend on which installation option you selected in step 2.

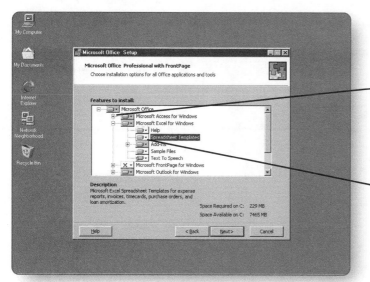

If you selected step 2b, you'll now get the option of which components you want to install.

4. Click on a **plus sign** (+) to expand a list of features. The features listed under the category will appear.

5. Click on the **down arrow** to the right of the hard drive icon. A menu of available installations options for the feature will appear.

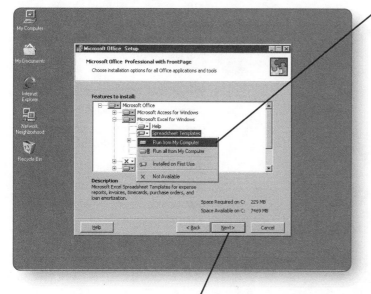

6. Click on the **button** next to the individual option and choose from the following settings:

- **Run from My Computer**. The component will be fully installed so you won't need the Office CD to run the application.

- **Run all from My Computer**. The selected component and all the components listed under it will be fully installed.

- **Installed on First Use**. The first time you try to use the component, you will be prompted to insert the Office CD to complete the installation. This is a good choice for those components you're not sure you will need.

- **Not Available**. The component will not be installed.

7. Click on **Next**. The Begin Installation screen will display.

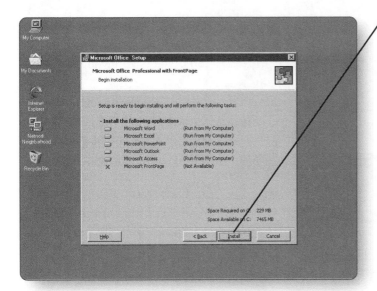

8. Click on **Install**. The installation process will begin.

NOTE

Be patient. This process can take several minutes to complete.

When the installation is complete, a dialog box will open.

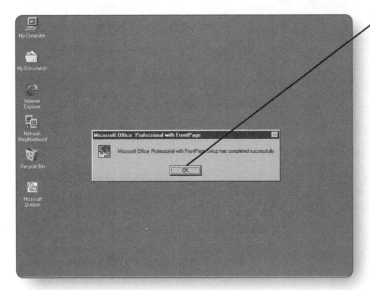

9. Click on **OK**. The installation will be complete.

When the installation is complete, you might be prompted to restart your system. Even if Office doesn't prompt you to restart, it is recommended you restart your computer after any software installation.

Working in Maintenance Mode

Maintenance Mode is part of the Setup program. After you've initially installed Office, when you need to add or remove features, repair your Office installation, or remove the Office XP applications, you'll work in Maintenance Mode. Office XP Maintenance Mode is accessed from the Windows Control Panel.

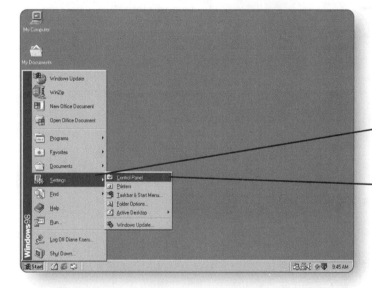

1. Click on **Start** from the Desktop. The Start menu will appear.

2. Click on **Settings**. The Settings submenu will appear.

3. Click on **Control Panel**. The Control Panel window will open.

4. Double-click on **Add/ Remove Programs**. The Add/Remove Programs Properties dialog box will open.

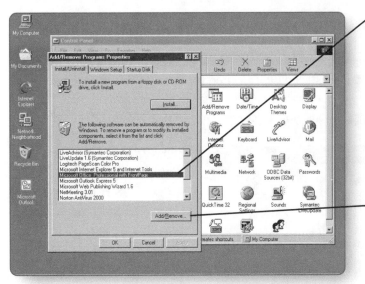

5. Click on **Microsoft Office Professional with FrontPage**. Depending on the variety of Office you have, the name you see might vary from the one shown, but the name will still contain the words Microsoft Office. The option will be selected.

6. Click on **Add/Remove**. The Office Installer will begin in Maintenance Mode.

Repairing or Reinstalling Office

If an Office application is behaving strangely, or refuses to work, most likely a needed file has become corrupted. Because you have no way of knowing which file is corrupted, you can't manually fix the problem. Office, however, includes options to repair Office or completely reinstall it. Both options are available from the Repair Office button in Maintenance Mode.

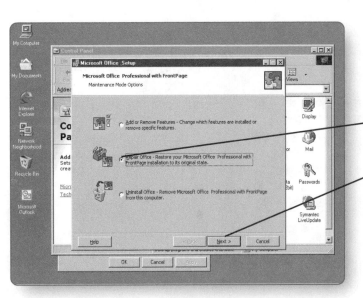

1. Click on **Repair Office**. The option will be selected.

2. Click on **Next**. An option will appear asking you what type of repair is needed.

3a. **Click** on **Reinstall Office** if you want the Office product to be reinstalled with the same settings you selected in the original installation. The option will be selected.

OR

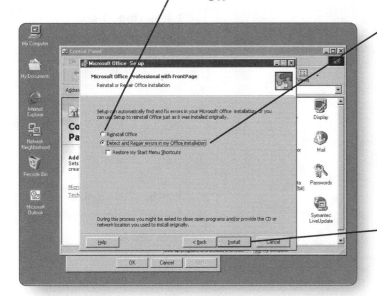

3b. **Click** on **Detect and Repair errors in my Office installation** if you want Office to search for any problems and try to fix them. In the interest of time, I suggest using this method first. If the problem is not resolved, try again using the Reinstall Office option. The option will be selected.

4. **Click** on **Install**. The reinstall/repair process will begin. Office will attempt to fix any application errors it finds or will repeat the last installation.

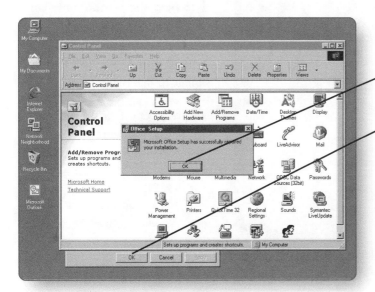

When completed, a dialog box will open.

5. **Click** on **OK**. The dialog box will close.

6. **Click** on **OK** again. The Add/Remove Programs dialog box will close.

7. **Click** on the **Close box**. The Control Panel window will close.

Adding or Removing Components

In order to add or remove components, you must also use the Office Installer Maintenance Mode.

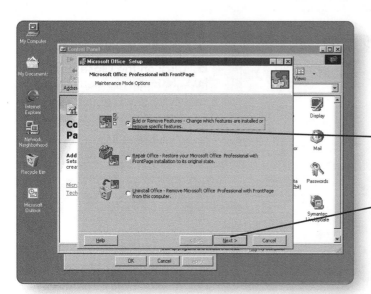

1. Follow steps 1-6 in "Working in Maintenance Mode" earlier in this chapter. The Office Installer will begin in Maintenance Mode.

2. Click on **Add or Remove Features**. The option will be selected.

3. Click on **Next**. You'll be asked which features you want to add or remove.

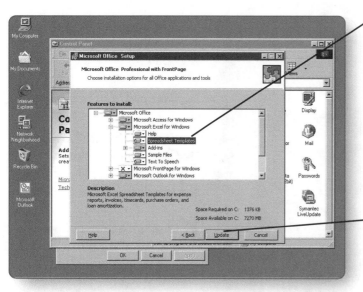

4. Select the **components** you want to add or remove. Selecting components to add or remove from the installation is similar to installing them.

See the section "Installing Office Components" earlier in this chapter for a instructions on installing specific features.

5. Click on **Update**. The Office Installer will update Office to your selections.

When completed, a dialog box will open.

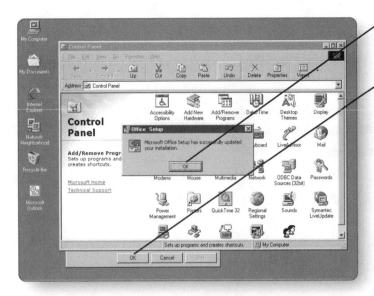

6. Click on **OK**. The dialog box will close.

7. Click on **OK**. The Add/Remove Programs dialog box will close.

8. Click on the **Close box**. The Control Panel window will close.

Uninstalling Microsoft Office

If you no longer want Office XP on your computer, you can uninstall it. Again, you'll use Maintenance Mode to remove the installation of Microsoft Office or any of its components.

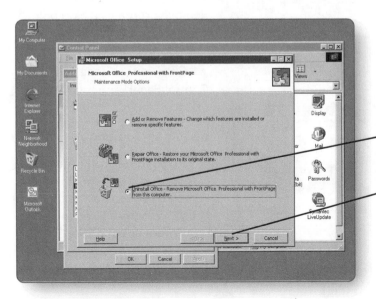

1. Follow steps 1-6 in "Working in Maintenance Mode" earlier in this chapter. The Office Installer will begin in Maintenance Mode.

2. Click on **Uninstall Office**. The option will be selected.

3. Click on **Next**. A confirmation box will open.

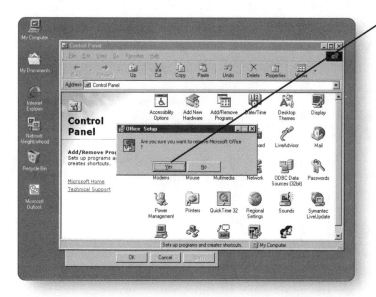

4. Click on **Yes**. The installer will begin removing the Office program and its components from your system.

When completed, a dialog box will open.

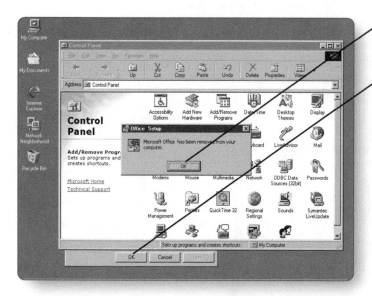

5. Click on **OK**. The dialog box will close.

6. Click on **OK**. The Add/Remove Programs dialog box will close.

7. Click on the **Close box**. The Control Panel window will close.

TIP

You might be prompted to restart your system. It is recommended you restart your computer after any software uninstallation.

Glossary

+ Addition operator used in spreadsheet formulas.

− Subtraction operator used in spreadsheet formulas.

= Initiates all formulas in tables and spreadsheets.

* Multiplication operator used in spreadsheet formulas.

/ Division operator used in spreadsheet formulas.

> Greater than operator.

< Less than operator.

<> Not equal to operator.

: Range operator; used to indicate ranges of cells in a spreadsheet.

=AVERAGE. An Excel function that calculates the average of a list of values. Syntax: =AVERAGE(*range of cells*)

=COUNT. An Excel function that counts the non-blank cells in a list of ranges. Syntax: =COUNT(*range of cells*)

=MAX. An Excel function that finds the largest value in a list. Syntax: =MAX(*range of cells*)

=MIN. An Excel function that finds the smallest value in a list. Syntax: =MIN(*range of cells*)

=SUM. An Excel function that adds a range of cells. See also *AutoSum*. Syntax: =SUM(*range of cells*)

A

Absolute reference. In a formula, a reference to a cell that does not change when copying the formula. An absolute reference always refers to the same cell or range. It is designated in a formula by the dollar sign ($).

Active cell. The selected cell in a worksheet. Designated with a border surrounding the cell.

Address. A named reference to a cell based on its location at the intersection of a column and row; for example, the cell in the fourth row of the second column has an address of B4. See also *cell reference*.

Address book. Stores names, addresses, and phone numbers in one handy location.

Alignment. The position of data in a document, cell, range, or text block; for example, centered, right-aligned, or left-aligned. Also called *justification*.

Animation. The adding of movement to text or images that are displayed on the screen.

Applet. A small software program provided with an application that enables the user to perform additional operations, such as WordArt, for enhanced text effects.

Appointment. An entry in the Outlook calendar that spans less than one day and to which no other individuals are invited.

Array. A contiguous set of cells in a worksheet.

Attributes. Items that determine the appearance of text such as bold, underlining, italics, or point size.

AutoCorrect. A feature of Office that automatically corrects common spelling mistakes (changes "teh" into "the" for example).

AutoFormat. AutoFormat enables users to apply pre-defined sets of formatting to a table's (or worksheet's) text, rows, and columns.

AutoSum. A function that adds a row or column of figures by clicking on the AutoSum button on the Excel toolbar. Same as *=SUM*.

AutoText. A feature of Word that enables the user to save text that is inserted into the document after a word or phrase is typed.

Axes. Lines that form a frame of reference for the chart data. Most charts have an x-axis and a y-axis. In a graph, one of two value sets. See also *x-axis* and *y-axis*.

B

Bar chart. A type of chart that uses solid bars to represent values. Normally used to compare items.

Bold. A style applied to text to make the font lines thicker.

Bookmark. Used to mark a place in a document to locate it quickly.

Border. A line surrounding paragraphs, pages, table cells, or objects.

Break. An instruction embedded into a Word document that indicates a change, such as a Page Break, which starts a new page. Other types of breaks include column and text wrapping breaks.

Browser. A software program especially designed for viewing Web pages on the Internet.

Bullet. A small black circle or other character that precedes each item in a list.

C

Cell. The area defined by a rectangle at which a row and column intersect in an Excel worksheet or a Word table.

Cell reference. A method of referring to a cell in a formula by listing the location of its row and column intersection. See also *address*.

Chart. A graphical representation of numerical data. Also called *graph*.

Choose. To use the mouse or keyboard to pick a menu item or option in a dialog box.

Circular reference. A cell that has a formula that contains a reference to itself.

Click on. To use the mouse to pick a menu item or option in a dialog box.

Clip art. Ready-made line drawings that are included with Office in the Clip Art Gallery. These drawings can be inserted into Office documents.

Clip gallery. A collection of clip art, pictures, and sound files that comes with Office.

Clipboard. An area of computer memory in which text or graphics can be temporarily stored.

Close button. Used to shut down or exit a dialog box, window, or application.

Column. A set of cells running vertically down a worksheet or vertical divisions of text on a page.

Comment. To add annotations to a document or spreadsheet cell. Comments do not print.

Compound formula. A formula, usually in a spreadsheet, that has multiple operators. An example is A2*C2+F4.

Contact. An entry that appears in an address book.

Copy. To duplicate a selection from the document onto the Clipboard, yet leave intact in the original.

Cut. To remove a selection from the document and move it to the Clipboard.

D

Data. Information, either numerical or textual, stored in a document.

Data form. A place where data, such as data used in a mail merge operation, is stored in individual records.

Data series. In charts, elements that represent a set of data, such as pie segment, line, or bar.

Data source. In a Word mail merge, the information that is used to replace field codes with personalized information, such as names and addresses.

Data type. The category of numerical data, such as currency, scientific, or percentage.

Database. A file composed of records, each containing fields together with a set of operations for searching or sorting.

Datasheet view. A view in a database where many records display in a table format.

Default. A setting or action predetermined by the program unless changed by the user.

Desktop. The main area of Windows where files and programs are opened and managed.

Dialog box. A box that displays warnings, messages, or requests information from the users.

Dictation. A speech recognition function that allows the user to use talk into a microphone to enable Office to translate the speech into text on-screen.

Document. A letter, memo, proposal, or other file that is created in an Office application.

Drag-and-drop. A method of moving text or objects by clicking on an object with a mouse, dragging it to a new location, and releasing the mouse button to drop it into its new location.

Drop caps A large dropped initial capital letter. Frequently used in the first line of newsletter articles.

E

E-mail. Messages sent electronically.

Equation. See *formula*.

Event. An entry in the Outlook calendar that spans an entire day.

Export. The ability to copy data from one program to another.

F

Field. In a form letter, a field is a placeholder for corresponding data. Also a piece of information used in a database.

Fields. Categories of information. For example, in an address book, the last name and phone number are fields.

File. Information stored on a disk under a single name.

File format. The arrangement and organization of information in a file. File format is determined by the application that created the file.

Fill. An action in Excel that automatically completes a series of numbers based on an established pattern.

Fill (color). A formatting feature used to apply color or a pattern to the interior of an object, such as a cell.

Fill data. A function that allows Excel to automatically complete a series of numbers or words based on an established pattern.

Fill handle. A block at the bottom-right corner of the active cell in a worksheet that is used to fill cells as it is dragged across them with a pattern of data.

Filter. To make settings so that only cells that meet certain criteria are displayed in the worksheet.

Financial functions. Functions (stored formulas) used to manipulate money, such as payments and interest rates.

Find. An Office feature used to locate characters in an Office document.

Flip. To turn an object on a page 180 degrees.

Font. A design set of letters, symbols, and numbers, also called a *typeface*.

Footer. Text repeated at the bottom of each page of a document or spreadsheet.

Footnote. Reference information that prints at the bottom of the page.

Form. A type of database document with spaces reserved for fields to enter data.

Form Design view. The view in a database that allows the structure of the database to be modified.

Form view. A view in a database where one record displays at a time.

Format. To change the appearance of text or objects with features such as the font, style, color, borders, and size.

Format painter. A feature of Word that enables the easy copying of all formatting that's applied to one set of text to any other.

Formula. An equation that instructs Excel to perform certain calculations based on numerical data in designated cells.

Formula bar. The location where all data and formulas are entered for a selected cell.

Freezing. Preventing sections of a worksheet from scrolling off the screen when the page moves down.

Function. A series of predefined formulas used in spreadsheets. Functions perform specialized calculations automatically.

G

General format. A numerical type applied to numbers in cells.

Go To. A feature that allows the quick movement to a page or cell of the document based on criteria provided.

Gradient. A shading effect that moves from lighter to darker in such a way that it suggests a light source shining on the object containing the gradient.

Graph. Also called a *chart*. A graph is a visual representation of numerical data.

Greater than. A mathematical operator that limits the results of a formula to be larger than a named number or cell.

Gridlines. The lines dividing rows and columns in a table or worksheet.

H

Handle. Small squares used to resize an object. They appear only when an object is selected.

Header. Text entered in an area of the document for display at the top of each page of the document.

Hide. A feature of Excel that temporarily prevents designated cells in a worksheet from being displayed.

Highlight. A feature that places highlighting on-screen for selected text.

HTML. The language used to create documents for publication on the Web.

Hyperlink. A screen element that consists of an address to a location, such as a folder on a computer or Web page. When a hyperlink is clicked, the document will jump to the location defined in the hyperlink.

I

Icon. A graphical representation used on toolbars to represent the various functions performed when those buttons are clicked with a mouse.

IF function. A pre-defined formula indicating that a result is to occur only when some criteria is met. For example, this function could be used to indicate that "if the result of a sum is greater than 10, the result should appear in this cell."

Import. The ability to receive data from another source.

Indent. To set text away from a margin by a specific distance; for example, at the beginning of a paragraph.

Italic. A font style that applies a slanted effect to text.

J

Justification. See *alignment*.

Justify. One type of alignment that spreads letters on a line or in a cell evenly between the left and right margin or across selected cells.

L

Label. A descriptive text element added to a chart to help the reader understand a visual element. Also refers to a row or column heading. Also any cell entry that begins with a letter or label-prefix character.

Landscape. A page orientation that prints a document with the long edge of the paper across the top. See also *portrait*.

Language Bar. The toolbar used to work with the Office speech recognition feature. See also *speech recognition*.

Legend. In a chart, a box containing symbols and text that explains what each data series represents. Each symbol is a color pattern or marker that corresponds to one data series in the chart.

Less than. A mathematical operator that limits the results of a formula to be smaller than a named number or cell.

Line spacing. The amount of space between lines of text.

Line style. Effects using width, arrows, and dashes that can be applied to a line.

M

Macro. A series of keystrokes that can be played back to perform an action.

Mail merge. A procedure that uses a form document, inserts placeholders for types of data (called fields), and merges that document with specific data to produce personalized mailings.

Maps. Represent data in charts with geographical maps rather than traditional chart elements such as bars and lines.

Margin. A border that runs around the outside of a document page in which no data appears.

Mathematical functions. Functions that produce mathematical results, such as SUM and AVG.

Meeting. An entry in the Outlook calendar that spans less than one day and to which others are invited.

N

Named ranges. Providing a name for a set of cells so that name can be used in formulas.

Notes (speaker notes). Additional text displayed alongside a printed slide to prompt the presenter.

O

Object. A picture, map, or other graphical element that can be placed in an Office document.

Office Assistant. A help feature of Microsoft Office products that allows the users to ask questions in standard English sentence format.

Office Shortcut Bar. A utility that ships with Microsoft Office. The Microsoft Office Shortcut Bar contains a series of toolbars that help speed up work by providing quick access to the resources most often used on the computer.

Open. To start an application, to insert a document into a new document window, or to access a dialog box.

Operator. The parts of a formula that indicate an action to be performed, such as addition (+) or division (/).

Orientation. The way a document prints on a piece of paper; landscape prints with the longer side of a page on top, whereas portrait prints with the shorter edge at the top.

Outline. A hierarchy of lines of text that suggests major and minor ideas.

Outlook bar. The panel that appears down the left side of the Outlook window. It contains shortcuts to the various sections in Outlook.

P

Page break. A command that tells the application where to begin a new page.

Page setup. The collection of settings that relate to how the pages of the document are set up, including margins, orientation, and the size of paper on which each page will print.

Passwords. A word selected by a user to protect a file from changes; once a file is protected, the correct password must be entered to modify that file.

Paste. To place text or an object previously placed on the Windows Clipboard (through cutting or copying) in an Office document.

Pattern. Shading and line arrangements that can be used to fill the center of an object.

Pie chart. A round chart type in which each pie wedge represents a value.

Plot. The area of a chart where data is drawn using elements such as line, bars, or pie wedges.

Point. To move the mouse until the tip of the mouse pointer rests on an item. See also *point size*.

Point size. A unit of measurement used to indicate font size. One point is 1/72 inch in height.

Portrait. A page orientation in which a document prints with the shorter edge of the paper along the top. See also *landscape*.

Print area. The portion of a worksheet that is designated to print.

Print layout. A view in Word that is commonly used for arranging objects on a page and drawing.

Print preview. A feature that allows users to view a document on the screen as it will appear when printed.

Properties. The characteristics of text, objects, or devices. Text properties include font, size, or color.

Protect. To enable settings so that only someone with the correct password can modify a document.

Q

Queries. Used in a database; a subset of data that meets certain criteria.

R

Range. A collection of cells.

Range name. An "English" name that identifies a range and that can be used in commands and formulas instead of the range address.

Record. The collection of multiple pieces of information about one particular subject. For example, Joe Smith's record might include fields such as name, address, and phone number.

Redo. A feature that allows users to restore an action that was reversed using the Undo feature.

Reference. In a formula, a name or range that refers the formula to a cell or set of cells.

Relative. In a formula, making reference to a cell relative to the location of the cell where the formula is placed; if the formula cell is moved, the cell being referenced changes in relation to the new location.

Replace. An Office function that locates text or formatting and replaces it with different text or formatting.

Reports. An Access database screen that summarizes data in a format suitable for printing. A mailing label is an example of a report.

Revisions. Highlighting effects applied to indicate any changes in text from one version of a document to another.

Right-aligned. Text that is lined up with the right side of a tab setting or document margin, as with a row of numbers in a column.

Rotate. To manipulate an object so that it moves around a 360-degree axis.

Row. A set of cells running from left to right across a worksheet.

Ruler. An on-screen feature used to place text and objects accurately on a page.

S

Save. To take a document residing in the temporary memory of the computer and create a file to be stored on a disk.

Save As. To save a previously saved document with a new name or new properties.

Scroll bars. The bars on the right side and bottom of a window that allow vertical and horizontal movements through a document.

Selection bar. An invisible bar along the left side of a document. When the mouse pointer is placed in the bar, it can be used to select a single line or multiple lines of text.

Shading. A color that fills cells or an object.

Shadow. A drawing effect that appears to place a shadow alongside an object.

Shape. Items such as a circle, rectangle, line, polygon, or polylines in the document.

Sheet. See *worksheet*.

Simple formula. A formula, usually in a spreadsheet, that has only one operator. An example is B4+B5.

Slide. An element in a PowerPoint presentation, equivalent to a page.

Slide layout. The term used to refer to the general appearance of a slide and the elements it contains; for example, a bulleted list layout, a chart layout, or a title only layout.

Slide Sorter view. A view in PowerPoint that allows the viewing of all slides together in one screen.

SmartTags. Small icons that appear throughout your document as you perform various tasks or enter certain types of text. SmartTags are used to perform actions in Office that would normally require you to open other programs.

Sort. To arrange data alphanumerically in either ascending (A–Z) or descending (Z–A) order.

Speech Recognition. The feature of Office that recognizes and translates voice patterns to screen text.

Spelling checker. A feature that checks the spelling in a document against a dictionary and flags possible errors for correction.

Spreadsheet. A software program used to perform calculations on data.

Start page. The first Web page to appear after logging onto the Web.

Status bar. An area at the bottom of a window that provides information about the document, such as what page, line, and column the pointer is currently resting in.

Style. A saved, named set of formatting such as color, size, and font that can be applied to text in a document.

SUM function. A saved, named function of addition that can be applied to cells by typing the term "SUM" in a formula.

Switchboard. In Access, the opening screen of a database.

Symbol. A typeface that uses graphics such as circles, percentage signs, or smiling faces in place of letters and numbers.

Syntax. The structure and order of the functions and references used in a formula.

T

Tab. A setting that can be placed along the width of a line of text that enables the pointer to quickly jump to that setting. Tab settings determine where the insertion point moves when the Tab key is pressed or the indent feature is used.

Table. A collection of columns and rows that form cells at their intersection. Used to organize sets of data.

Target cell. The cell into which the results of a formula should be placed.

Task. An entry that is made in Outlook's To Do section.

Task panes. A feature of Office in the form of an additional window on the right side of the screen to assist you with various tasks.

Template. A pre-defined collection of formatting and style settings on which to base a new document.

Text box. A floating object containing text that can be created with the drawing feature of Office programs to place text anywhere in a document.

Text wrap. Forces newly entered text to wrap to the next line when the insertion point reaches the right margin.

Themes. A collection of background colors/patterns, bullet styles, line styles, heading styles, and font styles. Frequently used when designing Web pages.

Thesaurus. A feature used to find *synonyms* (words that are alike) and *antonyms* (words that are opposite).

Titles. Descriptive pieces of text frequently used in charts and spreadsheets.

Tooltip. A help feature that displays the name of a tool in a small box when the pointer is over the tool.

Toolbars. They appear at the top of the application window and are used to access many of the commonly used features of the Office applications.

Transitions. In PowerPoint, elements that determine the type of transition from slide to slide.

U

Undo. A feature that allows users to reverse the last action performed. The user can undo multiple actions by repeatedly using this feature.

Unhide. To reveal rows or columns previously hidden in a worksheet.

Unprotect. To remove password safeguards from a worksheet so that anyone can modify the worksheet.

V

Value. An entry that is a number, formula, or function.

Variable. Cells that are changed to see what results from that change. For example, in a spreadsheet, you might enter an interest rate percentage (the variable) to calculate a loan payment. Each time you change the interest

rate percentage, the loan payment amount changes.

View. In software, various displays of documents or information that enable the performance of different tasks. Views also allow users to see different perspectives on the same information. One example is the Outline view in Word.

Voice command. A dictated command used with speech recognition to invoke a menu, menu command, or dialog box option.

Voice training. The process of teaching speech recognition the manner in which you speak.

W

Web page. A document that appears after logging onto the Web. Also called a Web document.

Web Page Preview. The feature of Office that allows users to view a document in Internet Explorer as it would appear on the Web.

What's This? A part of the Help system; once it is selected, the pointer changes to a question mark. The user can click on any on-screen element to receive an explanation of that element.

Wizard. A feature that walks through a procedure step by step, and helps the readers accomplish a task.

Word count. A tally of the number of words in a document.

Word processing. The ability to type, edit, and save a document.

Word wrap. To let text in a paragraph automatically flow to the next line when it reaches the right margin.

WordArt. An applet included with Office used for adding special effects to text, such as curving the text.

Workbook. A single Excel file containing a collection of Excel worksheets.

Worksheet. One of several pages in an Excel workbook.

World Wide Web. **(Also referred to as "The Web.")** A series of specially designed documents—all linked together—to be viewed over the Internet.

Wrap. See *text wrap*.

X

X-axis. In a chart, a horizontal reference line marked in regular intervals to designate chart categories with descriptive labels.

Y

Y-axis. In a chart, a vertical reference line marked in regular intervals to display the values of a chart.

Z

Zoom. To enlarge or reduce the way the text displays on-screen. This setting does not affect how the document will print.

Index

C

PRIMA TECH's *fast&easy* series

Fast Facts, Easy Access

Offering extraordinary value at a bargain price, the *fast & easy* series is dedicated to one idea: To help readers accomplish tasks as quickly and easily as possible. The unique visual teaching method combines concise tutorials and hundreds of screen shots to dramatically increase learning speed and retention of the material. With PRIMA TECH's *fast & easy* series, you simply look and learn.

Family Tree Maker® Version 8 Fast & Easy®: The Official Guide
0-7615-2998-5
U.S. $18.99 ▪ Can. $28.95 ▪ U.K. £13.99

Microsoft® Works Suite 2001 Fast & Easy®
0-7615-3371-0
U.S. $24.99 ▪ Can. $37.95 ▪ U.K. £18.99

Microsoft® Office XP Fast & Easy®
0-7615-3388-5
U.S. $18.99 ▪ Can. $28.95 ▪ U.K. £13.99

Microsoft® Windows® Millennium Edition Fast & Easy®
0-7615-2739-7
U.S. $18.99 ▪ Can. $28.95 ▪ U.K. £13.99

Microsoft® Access 2002 Fast & Easy®
0-7615-3395-8
U.S. $18.99 ▪ Can. $28.95 ▪ U.K. £13.99

Microsoft® Outlook 2002 Fast & Easy®
0-7615-3422-9
U.S. $18.99 ▪ Can. $28.95 ▪ U.K. £13.99

Paint Shop Pro™ 7 Fast & Easy®
0-7615-3241-2
U.S. $18.99 ▪ Can. $28.95 ▪ U.K. £13.99

Microsoft® Excel 2002 Fast & Easy®
0-7615-3398-2
U.S. $18.99 ▪ Can. $28.95 ▪ U.K. £13.99

Microsoft® PowerPoint® 2002 Fast & Easy®
0-7615-3396-6
U.S. $18.99 ▪ Can. $28.95 ▪ U.K. £13.99

Quicken® 2001 Fast & Easy®
0-7615-2908-X
U.S. $18.99 ▪ Can. $28.95 ▪ U.K. £13.99

Microsoft® FrontPage® 2002 Fast & Easy®
0-7615-3390-7
U.S. $18.99 ▪ Can. $28.95 ▪ U.K. £13.99

Microsoft® Word 2002 Fast & Easy®
0-7615-3393-1
U.S. $18.99 ▪ Can. $28.95 ▪ U.K. £13.99

PRIMA TECH
A Division of Prima Publishing
www.prima-tech.com

Call now to order
(800)632-8676 ext. 4444

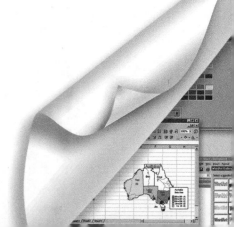